CLOTHES-
Part of Your World

MARGIL VANDERHOFF

Assistant Professor, Indiana University

Ginn and Company

The drawings were prepared by Contis Studios, Anna Marie Magagna and Erica Merkling.

The sewing diagrams were prepared by Barbara Corrigan.

Techniques used in the sewing diagrams were reproduced through the courtesy of Educational Bureau, Coats & Clark, Inc.; Simplicity Pattern Co. Inc.; Singer Sewing Machine Company; Talon Educational Services.

We extend our appreciation to the following for their valuable assistance in the preparation of the art for the pages listed below:

Page 10, Smithsonian Institution

Page 11, Museum of Fine Arts, Boston ("She Walks in Splendor," gift in memory of Gertrude Bickford Hutchings)

Page 31, National Dairy Council

Page 43 right, Seventeen Magazine

Page 133, Bruner Corporation

Page 134, The Dow Chemical Company

Page 138, E. I. du Pont de Nemours & Company, Inc.

Page 146, J. C. Penney Company, Inc. ("Storage for Clothes" from pages 20–21, *Penney's Fashions and Fabrics*, Fall/Winter, 1963)

Page 150, Elsie L. Seago

Contents

Preface

Clothes—Part of Your World is designed to serve as a guide for the study of clothing. It is planned particularly for secondary school girls, but other persons may find it useful as a reference.

One of the purposes of the book is reflected in its overall organization. Different aspects of clothing are included so that pupils may gain a broad concept of clothing as they encounter it in their everyday lives. A second purpose of the book is to encourage pupils to develop a positive attitude toward the study of clothing and an interest in further exploration of each topic.

The book was developed with close attention to the National Curriculum Study in Home Economics. The organization and contents are based on key concepts and generalizations which were selected and adapted from the Textiles and Clothing material. The Teacher's Manual includes a complete list of the generalizations on which each unit is based.

More than a dozen charts summarize important facts and examples. These detailed charts are highlighted in the book in order to encourage pupils to organize facts and examples into larger concepts, or ideas. The charts may also be used as ready references for specific types of information.

The illustrations in the book give it a truly distinctive character. Sketches are used, rather than photographs, in order to assure an undated appearance over a maximum period. Numerous illustrations throughout the book were planned very carefully to clarify important concepts for teen-age girls. Artists' drawings capture the typical characteristics of this age group—active, inquisitive, constantly developing. The delightful sketches in bright colors will appeal to girls everywhere.

The suggested learning experiences at the end of each unit are another outstanding feature of the book. Pupils are guided to analyze what they have read, to find more information, and to make some immediate applications of generalizations. In some instances, pupils are asked to consider future applications of the material. Suitable learning experiences are designated for individual study, for small groups, and for large class groups. The variety of learning experiences suggested makes it possible to adapt the ideas to different classroom situations.

Nine units outline different approaches to the study of clothing. Together, these nine units explain why clothes are a very real part of our world. For instance, after studying Unit One, "What Girls Wore Then," pupils may better understand how their clothes are influenced by styles of the past. Comparisons are made between girls' clothing "then" and "now." In order to inspire further investigation, ways to study the history of clothing are incorporated into this unit.

Unit Two, "Meanings of Clothing," will create an awareness of clothing as it is related to everyday activities. Pupils will gain an insight into clothes as one resource that can be controlled in order to achieve both immediate and long-range goals.

Unit Three, "Your Appearance Doesn't Depend Just on Clothes," attempts to show why this is so. If an attractive personal appearance is important, then other factors must be considered as well as clothing. Directions are included for analyzing and improving posture, for selecting foods, and for improving social skills.

Unit Four, "Making Choices about What to Wear," shows how to apply design principles in deciding what to wear. Many sketches show examples of design principles applied in clothing. Practical suggestions for choosing line, color, and texture are summarized in two useful charts for easy reference. Also, there are general guides for selecting appropriate clothes for different occasions.

Unit Five, "Making Decisions about Buying Clothes," is a guide for young consumers. The Shopping Experience Inventory may be used at the beginning of the Unit so that girls may discover their own need for more guidance in buying clothes. Pupils will find information about both natural and manufactured fibers which will be useful because the first clothing purchased by a young shopper may contain either type of fiber, or perhaps both. Directions for reading labels on ready-to-wear and yard goods are included. A descriptive chart summarizes characteristics of natural fibers. Another chart shows generic names of manufactured fibers commonly used in clothing, matched with examples of trademark names as they might be found on labels. General characteristics of manufactured fibers, as compared to natural fibers, are described. Also there are suggestions for buying some types of clothing, specifically sportswear, skirts, sweaters, blouses, and dresses.

Unit Six, "Learning to Care for Clothes," deals with a vital maintenance job—keeping clothes wearable. Girls are given direction in answering these questions: "What factors determine the care required by a particular garment?" and "What is my share in family clothes care?" Facts about fabric finishes which affect clothes care are compiled in the chart "Do You Know Your Fabric Finishes?" Illustrations and examples explain how management principles may be applied in arranging a closet, or any area used for clothes storage.

Unit Seven, "Learning as You Sew," begins with a plan for developing skill in clothing construction through a series of projects. The entire unit is outlined in a detailed chart, "A Guide to Sewing Skill," which relates construction techniques, vocabulary, management practices, and design principles which might be studied with each project. The sequence of projects is adaptable to different types of home economics programs. For example, the study of construction techniques is meant to be limited in scope in some programs. In other programs such a unit may be more extensive. Alternative projects are suggested to provide for differences in pupil interest and need. Other topics include equipment for sewing, selecting patterns and fabric, measuring, and learning to use the sewing machine. The personal progress record, toward the end of the unit, encourages pupils to review what they have learned about clothing construction before planning further experiences. In addition to the clothing-construction projects, other learning experiences are included at the end of the unit. For example, pupils are made aware of good management practices in clothing construction, but not by memorizing a list of do's and don'ts. Rather, they are guided to discuss illustrations which emphasize common management practices. If they study the sketches carefully, perhaps they will find themselves.

Unit Eight, "More Uses for Your Clothing Skills—Alterations and Repairs," is concerned with applying construction

vi

techniques to these two particular uses. Differences between simple and more difficult alterations and repairs are explained.

Unit Nine, "Vocations Which Require Clothing and Textiles Knowledge," directs girls in exploring different occupations. Pupils will gain an awareness of employment opportunities for individuals with specialized knowledge of fibers, fabrics, and clothing. Today's young teen-agers will become tomorrow's homemakers. And a large proportion of these future homemakers will have two jobs rather than one. For many girls, a realistic approach to the future includes both preparation for homemaking and preparation for paid employment. In Unit Nine pupils will learn what they can do now to prepare themselves for a vocation.

The contributions of the many individuals who aided in the development of this book are gratefully acknowledged. Special thanks is due to Dr. Mary Crenshaw, Dean of the School of Home Economics, University of Alabama, for her interest in the project and her encouragement throughout the writing of the manuscript. Dr. Crenshaw, formerly Chairman of the Department of Home Economics, Indiana University reviewed the statements concerning food needs of teen-age girls.

Thanks is extended to Lavina Franck and Leah Weidman, my colleagues at Indiana University, for their constructive suggestions about various parts of the manuscript.

Dr. Evelyn Davies, Professor of Physical Education for Women, School of Health, Physical Education and Recreation, Indiana University, made helpful suggestions regarding posture analysis and posture improvement.

Three young women have made unique contributions to the unit, "Vocations Which Require Clothing and Textiles Knowledge." Jeanne Golly, Joyce Poling, and Mary Anne Pope wrote their personal stories to illustrate how specialized knowledge of clothing and textiles is applied in different vocations.

Virginia Winston, Supervisor of Home Economics, Cincinnati, Ohio, made valuable comments on parts of the manuscript. Miss Winston has shared her thoughtful views on teaching, learning, and home economics during our many informal discussions extending over a period of seven years.

Many other persons assisted either directly or indirectly in the preparation of this book. Although their names are not listed here, their help is sincerely appreciated.

Margil Vanderhoff
Indiana University
Bloomington, Indiana

UNIT ONE

What Girls Wore Then

I. Clothing for Girls — Then and Now

Were girls of a hundred years ago interested in clothes? What kinds of clothes did they wear? Were new fashions important to them? Were their clothes more or less feminine and prettier than today's styles? What were the fads?

Unless human interests have changed drastically, we can assume that girls of every era have enjoyed the fashions of the day. And each historical period has had its own modes of dress.

Clothes for Active Sports

Picture the prim miss of the 1860's enjoying suitable sports for young ladies. A game of croquet was possible even though she had yards and yards of skirt to control. Perhaps the competition was not serious.

Fashionable riding costumes, too, featured full skirts and fitted bodices. They seem very restrictive and awkward when compared with the comfortable riding outfits for girls today.

Girls practiced archery one hundred years ago just as they do now. However, you might feel handicapped in using a bow and arrow wearing a full-length dress, as they did. Ladies were well covered while taking exercise. Today we think that ideal sportswear is designed for action.

Walking dresses for girls then looked very much like adult styles of the time. The voluminous dresses with elaborate details seem to have been suited only to casual strolling. Perhaps walking was meant chiefly to be sociable rather than to provide exercise.

Today's swim suits have no resemblance to the swimming costumes of fifty years ago. Of course, there was no need for specially designed swimming clothes until swimming became popular as public recreation. The early swimming outfits covered the body almost completely. Such a costume seems better suited for beach sitting than for swimming. In the early 1900's the widespread development of public swimming pools in recreation parks

was still in the future. Today, backyard swimming pools, skin diving, and surfboarding show that there is no longer a cautious attitude toward swimming.

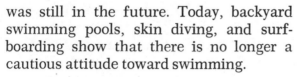

Dressy Clothes

In the 1860's young ladies' afternoon dresses were frilly and feminine. Some of the same types of decorative trim are used today. Laces, braid, buttons, sashes, and embroidery are still familiar types of dress trim. The bell-shaped skirt caused the wearer to step about daintily. Dresses covered one to the throat and ended at the floor. A parasol, a feminine accessory used as a sunshade, or just to carry, might have been added to complete an outfit.

Very young girls' dresses were shorter, with pantaloons (trouser-type underwear), showing below the skirt. Nevertheless, dresses for young girls closely resembled adult dresses of the day. Clothing especially designed for children developed later. Now children's clothes further comfort, encourage activity, and are often designed to accommodate some of the rapid growth

characteristic of childhood. The chances are that a young lady's formal evening dress had a low neckline showing her bare shoulders. Her fashionably small waistline, already emphasized by the full skirt, was bound even tighter by a waist-cinching corset. She went to the grand ball in splendor with her skirt rustling and swaying over lacy petticoats.

3

II. Why Learn about Clothes from the Past?

You Gain Insight into an Everyday Human Need

A study of historic clothing can give us a better understanding of clothing today. The history of clothing is actually a history of your clothing. Consider, for example, that not all contemporary clothing styles are entirely original. Many of our currently popular fashions are modeled after designs from the past. A few examples will illustrate the re-use of fashion designs.

High-waisted dresses, so popular in 1965 and 1966, were also fashionable about 1810. And many centuries before, during the Greek and Roman civilizations, a similar line in women's dress was worn, with emphasis under the bust. In the fashion world this high-waisted silhouette is sometimes called the empire line.

The "dropped" waistline, which emphasizes the hipline rather than the waist, was a predominant style in the 1920's. At the same time fashionable skirt lengths ended above the knee. Both the dropped waistline and short skirts were popular again in 1965 and 1966.

Excessively full skirts have been popular at various times down through the centuries. As early as the time of Queen Elizabeth I, in the late 1500's, when the colonization of North America had barely begun, the women in England were wearing great hoops under their skirts to make them stand away from their bodies. About two hundred years later, between 1750 and and 1790, the time of the French Revolution in Europe and of the Revolutionary War in this country, hooped skirts were again popular. And in the next century, be-

4

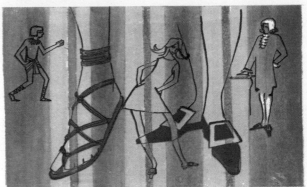

Designs in footwear have been repeated, too. Large metal buckles decorated shoes in the seventeenth and eighteenth centuries and again in 1966. Egyptians wore sandals more than 3000 years ago. Do you?

Next time you read about new styles and fashions, stop to ask, "Is it really new?"

You Increase Your Understanding of History, Literature, and Art

The history of dress is more than a story of changing fashions. Through the study of clothing you can better understand other aspects of history. The changing status of women, particularly over the last century is reflected in clothing. Women's everyday activities are no longer centered entirely in the home; today women participate more freely than ever before, as individuals, in public activities. As women have become more active, women's clothing has become more casual, comfortable, and nonrestrictive. Everywhere women are involved in community organization. They help at the polls on election day and preside at P.T.A. meetings. They join study clubs and recreation groups. Many have paid employment outside the home. Many women have more leisure time to travel. Furthermore, it is not uncommon for a woman to travel a long

tween 1830 and 1870, full skirts were again popular. During this time hoops were sometimes used to hold the skirt out, and also bulky petticoats called crinolines. These were sometimes padded.

These massive hooped skirts and bulky petticoats must have been very inconvenient for sitting, clumsy for walking, and difficult to store or pack. The yards of fabric certainly would have made a dress uncomfortable in warm weather. However, full skirts and crinolines were popular once again during the late 1940's and the early 1950's. So even in as recent times as these girls and women have sacrificed comfort and convenience in order to be fashionable. Skirts in the late 1940's were not quite as billowy as those of the 1850's and they were not quite floor length, as they were a century ago, but some skirt styles, those of "ballerina length," ended only slightly above the ankle.

Toques and berets, two popular hat shapes in recent years, date back to the sixteenth century.

distance alone by plane, train, bus, or in her own car. Versatile clothing, easily packed, makes it possible for her to take all the clothing for her trip in a single piece of luggage.

Do you believe there are any girls and women who want to return to steel corsets, hoops, and cumbersome yards of fabric?

Let's consider now another aspect of history that is related to the clothing we wear.

Technological developments, inventions and discoveries, as well as social changes, bring about changes in clothing. Until man-made fibers were developed textile fabrics were manufactured only from natural fibers. Women wore stockings, for example, of cotton or wool. Nylon stockings have been manufactured for less than thirty years; they were first available to consumers in 1940. Sheer hosiery manufactured from olefin is a still more recent development, coming after 1960. Stretch fabrics, made of spandex fibers, also have been introduced only since 1960. Fabric finishes which control such problems as shrinkage, wrinkling, and static electricity have only recently resulted in clothing which is more useful and easier to take care of.

The invention and improvement of the sewing machine took place during the thirty years from 1830 to 1860. This resulted in the mass production of ready-made clothing. In the 1860's the sewing machine was used in large-scale production of ready-mades. As a result of the invention of the sewing machine the everyday life of the homemaker changed. First, she could buy some ready-made clothing for the family. Second, she could buy a sewing machine for use in her home. Either action tended to lighten the physical work of homemaking.

A general knowledge of clothing history will help you understand some of the things you read, and so make them more enjoyable. Clothing is so much a part of everyday life that few stories can be written without some reference to it. Next time you read a story, watch for references to clothing. Try to picture it as the author describes it. Study the specialized vocabulary which tells you about clothing. For instance, "panier," "farthingale," "watteau gown," "redingote," "batteau neckline," "ruff," and "hennin" are only a few of the many terms related to clothing which you may find in stories you read, especially in historical novels.

Paintings too will have greater interest for you if you understand the details of costume. Portraits of the fifteenth and sixteenth centuries may seem less strange if you can recognize clothing details of the particular period.

It May Be Useful in Various Occupations

To theater costume designers

The work of theater costume designers is described in the unit, "Vocations which Require Clothing and Textiles Knowledge." In order to create authentic costumes, professional designers must understand historic trends in clothing. These specialists need to know where to find descriptions of the clothes and accessories for any historic period. They must be able to use various sources to compile information about all details of dress including hats, shoes, and jewelry.

Occupational opportunities in the theater may increase as our leisure time increases. Drama, ballet, and musical plays provide recreation at every stage of life— from the very young to the aged. If you have an interest in history and drama, as

6

well as clothing, you may want to learn more about this vocational area with a promising future.

To fashion designers

Our clothing today reflects ideas from historic costumes. Some examples of recent styles inspired by the past have been described (see pages 4–5). Clothing designers search in the clothing of the past for ideas that might be applied in creating new fashions. Designers of accessories and of jewelry also find ideas in the designs of historic articles. For a more complete description of the occupational field of clothes designing see "Vocations which Require Clothing and Textiles Knowledge."

To museum curators

The work of a museum curator is concerned with overseeing the articles, or collections of articles, in a museum. In addition, a curator is sometimes required to describe articles for the public. Historic costumes and accessories are often preserved and displayed in museums. Therefore, knowledge about historic clothing is useful to the museum curator. The important work of museum curators makes it possible for us to have a direct source of information about the past.

It May Lead to Hobbies and Personal Interests

Clothing history is specialized knowledge which has still other uses. Many different kinds of specialized knowledge can be put to use in leisure-time activities. The history of clothing is one type of knowledge that might be used this way. It can lead to hobbies for leisure hours. Explore your abilities and develop some personal interests.

Here are some suggestions for hobbies based on historic clothing.

Collecting antique jewelry[1]

Clothes and jewelry complement each other. From ancient times people have decorated themselves and their clothing with various ornaments. Familiar types of jewelry and other ornaments that are commonly worn at the present have interesting origins. There is jewelry of great value and of historical worth in museums and private collections. Enjoy some of these whenever you have an opportunity to visit a museum. There are also many old pieces of jewelry from the recent past. Your family may

[1] Data on historic jewelry from Carolyn G. Bradley, *Western World Costume*, Appleton-Century-Crofts, Inc., New York, 1954.

7

have some heirlooms of this kind which have been handed down from your great-great grandmother or other ancestors.

Collecting antique jewelry can be a great deal of fun as well as being educational. Antique shops are a source of old jewelry and ornamental items. Not all old jewelry is precious or expensive, but it may be interesting. Non-valuable old pieces can often be purchased rather inexpensively. Well-designed and interesting old jewelry can add individuality to your outfits.

However, there is no reason to limit such a hobby to collecting articles. Learning about them is part of the fun. Also, good contemporary designs in jewelry based on old designs can be found. Perhaps you have some such pieces but are not aware of it. For example, watches were worn on long neck chains in the early 1700's and again in the 1800's. Pendant watches are being worn again today.

Lockets, whether treasured heirlooms or modern copies, are favorite possessions of many girls. Lockets have a long history dating back at least to the early 1800's.

Cameo brooches and bracelets are another type of jewelry which can be traced into the past. Cameos were worn by ladies of the late eighteenth century. However, cameo jewelry is believed to have appeared much earlier than that, even before the Middle Ages. It was worn during the later period of the Greek civilization 336–146 B.C. Women of ancient Egypt, about 3500–3000 B.C., wore magnificent earrings, necklaces, bracelets, and armbands fashioned of gold with stones of garnet, amethyst, turquoise, and carnelian. Elaborate ornaments were fashioned for women to wear in their hair.

Do you wear a ring on a long chain around your neck? This idea seems very young and modern. Actually, it dates back to the 1700's. So, what's really new?

Making costume dolls

Another hobby for girls with special interests is designing and making historical clothing in miniature. Costume dolls become your own works of art if you can reproduce details accurately. These miniatures might be planned to represent well-known persons of a particular historic era. Or costume dolls might be inspired by characters in stories and plays.

You have an opportunity to apply your knowledge of history and art and your sewing skill. Study illustrations and descriptions of historic dresses. Notice fabrics, colors, and accessories. Make sketches in planning a costume. Commercial patterns for doll clothes might provide the bases for original designs. Dolls about twelve inches high, with movable arms and legs, are easier to costume than smaller ones.

Sewing

If you can sew, you may want to try some simple designing for yourself. Try adapting good ideas from the past into individualized features for your clothes.

8

This hobby will help you to learn something about historic dress. A study of illustrations will provide you with ideas.

Your own unique designs do not have to be complex, nor do they need to involve an entire outfit. Often, simple but original decorative trims are all that are necessary to add individuality to your wardrobe. Notice placement of buttons on bodices, skirts, and sleeves. Interesting uses for ruffles, lace, braid, and embroidered trim can be adapted from old, but excellent, designs.

This hobby might help you to understand one source of ideas for contemporary clothing designers. Designers actually do find inspiration in historic costumes. Also, in a limited way, this hobby will lead you to explore your interests and talent in the occupational area of clothes design.

Photography and sketching

If amateur photography is already your hobby, then you may want to concentrate on a specialty. Collections of good snapshots can be based on favorite subjects. Birds, animals, and flowers are examples of favorite subjects for photographers. Historic costumes might be another.

Sketching is another hobby which can be applied to the history of clothing. Making detailed sketches of historic costumes can be both recreation and a way to learn clothing history. In this hobby, portraying colors and textures accurately may be a challenge.

Reading biography and autobiography

Reading biographies and autobiographies is pleasant recreation in itself. It also is a way to build your knowledge of people and events. Although major events may be emphasized, anecdotes of ordinary activities are often included in life stories. Notice incidents related to the clothing.

9

III. How Can We Learn about Clothes from the Past?

Resources in Your Community

Periodicals and references

Today's clothing did not just happen. We have seen that it has a history. Close around you in your own community there are resources for studying the history of dress. As you read newspapers and magazines, notice news items and feature stories. From time to time interesting stories related to the history of clothing appear in the news. Fashion news provides a continuous source of information about the subject.

Your school library and city library may have some good references on the subject. Librarians are able to help you find information on specific topics. The history of clothing is a subject that is very much

alive. It is being investigated constantly. Therefore, there are attractively illustrated references published in recent years.

Biography and autobiography have already been mentioned as other resources.

Hobbies

In addition to reading, hobbies are another resource for learning. We learn in various ways. Collecting things and constructing things are only two ways. Each of the hobbies described suggests ways to explore the same subject. (See "Why Learn about Clothes from the Past?" pages 4–9.)

Movies, television, stage plays

Besides hobbies, other recreation activities are available in your own community. Read the television program schedule to locate historic plays and dramatized events from history. The costumes may give you some clues about clothes of the period.

Movies and stage plays with historical settings will provide this opportunity. As you watch and listen, think about the things you see and hear.

Costume Collections

Museums

Why limit yourself? Why not see actual examples of historic clothing? There are various opportunities to do this—if you know where to look. Public museums are places to look for historic dress collections.

One of the best-known museums in our country is the Smithsonian Institution in Washington, D.C. It includes several types of museums housed in separate buildings. It is in the Museum of History and Technology that displays of historic clothing are located.

The First Ladies Hall is a collection of dresses worn by Presidents' wives. Also, a few dresses represent Presidents' daughters, sisters, and other women relatives who lived in the White House.

The dresses are displayed on mannequins and arranged in groups. For instance, one group represents the period from 1787 to 1809. The First Ladies are shown in a room of the Executive Mansion in Philadelphia, the capital from 1790 to 1800. The other groups are arranged in settings similar to different rooms in the White House. These room backgrounds are furnished as they actually were at the times when the various First Ladies lived in the White House. Therefore, in each exhibit you may see styles both in dress and in home furnishings.

The Museum of History and Technology has a second exhibit showing historic trends in clothing. This is the Hall of American Costume. Here, you can see children's clothing of the 1800's. Also, more women's clothing is displayed on mannequins. The mannequins' hair styles fit the historic periods of their dresses.

In addition to the Smithsonian Institution, some other public museums in large cities have exhibits of historic dress. These museums are located in different parts of the United States. A few examples are the Metropolitan Museum of Art in New York City; the Philadelphia Museum of Art; the Cincinnati Art Museum; the Chicago Art Institute; the Kansas City Museum in Kansas City, Missouri; and the Los Angeles County Museum.

If your state has an historical museum, find out whether clothing is among the exhibits. You may discover examples of dress closely related to the history of your state.

There are still other places to see historic clothing. Within your state, perhaps in your own community, may be an historic house which is maintained as a museum. Clothing is sometimes included in the original objects preserved in historic homes. The Robert Campbell House Museum[2] in St. Louis, Missouri is an example of a private home museum. The Costume Room contains an exhibit of clothing fashionable in the period 1850–1880.

College and university Home Economics departments

A few college and university Home Economics departments located in various parts of the country have collections of historic clothing. These costume collections are usually supervised by a faculty member who is a textiles and clothing specialist.

The University of Rhode Island at Kingston has a collection of historic clothing. Another is located at Drexel Institute in Philadelphia. In the Midwest there is a collection in the Home Economics Department at Indiana University, Bloomington. Other collections are located in the College of Home Economics at Michigan State University, East Lansing and, in the Far West, at the University of Washington in Seattle. Although only a few places are mentioned here, historic clothing exhibits are maintained at many other colleges and universities in the United States. Perhaps your community has such an exhibit.

These historic collections are used to investigate origins of clothing design. Furthermore, the systematic study of clothing provides clues about the social and economic conditions of a given period. Costume collections provide inspiration for garments designed by students.

IV. What Will Clothes of the Future Be Like?

If we could look into the future, what kind of clothing would we see? We cannot be certain. However, a few very general predictions can be based on current trends.

It seems probable that casual clothes for leisurely living will continue. Shorts of various lengths have been popular for a long time. Also, long pants and pant suits are generally accepted casual wear for girls and women. Loose-fitting dresses are another way that a casual feeling is obtained. Comfort has become a very important characteristic in clothes. This suggests a guide for selecting clothes. If your appearance is as important to you as comfort, then select casual clothes as carefully as you would others. This may be a major challenge as you select clothing in the future.

Each year more people travel more often. Because of this, the demand for clothing specially planned for travel is likely to increase. Ideal travel clothes are lightweight, non-bulky, and wrinkle-resistant. Man-made fibers have helped to make these characteristics possible. For instance, featherweight fabrics are produced from polyester and polyester-cotton blends. An adequate travel wardrobe need weigh only a few pounds.

Ideally, travel clothes will require little maintenance. Again, man-made fibers produce washable fabrics which are wrinkle-resistant and fairly durable.

[2] The Robert Campbell House Museum is located at 15th and Locust, St. Louis, Missouri. It is operated by the Campbell House Foundation of St. Louis.

durable. Rips in these paper dresses can be repaired with transparent mending tape. Of course, they cannot be washed. After several wearings, a paper dress of this type is no longer wearable.

Very low-cost clothing might be economically discarded after several wearings. Perhaps disposable clothing would become more practical if it could be made more durable.

Do you prefer fur? Or would you like fur-like fabrics instead? Man-made fibers have made it possible to have synthetic fur fabrics on a limited clothes budget. For several years these furry fabrics have been made from Dynel, a modacrylic fiber.[5] Because their textures are deep and soft, these fabrics look very much like real fur. Synthetic fur fabrics can be purchased by the yard or in ready-mades such as jackets and coats.

[3] John Carr Doughty, "The Future of Knitting," *American Fabrics*, No. 70, Winter 1965–66, p. 51.
[4] Paper dresses by Scott Paper Company, Philadelphia, Pennsylvania. Another throw-away dress is made by Mars Manufacturing Company of Asheville, North Carolina.
[5] Dynel® is the trade name for the modacrylic staple fiber produced by Union Carbide Chemicals Company.

Knit clothing is increasing in popularity. We can easily understand this when we consider its advantages. Knit fabrics are comfortable. They adjust to fit the shape of the body. They resist wrinkling. For these reasons, knits are good travel clothes.

Knit clothes, depending on the fiber content, are suitable for all seasons. A wool knit dress would be comfortable only during cool weather. But knits of man-made fibers would be reasonably comfortable for warm weather also. For example, an all-polyester knit dress would be wearable in all seasons.

We may see more knit clothing in the future. The prediction has been made that during the next fifty years more fabric will be produced by knitting than by any other method of fabric.[3] At the present time woven fabrics are most common.

In future years, we may expect some different materials to be used for clothing. In 1966, simple paper dresses were introduced.[4] They are inexpensive but not very

Suggested Learning Experiences

Individual or Group Projects

1. Do our present-day fashions reflect styles from the historical past? Make a bulletin-board display and pair some currently popular fashions with similar styles from the past. How many of our present-day fashions are inspired by designs out of the past?

2. Find facts and give reports about the history of particular types of garments. Topics to investigate: hats, shoes, handbags, gloves, capes, blouses, petticoats, muffs.

Art

3. Ask your art teacher to tell about a masterpiece by a well-known painter. Ask your resource person to select for this lesson a painting in which details of clothing can be clearly seen. Inexpensive prints of many fine masterpieces are available. Also, slides of some well-known paintings might be used.

History

4. Have you learned to associate certain styles of dress with particular periods in our history? Compile a report of fashions worn by Presidents and Presidents' wives. A booklet on this subject may be obtained from the Smithsonian Institution, Washington, D.C. Class members who have toured the exhibit of inaugural gowns of Presidents' wives may want to report on this.

5. Do you live near a college or university which has a Home Economics department? Find out whether the department has an historic costume collection. Ask the person in charge of the collection to tell your class about one or two outstanding items in the collection.

6. Contact the director of your state historical museum to determine whether any historic clothing is included in the exhibits. If there is one, have a committee find out more about the collection and report to the class.

Literature

7. Notice the descriptions of clothing next time you read a biography or an autobiography. When you are making a book report for literature class include an accurate description of clothing worn by the characters in the book. Or illustrate your report with sketches of the clothing.

References for Pupils

LESTER, KATHERINE MORRIS, and ROSE NETZORG KERR, *Historic Costume*, Fifth Edition. Chas. A. Bennett Co., Inc., Peoria, Ill., 1961.

SEIDLER, NED, *Gems and Jewelry*. The Odyssey Press, Inc., New York, 1964.

Smithsonian Institution, *The First Ladies Hall, Smithsonian Institution*, Smithsonian Publication 4640, 1965. Editorial and Publication Division, Smithsonian Institution, Washington, D.C.

WILCOX, R. TURNER, *Five Centuries of American Costume*, Charles Scribner's Sons, New York, 1963.

References for Teachers

CONTINI, MILA, *Fashion*. The Odyssey Press, Inc., New York, 1965.

LAVER, JAMES, *Costume*. Cassell and Company, Ltd., London, 1963.

PAYNE, BLANCHE, *History of Costume*. Harper & Row, Publishers, New York, 1965.

WILCOX, R. TURNER, *The Mode in Costume*. Charles Scribner's Sons, New York, 1958.

UNIT TWO

Meanings of Clothing

I. Your Clothing Reflects You

Clothing and Personality

To some extent clothing may express one's personality traits. In other words, an individual's clothing tells others what he is like. Let's look at an example of this. Theater costumes are specially designed for stage plays, operas, and movies to help the actors represent their parts. In a brief time the audience must become acquainted with the characters in order to understand the play. One way in which they may come to understand the personalities of the different characters is by observing the clothing they wear. A professional costume designer must study the characters created by the author and then try to design costumes that will present them accurately to the audience.

In the paragraphs below, a college student who was studying costume production explains how personality traits and costumes are related. Sketches of her original costume designs show some of the details which she describes for you.

"A stage costume helps the player to become a character in a play. Before an actor or an actress says a word, something about his or her personality and age should appear in the costume. The costume designer uses color and styles to create an impression for the audience.

"These sketches show costume designs for the play *The Barretts of Wimpole Street* [by Rudolph Besier]. This famous story tells how the poet Robert Browning won Elizabeth Barrett as his wife. The play is set in London in the 1840's. The Barretts were a real family who actually lived at 50 Wimpole Street during that time.

"Certain clothing styles had to be observed in the play in order to present the characters authentically. The costumes and hair styles show the fashions of the middle 1840's. During this period men commonly wore long sideburns called 'piccadilly weepers.' Women wore fitted bodices with the waist forming a point at the center. Skirts were bell-shaped and floor-length. Generally, women wore their hair parted in the center.

"Robert Browning was a dandy and therefore is smartly dressed in rich fabrics. He has on a cutaway coat depicting his young age. Subtle colors are used for his costume. Men did not wear bright colors in the 1850's.

"Elizabeth is a frail person. Because of her poor physical condition she has been confined to her room for many years. Pale colors and soft, rich fabrics are used in her dress to give a feeling of weakness in body but not necessarily in mind. Elizabeth has a strong mind of her own. She achieves her scheme through a carefully thought-out plan.[6] The color and finish of the pale blue moiré taffeta helps achieve a feminine appearance for Elizabeth.

"Elizabeth's sister Henrietta is as rebellious as it is safe to be in dealing with Papa, their tyrannical father. She is wearing a daytime dress of green gingham with bell-shaped sleeves and a white underblouse. A peplum is added at the waistline for additional style. The dress is completed with bright green trim at the sleeves and down the front. Henrietta has a fashionable outfit for the day.

[6] Read the play and discover for yourself Elizabeth Barrett's clever scheme.

16

The BARRETTS of WIMPOLE STREET

A Play by Rudolph Besier

Robert

Elizabeth

Henrietta

Papa

Bella

Now Playing

"Papa is dressed completely in somber gray and black to show his age and personality. Papa is a depressing individual who thinks only of himself. He wears a black tail coat, which was the formal attire of that day. Papa thought of himself as conservative. Changes and new ideas were not for him.

"Bella, the cousin of Elizabeth and Henrietta, wears a burgundy velvet visiting dress with gray fur trim to soften the lines. The bell-shaped sleeves and skirt are tiered. Balls of fur and bows have been added as decoration on the skirt. Most women of that time would not have worn a dress with this saucy detail of fur trim. It would have been considered daring and frivolous. Bella had a winning way with the men, including Papa. She was considered a flirt because of her sweet baby talk.

"Bella's costume contrasts with Elizabeth's simple dress. These two costumes point out extreme personality differences between vivacious Bella and quiet Elizabeth."

Mary Anne Pope
Senior, Indiana University
1966

This was the Barrett family and Robert Browning. The drama tells about one remarkable event in the lives of these people. Delicate, but strong-willed Elizabeth shows her determination. Henrietta is at the same time rebellious, yet a reluctantly dutiful daughter. Papa dominates his household like a stern master. The author pictures Bella Hedley as vivacious, somewhat daring, and frivolous. Robert Browning appears as a suave gentleman devoted to Elizabeth. Impressions made on the audience by the colors and styles of their clothing aid us in understanding each of these different characters.

17

There are stage personalities and real-life personalities—like yours. In actual everyday situations as well as in the theater impressions are made by clothing. Your clothing is one of the obvious ways you reflect your personality; your clothes are an expression of yourself to other persons. Words and actions are other ways in which you express yourself. Clothes, words, and actions—all these together tell others about yourself. What is the impression you want to leave with other people? (For suggestions about clothing and appearance, see "Your Appearance Doesn't Depend Just on Clothes," and "Making Choices about What to Wear," pages 29–50, and 51–80.)

II. Clothing and Roles

What Does "Role" Mean?

We tell others about our roles by the clothing we wear. In the same way, through clothing, we know something about the roles of other persons. A role can be defined as what one does or what one is expected to do in a particular situation. Your roles can be defined as the parts you play in real-life situations every day. Each individual, like yourself, has several roles. You have roles at school, at home, and in your community.

Your Roles at School

Since a role is what one does or what one is expected to do in a particular situation, it seems reasonable for you to think of your main role at school as that of a stu-

dent. Furthermore, you are a specific student in a particular school enrolled at a particular grade level. Although there are many students besides yourself in your school, each one is an individual with a unique combination of roles.

The responsibilities of your role as a student are varied. You are a member of several subject-matter classes. You participate in group work in several different ways. You recite, give reports, and contribute your comments to group discussions. On some days your role is simply that of being a good listener. You read assignments and write examinations. You are sometimes in charge of bulletin boards and exhibits.

However, it is probable that you have other roles in your school besides that of student. Are there other phases of school life in which you play a part? How do you participate in these phases?

Within every school are some special-interest groups, clubs, and teams. Teams need cheerleaders, majorettes, and fan clubs. For the music-minded there are choruses, glee clubs, bands, and orchestras. Although girls can't do much about football, there may be archery teams, tennis clubs, and organized swimming groups. There are drama clubs, folk-dancing and ballet organizations. Also, there are Future Homemakers, art groups, photography, and science clubs. Belonging to a club is a role. Being a group member means sharing common interests because you want to. Depending on your interests, you may have more roles than you realized.

Frequently an organized group uses a certain article of clothing or uniform to identify itself. Clothing is used in this way to communicate to others that the group exists. You identify yourself with a special

19

Eventually, if you are a success in your role as student, you will become a high-school graduate. Special ceremonial clothing is sometimes used to identify the role of graduate. The familiar mortarboard and gown tell everyone that the wearer has graduated from a school or college.

Belonging is a very human need. Being a part of a group which has real value to you is somewhat like having a treasure. A role worth having should be treated like a treasure. Guard it and care for it so that you do not lose it.

Your Roles in Your Community

Being a student is a major role you have in your community. It can not help but be the main part of your life as a young teenager. "Where do you go to school?" and "How are you doing in school?" These are typical questions which tell you that the community knows you are a student.

However, being a student is only one aspect of your life in your town or neighborhood. You will find various opportuni-

organization when you wear the uniform of the group. For example, you know your school band anywhere because of its uniform. Furthermore, an individual band member can be identified when he is apart from the band if he is wearing his uniform. The uniform tells everyone that he is a part of that special group. Everyone can recognize cheerleaders and majorettes by their special outfits. School letters and school colors tell us whom they represent. Chorus members may wear similar robes when they perform as a group, though group clothing need not always be so formal for choruses—a girls' chorus may dress in white blouses and dark skirts, to identify itself.

Of course, all students in a particular school belong to one special group. They are members of the student body of their school. Each individual student can, if he wishes, identify himself with his school by some symbol or article of clothing—a sweater, a jacket, an emblem, letters, the school colors.

ties to take part in activities and events outside your home and school. Chief among these activities may be membership in organizations of persons your own age and in some for both teens and adults. Your regular schedule may include church choir rehearsals and presentation of music at the services. A choir robe may identify this role. The girl scout uniform represents another way in which you may be sharing life in your community. The volunteer Candy Stripers uniform shows that concern for others is important to the girls who wear them. Hospitals in many cities benefit from the services provided by girls who give their time as Candy Stripers.

You are an individual with a combination of personality traits and capabilities. If you like small children and understand them you may make one of your roles that of a reliable baby-sitter. If you are interested in helping others, you will find more opportunities for occasional employment as you mature. With some training you may qualify as an aide in a day nursery. When you assist in a child care center you provide a valuable service for mothers who work outside the home. Can you set a table and serve food attractively? These basic skills can lead to a summertime job in a restaurant or cafeteria. Can you sing, ride a bicycle, clip a hedge, swim, make a salad, or play badminton? Your abilities may be of value to others as well as to you. Growing up means finding your place in the community. And part-time jobs can help you to learn about your future roles.

Your Roles at Home

Living with your family at home is a real-life situation, too. You probably have several roles in your home. You will participate in everyday family activities, such as housekeeping, recreation, and meals. You may be a housekeeping assistant to

your mother with some regular responsibilities in maintaining the home. You may be chief cook on Sunday night and salad girl during the week.

How you dress for your various activities at home is affected very much by your family's ideas regarding suitable dress. Families differ in what they consider suitable dress for various activities at home. For example, they differ in what they consider acceptable dress for mealtimes. Family mealtime atmosphere may range from the very casual and relaxed to the very formal.

Families differ too, in the recreations they prefer. Therefore, what a particular family considers suitable dress for leisure time is affected by the type of leisure activity they prefer. Some families are enthusiastic campers and so they are likely to dress for it. Other family groups prefer swimming, and still others like conversation and music. The roles you have in your family and how you dress at home are both related to family preferences.

Clothing Identifies Occupational Roles

Clothing identifies certain occupational roles. We can tell something about a person's vocation by the clothing he wears at work. While you were still very young you learned to associate uniforms with some types of occupations. You learned to recognize nurses, policemen, elevator operators, bus drivers, and firemen by their uniforms. Uniforms also identify professional baseball players, airline stewardesses and stewards, waiters, armed forces personnel, and forest rangers.

For some other occupations, although a specific uniform may not be required, particular types of dress are considered appropriate. Durable clothing is important to farmers, railroad maintenance workers, miners, and employees in other active occupations. Working clothes, then, can tell us something about types of employment.

Conservatively styled clothing is recognized as appropriate for both men and women in a wide range of business occupations. Faddish styles and extreme combinations of clothes appear out of place in a business environment. For instance, a secretary might consider the suits and dresses she wears to work as her "uniforms." This does not mean that her clothing lacks individuality. It means that she selects her working clothes so that she appears appropriately dressed for her particular occupational role. Perhaps you have seen a "career shop" in a large department store. The "career girl" clothes displayed in such a shop illustrate that certain types of clothing are associated with the occupational roles of career girls.

How We Learn New Roles

We learn about roles by watching others. A youngster parading about in her mother's hat, gloves, and high-heeled shoes imagines herself in a grown-up role. She is pretending to be a "grown-up lady." As long as she wears her proper costume, she is Mom, Mrs. Flossy, or any other grown-up lady she wants to be. Ladies, she has noticed, wear certain kinds of clothes— such as hats and high-heeled shoes. Of course, there is also grown-up behavior and adult responsibilities that must accompany grown-up clothes. So she goes shopping and makes a friendly call on the neighbors.

The little girl playing at "grown-up" roles now will, as time goes on, have roles which become more and more mature as she grows older. She will learn to be a cheerleader, a committee member, a high school sophomore, a date at a high school dance and, in time, the lady she is now pretending to be. Naturally, she will learn the appropriate dress for each new role.

Through appropriate dress she can more easily find a place for herself in each new situation she encounters.

Another way we learn new roles is by deliberately setting goals, then working toward them. One can enter most occupational fields only after some specialized study. This preparation may consist of developing necessary skills, or acquiring a broad background of knowledge, or both. Part of the preparation for a particular occupation may include observation of workers already employed. This provides an opportunity to observe the accepted mode of dress for the occupation.

Preparation for successful entry into an occupation may mean accepting and developing the expected standard of dress. High standards of cleanliness in dress and grooming are generally expected of food service workers for sanitation.

Success as a secretary, receptionist or cashier depends on standards of personal appearance as well as specialized occupational skills. Your clothing standards, then, may become an important step in reaching an occupational goal.

III. Your Clothing and Your Goals

Your Goals

Goals are guides that help determine your actions. One value in having a goal is that you have a good feeling of success when it is reached. Also, you are more likely to make wise choices about the things you do if you know what it is you really want to accomplish—where you want to go. The more important goals are usually reached gradually through success in reaching smaller goals.

You probably have some immediate goals and some long-distance goals. Immediately, you may be concerned about achieving reasonable success in school from day to day. This may mean passing a test this week, presenting a good report, or completing a project. The more distant goal you want to reach is a high-school diploma. You can see how short-range goals lead to success in reaching the goals that are farther away.

Making new friends and keeping those you have is an important goal at any stage of life. It is worth while as an immediate goal and as a long-range goal.

Living harmoniously in a family is both an immediate goal and a long-range goal for many persons. This involves living with your parental family now. The long-range goal may mean establishing your own home apart from your parental family. Understanding other persons is involved in achieving this goal.

Perhaps you want to learn more about occupations soon so that you can plan your school course better. Or an immediate goal may be getting some occasional paid employment so that you can try out your tal-ents and skill in it. A long-range goal may be preparing yourself for a specific occupational field.

Developing skills in money management is another goal that deserves attention. Financial security is a long-range goal that is more likely to be accomplished after you have first developed some ability to manage money.

Clothing Can Help You Reach Your Goals

Understanding and skills are needed

Whatever your goals clothing can help you reach them. However, you must plan for that to happen. You will be able to use clothing to reach your goals if you:

1. acquire an understanding of appropriate dress for different roles.
2. develop some knowledge and skills so that you can solve your clothing problems.

Think about the first suggestion. An understanding of appropriate dress can be applied as you change from one role to another during a usual day. On a weekday morning you are off to school in a skirt, blouse, sweater, and flat shoes. This outfit looks very much like the type of clothes other girls are wearing. However, you have shown your individuality in your choice of colors and details. You feel comfortable in them because you like their design and because they fit you. Another reason you feel comfortable in them is that they look right for the situation.

After school, at home, you may change into Bermuda shorts and a casual blouse.

24

For a brief time you are an assistant cook; you prepare the salad for the evening meal. But, as you work you are already thinking ahead to the next event of the day.

The annual spring concert is to be presented that night in the school auditorium. The chorus, of which you are a member, will sing at 7:30. Two weeks ago the chorus had a special meeting after practice to discuss their part in the concert. It was agreed that each member would wear a dressy pastel dress and low-heeled pumps. After the meeting you and two of your close friends discussed among yourselves the dresses that you would wear. Still later, there were some telephone calls among you and your friends. If we might have listened we would have overhead something like this: "What is everybody wearing? What are you going to wear? Amy and Carol are going to wear blue dresses and Kay is wearing a pink one. I have a pale green dress."

Why all the concern over what to wear to sing at a concert? Could it be that looking right and feeling comfortable about it is a part of success?

Adjusting to new roles

As you look ahead to your future, an understanding of appropriate dress has still other uses. Everyone can expect to acquire new roles from time to time. A common example of this can be seen when a high-school graduate, or a college graduate, changes from a student to a full-time employee in an occupational field.

Moving on to a new role in the world of work means making some changes in how you dress. The clothing you wear adds to the impression you make. Your standards of dress, including appropriateness, may affect your opportunities to be employed. Fads and extreme styles may need to be discarded. Badly fitted clothes and clothes in need of repair will leave an unfavorable impression.

Personal preference cannot be the only consideration in dressing for a job. In personal stituations, such as relaxing at home or shopping, you represent only yourself and your family. On the job, as employee, you will represent not only yourself but also your employer, the business, or the company. On a larger scale, an employee represents his entire occupation or profession.

Your success in a particular vocation may be affected by your willingness to follow certain standards of dress. Appropriate dress may add to the confidence you need to do a job or fill an important role. Looking right and feeling comfortable about your appearance is part of success in any role.

The type of employment you prefer may put some restriction on the clothing you wear to work. If a uniform is the expected dress this will restrict your clothing choices. Certain types of jobs may give you the opportunity to dress as you want to dress—an advantage for you to enjoy.

Solving your clothing problems

Let's consider the second suggestion: you need some knowledge and skills in order to solve your clothing problems and reach your goals. Just wishing won't make it so.

Skill in buying clothes can lead to better money management. Furthermore, appropriate clothing may help you adjust in social situations and in entering an occupational field. Even though you have limited funds for clothes you do not need necessarily to limit your goals. Rather, you may work harder to become an expert shopper. Learn to select clothing so that everything you buy is useful. Fewer clothes that can be worn many places are better than many items that can be used only occasionally. Skill in buying clothes is not developed in one easy lesson. You will want to learn how to check the fit of ready-made clothes; how to read labels; how to judge the wearing qualities of different fabrics.

Some sewing skill is an asset. If you know how to operate a sewing machine and use a simple pattern, you can solve many clothing problems. Getting clothes to fit right is a common problem. You can have better-fitting clothes if you learn how to alter garments and to sew some of your own clothes.

Your appearance is affected by your ability to maintain your clothes in wearable condition. Will your clothes be ready to wear when you are ready to go? If you have some sewing skill, you can repair your clothes. Also, a knowledge of fabrics and fabric finishes is useful in keeping your clothes clean.

You can learn how to combine your clothing into outfits that complement you. You will need a knowledge of design principles and how to apply them to the way you dress. Next you will need to study your own characteristics because you are the subject.

Clothing can help you reach your goals. The clothes you wear add to the impression you make. Also, they may contribute to the confidence you need to do a job or fill an important role. Deciding how you want to look is only the first step. The second step is doing something about it.

26

Suggested Learning Experiences

1. Discuss the topic "How does clothing help us reach our goals?"
2. How many occupations can you identify by clothing? Do you believe there are advantages in being able to do this? Explain.
3. Make a bulletin-board display showing typical dress that we associate with certain occupations.
4. Sometimes we use the term "uniform" when referring to certain types of clothing. Write a definition of "uniform." Then, use the dictionary to check the accuracy of your definition.
5. Can you explain the meaning of the term "role"? How many roles do you have? Do you wear special kinds of clothing for some of these roles?
6. Can you describe your personality? How does your clothing reflect your personality?
7. Describe a character in a T.V. program or a movie you have seen recently. Did the character's clothing tell you something about his personality traits? Did clothing help to explain his role in the story? Try describing the character without mentioning clothing.
8. Join the dramatics club or the theater arts group in your school and volunteer for the costume committee. Here is another way to apply what you have learned about personality and clothing. Planning authentic costumes can be as much fun as acting, and there are no lines to memorize. But you will need to understand the personality traits of the characters and choose costumes to fit these traits.

References for Pupils

GEHMAN, RICHARD, "Pennsylvania Amish Folk," *National Geographic*, Vol. 12, No. 2 (August 1965), pp. 227–253.

SUGARMAN, DANIEL A., and ROLLIE HOCHSTEIN, "What It Means To Be A Girl Now!" *Seventeen*, Vol. 25, No. 5, May 1966, pp. 172–173, 254–257.

References for Teachers

"Clothing Concepts—A New Approach," *Fashions and Fabrics*, Fall/Winter, 1965, pp. 6–9, J. C. Penney Company, New York.

COMPTON, NORMA, "Significant Ideas for Textiles and Clothing from Social Psychology," in *Proceedings of National Meeting, College Teachers of Textiles and Clothing, Detroit, Michigan, June 18–20, 1964,* pp. 34–37.

DOUTY, HELEN I., "Influences of Clothing on Perception of Persons," *Journal of Home Economics*, Vol. 55, No. 3 (March 1963), pp. 197–202.

ERWIN, MABEL D., and LILA A. KINCHEN, *Clothing for Moderns*, Third Edition. The Macmillan Company, New York, 1964. Chapter 5, "One World of Women and Dress"; Chapter 3, "Toward a Philosophy of Dress."

EVANS, S. EVELYN, "Motivations Underlying Clothing Selection and Wearing," *Journal of Home Economics*, Vol. 56, No. 10 (December 1964), pp. 739–743.

GEHMAN, RICHARD, "Pennsylvania Amish Folk," *National Geographic*, Vol. 12, No. 2 (August 1965), pp. 227–253.

KEANE, HELEN FAITH, "Why We Dress as We Do: The Story of Fashion," *Forecast for Home Economists*, Vol. 77, No. 2 (February 1961), pp. 33–39.

LINN, ALICE, "Meanings of Clothing," *Fashions and Fabrics*, Spring/Summer, 1963, p. 13, J. C. Penney Company, New York.

ROACH, MARY ELLEN, and JOANNE BUBOLZ EICHER (editors), *Dress, Adornment, and the Social Order.* John Wiley & Sons., Inc., New York, 1965.

Rosencranz, Mary Lou, "Clothing Symbolism," *Journal of Home Economics*, Vol. 54, No. 1 (January 1962), pp. 18–22.

————, "Social and Psychological Approaches to Clothing Research," *Journal of Home Economics*, Vol. 57, No. 1 (January 1965), pp. 26–29.

Ryan, Mary Shaw, *Clothing: A Study in Human Behavior*. Holt, Rinehart and Winston, Inc., New York, 1966. Of particular interest to junior-high- and high-school teachers should be Part III: "Social-Psychological Aspects of Clothing Related to the Age of the Wearer."

Ryan, Mildred Graves, "Project: Communications," *Practical Forecast*, Vol. 11, No. 7 (March 1966), pp. F-38–F-41.

Sugarman, Daniel A., and Rollie Hochstein, "What It Means To Be A Girl Now!" *Seventeen*, Vol. 25, No. 5 (May 1966), pp. 172–173, 254–257.

Sybers, Ruth, and Mary Ellen Roach, "Clothing and Human Behavior," *Journal of Home Economics*, Vol. 54, No. 3 (March 1962), pp. 184–187.

Tate, Mildred Thurow and Oris Glisson, *Family Clothing*. John Wiley & Sons, Inc., New York, 1961.

UNIT THREE

Your Appearance Doesn't
Depend Just on Clothes

I. What Is an Attractive Appearance?

Your appearance is the total impression you make on others. Attractive clothing can help you create a pleasing appearance, but clothing alone cannot make you an attractive person. What else is there to consider in describing personal appearance? Clothing, health, and behavior affect personal appearance.

Physical attractiveness begins with good health. This can be furthered by the selection of correct foods, by cleanliness, by exercise, and by the way you carry yourself.

Add to these the knowledge and skills of clothing selection and clothing care and you will have resources to develop and sustain high standards in your physical appearance. Part of your task of growing up successfully is to develop personal habits that will help you maintain an attractive appearance throughout life. Maintaining

your physical appearance the way you want it to be will mean lifelong concern for good health, independent food selection, cleanliness, and exercise. To a great extent you can control your appearance through the everyday decisions you make about the things that influence it.

But physical attractiveness is only part of a pleasing personal appearance. Actions and behavior also are part of one's total appearance. Your behavior toward others, and with others, can add or detract from your personal attractiveness.

All these together—your actions, your physical appearance, your clothes—make up your appearance. You feel good to be yourself when your appearance is pleasing to you. You feel good about your appearance when you know that others approve of it, too.

II. The Foods You Need

Ways to improve your appearance can be learned. Let's start with food. The foods you eat every day affect how you look and how you feel. A healthy condition of your skin, eyes, teeth, and hair depends on the foods you eat. Your body weight can be controlled to a great extent by careful selection of food. Energy and enthusiasm are immediate results of good eating practices.

In order to develop sound ideas about eating you need to know the types of foods your body needs. It is easy to learn these four groups of foods and the recommended amounts to eat each day:

1. Milk group—4 or more glasses for teen-agers
2. Meat group—2 or more servings
3. Vegetables and fruits—4 or more servings (include dark-green and yellow vegetables, citrus fruits, and tomatoes.)
4. Breads and cereals—4 or more servings

Foods made with large amounts of milk can provide part of the four glasses of milk you need. If you do not care to drink the total amount of milk you need, good substitutes are cheese, ice cream, ice milk, and puddings made with milk.

You need two or more servings daily from the meat group. Traditionally the "main dishes" of many meals consist of foods from this group. Lean meats, fish, poultry, eggs, and cheese supply a wide range of choices, and each of these foods can be prepared in a variety of appetizing ways. Dried beans, peas, nuts, and peanuts are also included in this group. When you eat one of these four choices, add to it a glass of milk, or an egg, or a piece of cheese, or other similar foods, and the combination will probably substitute for one of the other foods in the meat group.

Include a dark-green or a deep-yellow vegetable or yellow fruits in your four servings of vegetables and fruits each day. You can learn to recognize fruits and vegetables which are considered dark green or deep yellow. Apricots, carrots, pumpkin, cantaloupe, mangoes, sweet potatoes,

THE FOUR FOOD GROUPS
Every day you need:

MILK
4 or more glasses
to drink and in foods like these

MEAT and EGGS
2 or more servings
or some of these alternates

Have one dark green or yellow vegetable
VEGETABLES and FRUITS
4 or more servings
Have one citrus fruit

BREAD and CEREALS
4 or more servings
enriched or whole grain

31

squash, and persimmons are deep yellow. Kale, chard, spinach and other leafy greens, and broccoli are considered as dark-green vegetables.

An orange or grapefruit or the juice of either of these fruits will fulfill your need for a serving of citrus fruit every day. A large serving of tomato juice, or tomatoes, or cantaloupe, broccoli, or strawberries would be substitute choices for citrus fruits.

Foods in the breads and cereals group can be recognized in many familiar forms. Classified as bread or cereal products are cooked or ready-to-eat cereals for breakfast, a sandwich bun, a slice of bread, toast, rice, crackers, noodles, macaroni, and spaghetti. You need four or more servings daily. Enriched or whole-grain products are recommended. When you help with the food shopping, read labels. They will tell you whether or not the product is enriched or whole-grain.

Foods from these four groups, eaten in adequate amounts, are the basis of good eating habits.

Additional servings, but not excessive amounts, of the foods in these four groups may be eaten to satisfy your hunger. Eat moderate amounts of other foods, not included in any of the four groups, to satisfy your appetite and to vary meals and snacks. What types of "other" foods to eat is a matter of good judgment based on knowledge. Examples of other foods are spreads such as jams and honey; sauces, nuts, and whipped cream added to ice cream; tomato catsup and relishes used on hamburgers; dressings on salads, and gravies added to potatoes and meat.

People vary in the exact amount of food they need daily. An adequate amount of food for each person depends on age, physical activity, body size and other conditions. Frequent eating of more food than your body can use immediately is likely to result in a gradual gain in excess weight.

A small snack during the day can keep you from becoming so hungry that you overeat at mealtime. You can learn to control the snacks you eat if you plan them as part of the food you need. The result will

Eat this for ENERGY if you prefer but add other foods you need.

32

be better than eating more food than your body can use. A few good snacks that can be counted as part of your body's total daily food needs are a glass of milk, ice cream, raw fruits, or a meat sandwich. Examples of snacks which will not take care of your daily food requirements are carbonated drinks and candy. They do provide immediate energy, however, which your body can use if you are active physically.

Eating too little food can have the immediate effect of leaving you without enough energy, too tired to carry on your activities. Long-time results of eating too little food are lowered resistance to disease and infection, and poor body development.

Study the table which shows desirable weight in relation to height for girls 9 to 18.

Right now, from day to day, you are forming habits of eating particular types of foods in particular quantities. Eating patterns which are based on the foods you need will help you maintain general good health and desirable body proportions.

Desirable Height and Weight for Girls 9 to 18[7]

Age (years)	Weight (pounds)	Height (inches)
9–12	72	55
12–15	103	62
15–18	117	64

If your appearance is important to you, there are two basic ideas about food which you can use immediately:

(1) Include foods from each of the four groups of foods.

(2) Eat the amounts of each type of food you need.

What have you eaten today? Do you usually include foods from each of the four food groups each day? If you have had poor food habits for a long time it may take you a period of time to bring your body to good condition.

III. A Graceful You

There is beauty in the graceful movements of a well-coordinated body. Perhaps this is the reason why almost everyone enjoys seeing the elegant actions of a ballet dancer, an accomplished skater, or a relaxed hiker who strides along effortlessly.

No one is born with the ability to move about gracefully. A baby's first attempts at crawling and walking may be enthusiastic but they are not graceful. In fact, you may have noticed that a young child's movements appear awkward until he learns how to control his arms and legs. From an awkward beginning like this, the skater, the dancer, and the hiker had to learn to be

graceful before others admired their expert body coordination.

Just as important as grace of movement is the grace with which one holds one's body when at rest. "Posture" is the word used to describe the way you hold and control your body when you stand or sit, walk or otherwise move about in the course of your daily activities. How is *your* posture? How was it before you straightened up in your chair just now? Take a careful look at your usual posture and see whether or

[7] Figures from Food and Nutrition Board, National Academy of Sciences—National Research Council. Recommended Daily Dietary Allowances, 1963.

33

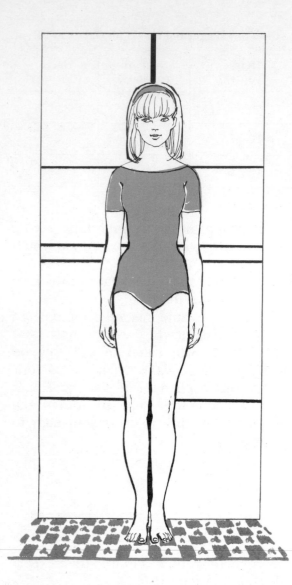
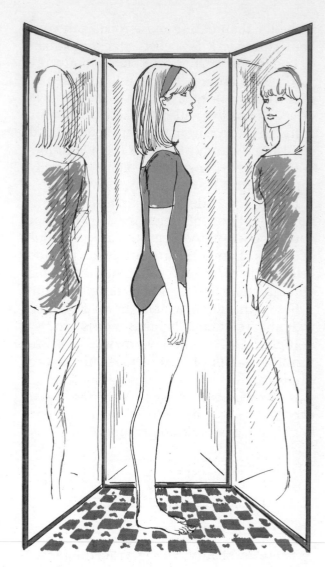

not it is an asset to your appearance. Here are two easy ways to analyze your standing and sitting posture right in the classroom. Pairs or groups will need to cooperate to carry out these simple procedures.

Try this method first. Align your body with vertical and horizontal lines in the room. A window or chalk-board frame, if available, will provide straight lines. Or a committee could draw, on a large sheet of white paper, several horizontal black lines. Space the lines at approximately shoulder, waist, hip, and knee level. Use a yardstick to make the lines parallel with each other and exactly horizontal on the paper. Also, draw a vertical line down the center of the sheet. Colored Scotch tape might be used to make the lines wider and darker so that they can be seen easily. Stand so that you align your body with the vertical line and the horizontal lines. Both front view and side view may be checked this way. Partners can help each other answer these questions:

1. Are my shoulders and head centered over the rest of my body?

34

2. Are my shoulders level—parallel with the horizontal line?

3. Are my shoulders aligned directly over my waist?

4. Is my waistline level—parallel with the horizontal line?

5. Is my waist centered over my hips?

6. Is my hipline level, with neither hip higher than the other—parallel with the horizontal line?

7. Are my knees of even height—pointed straight ahead?

8. Are my feet pointed straight ahead?

A second way to analyze your posture requires a full-length, three-way mirror. Or three separate free-standing mirrors can be placed so that both sides of the figure can be viewed as well as the front of the body. We can never actually see ourselves as others do, but this arrangement may give you a good idea of the way you look to others. Answer the questions as you observe yourself in the mirrors.

When you sit, practice posture that would be graceful enough for a portrait. Sit with your hips touching the back of the chair and your neck in line with your upper back. Analyze your sitting posture in the three-way mirror arrangement checking these points:

1. Do my hips touch the back of the chair?

2. Are my head and shoulders centered over my hips?

3. Is my neck in line with my upper back?

4. Do I lean forward from the hips to work at my desk?

5. Are my feet on the floor?

The size and depth of a particular chair will affect your sitting posture. The chair should be of suitable height so that your feet rest comfortably on the floor. Also, the seat of the chair should be of suitable depth so that it is possible for you to sit comfortably with your hips touching the back of the chair.

Your posture shows when you move about as well as when you are standing or sitting. When you walk swing your legs forward from the hip joints, keeping your toes pointing straight ahead and your head and chest high. Practice walking with a light and limber step until it is natural.

35

For good results the exercises should be done five times a week. Try to do all of them without stopping to rest. Perform each exercise correctly to get maximum benefit.

1	Run in Place . .	50 slow
2	Twister	5 each way
3	Robot	20
4	Windmill . . .	10
5	Run in Place . .	50 moderate
6	Wing Stretcher .	15
7	Propeller . . .	10 each way
8	Knee Pushup . .	10
9	Run in Place . .	25 slow, 50 fast, 25 slow
10	Airlift	10
11	Situp	15
12	Sidewinder . .	10 each leg
13	Run in Place . .	50 slow

1–5–9–13—Jog in place, raising each foot at least 4″ off floor. Count one repetition each time left foot strikes floor.

2—**Starting position:** Stand erect, hands on hips, feet shoulder-width apart. **Action:** Count 1—bend forward from waist. Count 2—Twist trunk to right. Count 3—Bend trunk backward. Count 4—Twist trunk to left. Repeat specified number of times.

3—**Starting position:** Stand erect, hands on hips, feet shoulder-width apart. **Action:** Count 1—Bend trunk to right, reaching hand as far down right leg as possible. Count 2—Return to starting position. Counts 3 and 4—Same action to left side. Repeat specified number of times.

4—**Starting position:** Stand erect, feet spread apart, hands extended sideward at shoulder level, palms down. **Action:** Count 1—Bend and twist trunk, touching right hand to left toe. Count 2—Return to starting position. Counts 3 and 4—Same action to other side. Repeat specified number of times.

6—Starting position: Stand erect with elbows at shoulder height, hands clinched in front of chest. **Action:** Count 1—Thrust elbows back vigorously without arching back. Keep head up, elbows at shoulder height. Count 2—Return to starting position. Repeat specified number of times.

7—Starting position: Stand erect, arms at sides, feet parallel and 1' apart. **Action:** Swing arms sideward and upward in full arcs, crossing them at height of swing and continuing around to starting position. Count one repetition for each complete revolution. Do specified number of repetitions in one direction, then reverse action.

8—Starting position: Lie face down, legs together, hands on floor under shoulders with fingers pointing straight ahead. Knees should be bent at right angle with feet raised off floor. **Action:** Count 1—Push upper body off floor until arms are fully extended and body is in straight line from head to knees. Count 2—Return to starting position. Repeat specified number of times.

10—Starting position: Stand erect, feet together, arms at sides. **Action:** Count 1—Lift arms sideward and upward while rising on toes and taking a slow, deep breath. Count 2—Exhale slowly while returning to starting position. Repeat specified number of times.

11—Starting position: Lie on back, legs straight and together, arms extended beyond head. **Action:** Count 1—Bring arms forward over head, rolling up to sitting position and sliding hands along legs to grasp ankles. Count 2—Roll back to starting position. Repeat specified number of times.

12—Starting position: Lie on right side, head resting on right arm. **Action:** Count 1—Lift leg as high as possible. Count 2—Lower leg to starting position. Do required number of repetitions, then reverse position and repeat exercise on other side.

37

Tall or short, big or little, you can improve your figure. Proper exercise can help you take pounds off—or put them on where you need them. The following exercises are especially designed to smooth out your figure trouble spots:

For the Bustline

1. The Press
Starting position: Stand or sit erect. Clasp hands, palms together, close to chest. **Action:** Press hands together hard and hold for 6–8 seconds. Repeat three times, resting briefly and breathing deeply between repetitions.

2. Pullover
Starting position: Lie on back with arms extended beyond head. Hold books or other objects of equal weight in hands. **Action:** Count 1—Lift books overhead and down to thighs, keeping arms straight. Count 2—Return slowly to starting position. Repeat 3–6 times.

3. Semaphore
Starting position: Lie on back with arms extended sideward at shoulder level. Hold books or other objects of equal weight in hands. **Action:** Count 1—Lift books to position over body, keeping arms straight. Count 2—Lower slowly to starting position. Repeat 3–6 times.

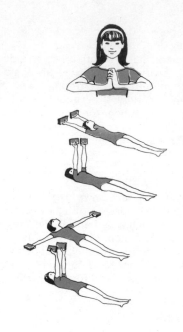

For the Waist

1. Knee Lifts
Starting position: Lie on back with knees slightly bent, feet on floor and arms at sides. **Action:** Count 1—Bring one knee as close as possible to chest, keeping hands on floor. Count 2—Extend leg straight up. Count 3—Bend knee and return to chest. Count 4—Return to starting position. Repeat 5–10 times, alternating legs during exercise.

The double knee lift is done in the same manner, raising both legs at the same time. Do 5–10 repetitions.

2. Crossover
Starting position: Lie on back, arms extended sideward, palms down. **Action:** Count 1—Raise right leg to vertical position and move slowly to left until almost touching floor. Keep arms, head and shoulders on floor. Count 2—Return to starting position. Counts 3 and 4—Same action to other side. Do 5–10 repetitions.

38

For Hips and Thighs

1. Cheerleader
Starting position: Kneel on floor, back straight, hands on hips. **Action:** Count 1—Bend backward as far as possible, keeping knees on floor and body straight. Count 2—Return to starting position. Repeat 10–15 times.

2. Bicycle
Starting position: Lie on back with hips and legs supported by hands. **Action:** Simulate bicycle pumping action with legs. Pump 50–100 times.

3. Ballet Stretch
Starting position: Stand erect with left hand resting on back of chair for support. **Action:** Count 1—Raise right leg sideward as high as possible. Count 2—Return to starting position. Count 3—Swing right leg forward as high as possible. Count 4—Return to starting position. Count 5—Swing right leg back as high as possible. Count 6—Return to starting position. Do 5–10 repetitions, then repeat exercise with left leg.

4. Two-Way Stretch
Starting position: Kneel with hands on floor, back straight. **Action:** Count 1—Arch back, bend head down and bring left knee as close as possible to chin. Count 2—Lift head high and extend left leg as far backward as possible. Repeat 6–10 times with each leg.

For Calves and Ankles

1. Rocker
Starting position: Stand erect, feet together, hands on hips. **Action:** Count 1—Rock back on heels, keeping legs straight and raising toes off floor. Count 2—Rock forward on toes, lifting heels off floor. Repeat 10–20 times.

2. Hop
Starting position: Stand erect, feet close together, hands on hips. **Action:** Hop lightly on both feet 50 times, on the right foot 25 times, on the left foot 25 times, on both feet 50 times.

3. Stemwinder
Starting position: Stand erect, left foot lifted clear of floor. **Action:** Rotate left foot in small circles 20 times. Repeat with right foot.

39

Are you interested in keeping your figure flexible and firm? If so, you will want to learn a few good exercises and use them every day. Several years ago the President of the United States appointed a group of authorities on health and physical fitness to be known as the President's Council on Physical Fitness. They developed exercise plans for girls 12 to 18, boys 12 to 18, and adults. The Council's "Basic Workout" for girls is meant to keep you flexible if you do the exercises regularly. The "Figure-Builders" is a group of exercises especially selected to smooth out your figure trouble spots. (See pages 36–39.)

If you keep your body firm and flexible you are likely to look alert. Also, if your body is aligned symmetrically, you and your clothes will look well together. But you will need to persist if you expect rewards. Any worthwhile achievement requires persistence.

IV. Make the Scrubbed Look Routine

Cleanliness is basic to all other grooming procedures. Keeping clean is a personal maintenance job that needs to be done every day. Take time in your busy schedule to have a daily bath or a shower. After a bath it is well to use a deodorant. Using a deodorant is one of the standards of personal grooming that is generally accepted today. Deodorants come in several forms and are relatively inexpensive when their cost is compared to that of other grooming aids.

In addition to an overall scrub, wash your face thoroughly at least twice each day. On days when you are away from home at school, it may be most convenient to do this in the morning when you get dressed and again in the evening. If you train yourself to keep your hands away from your face, it is likely to stay clean longer between washings. Because your hands become very dirty from everyday activities try to wash them often. When your hands are clean you will find that it is easier to keep your clothes clean, too.

Give some special attention to your teeth in your clean-up schedule. A good toothbrush, dental floss, and some type of dentifrice are necessary tools. Brush your teeth after your evening meal, in the morning after breakfast, and more often if you can manage it. Many drugstores and variety stores sell a type of toothbrush which can be folded into a case and carried in a purse easily. A dental examination once or twice a year is a good investment in both

health and appearance. Only a dentist can provide the professional services that are needed to keep teeth repaired.

In addition to an obvious effect on your appearance, the condition of the teeth is related to your ability to digest food. Dental care is important to your general good health. Some expenses involved in maintaining a good personal appearance may be considered optional, but adequate care of the teeth is a necessary expense.

Your fingernails deserve a place in your grooming schedule. Grooming your nails is called a manicure. A few pieces of inexpensive equipment will help you to do this well. Start with an orangewood stick, an emery board, a fine-grained nail file, and a small hand brush. Scrub under and over your nails with the hand brush. Use the orangewood stick to push back cuticle around the nails carefully. This improves the shape of the nails and helps to keep the cuticle from splitting. Use the fine-grained file and the emery board to shape the nails and maintain them at an attractive length. Nail polish is optional in grooming. If you use it, and if you prefer only a shine on your nails, use a colorless polish or a base coat. If you like a polish with some color, natural or very pale pink colors are good for daytime use such as school. If you use polish, try to keep it repaired. Chipped polish looks as worn out as socks with holes.

Rough hands and sensitive skin may need attention between manicures. Body lotions and hand creams come in a wide range of prices, colors, and fragrances, but the inexpensive ones can reduce roughness and make skin less sensitive.

You will want to care for your feet as carefully as for your hands. When you run about in open sandals your feet show how much you care. Neat feet look better at the swimming pool than scraggly ones. Scrub your feet all over with a brush every time you take a bath. Use your orangewood stick and nail file on your toenails. If your heels become rough in cold weather, use a lotion or cream on them every night. Callouses or sore spots on your feet may indicate that you are not wearing the correct shoe size. Have your shoe size checked carefully each time you purchase shoes. You will feel better all over if your shoes are comfortable.

V. Your Hair Is Special

Your hair is one of your more noticeable features, and it is worth learning how to keep it attractive. Like a daily bath, keeping your hair clean is basic grooming. Because your hair collects perspiration and dust just like the rest of your body it needs to be washed regularly. Hair that needs to be shampooed is apt to appear dull, or it may look streaked and oily. Your scalp may feel irritated. You can soon learn to recognize how often your hair needs to be washed. This may be every three or four days, once a week, or even less frequently. There is no one rule that all girls can follow about how frequently to shampoo their hair.

Regular brushing and combing is necessary hair care, too. If you are interested in having attractive hair, consider a hair brush and comb two of your most valuable possessions.

Hair is likely to appear neater and will be easier to arrange if it has been shaped well by an expert haircutter. Although you may wash and set your hair yourself, you may consider it worthwhile to pay for haircutting services at a beauty shop. Everyone does not have the time and patience to develop skill in cutting hair. If you are not skilled in cutting your own hair, it is usually wise to let a trained person do this. A well-shaped cut is easier for you to wash and set. It may do more for your self-confidence than an extra malt, a movie, a spare lipstick, or even the latest record. Plan to have a haircut as often as needed.

A permanent or end curl may be preferred, or is sometimes needed to improve appearance. A "body-permanent" is meant to add a soft look.

Experimenting to discover hair styles that are becoming to you can be a great deal of fun. Pictures in magazines and newspapers are a source of current ideas for arranging hair. You may want to try arranging your hair several ways in order to

Which Style is Best for You?

Face Shape	Good	Needs Improvement
Oval		
Square		
Round		
Oblong		
Heart		

Try to arrange your hair in several ways so that you can find the most attractive hair style for your height, body proportions, and facial features.

Choose a hair style and frame which will complement the shape of your face.

If your face is square, your hair style should be rounded. Choose an upswept frame at least as wide as the broadest part of your face.

If your face is triangular, your hair style should be widest at the temples, with a poufy crown. Choose a frame that curves up slightly at the bottom and adds width to the top part of your face.

If your face is heart-shaped, your hair style should have fullness at the lower part. Pick a frame with straight lines that is narrower than the width of your forehead.

If your face is oblong, your hair style should have a rounded crown with fullness at the sides. Choose a softly rounded frame that is just as wide as the widest part of your cheekline.

If your face is round, your hair style should have a bouffant crown and sides that are close to the head. Pick a square frame that is wider than the widest part of your cheeks.

43

compare the effects that different hair styles have on your appearance. Your height, your body proportions, your facial features—the impression made by all these is affected by your hair style. A hair style can make the shape of the face more pleasing. Good facial features can be accented and less attractive features can be made less noticeable by your hair arrangement. If you wear glasses, the size and shape of the frames are part of the total design formed by your face and hair. Glasses can become a complementary accent to the face when they are combined well with a flattering hair arrangement.

Ask yourself these questions:

How much time do I have for arranging my hair, especially in the mornings?

How much time am I willing to spend on hair grooming each day?

What expenses are involved in maintaining a particular hair style?

If you have limited time for personal grooming, a simple hair style which requires minimum care will probably be a suitable choice. If you need to limit your grooming expenses, then you can plan a hair style which you can maintain yourself, or which will require minimum upkeep by a trained operator.

VI. What Can Cosmetics Do?

Have you ever stopped to ask yourself, what is a cosmetic? According to the Food and Drug Administration, an agency of the United States government, a cosmetic is "an article (except soap) used for cleansing, beautifying, promoting attractiveness, or altering the appearance."

Many different cosmetic products are available in the stores today. If you prefer to be experimental in learning to use cosmetics, inexpensive brands which are packaged in small amounts are available. Find out how the product is meant to be used. The label on the container will tell you

DIRECTIONS

Wash affected area with mild soap and water. Clear Skin Soap is especially formulated for this purpose. Squeeze a small amount of Clear Skin Medication onto fingertips and apply thinly and evenly to blemished area. Do not rub in. Smooth edges to blend with skin. For larger areas of blackheads or excess oiliness, apply a thin coat over entire area, avoiding eyes and eyelids. Use at least once a day. Wash as directed before each use.

CAUTION: For external use only. Do not get into eyes.

IMPORTANT: Do not use if skin is irritated or sore.

Mixing CREAM with cosmetic bleaches may lead to dangerous skin irritations. For best results, use only CREAM.

Some individuals are allergic or sensitive to certain foods, drugs, or cosmetics. If irritation appears, discontinue use of this cream.

DIRECTIONS FOR USING

The manufacture and sale of this product are under the provisions of the U.S. Food, Drug & Cosmetic Act which requires preliminary skin testing before all applications.

The Preliminary Skin Test

In order to ascertain whether an individual is allergic or supersensitive to this product, the following test should be made before every application, including retouch applications: . . . . . .

Cleanses hair and scalp thoroughly. Suppresses growth of germs when used regularly. Forms hidden, anti-bacterial film . . . Loosens and dissolves flakes and scales . . . Eliminates dandruff associated with dry or oily scalp. Preserves natural "acid mantle" of skin and restores the protective coating . . . Does not irritate. May be used as often as necessary.

IMPORTANT — What you need to know about Curl Relaxer:

Use only if hair and scalp are in good condition. Do not use if hair is dry or brittle, or scalp is sensitive or sore.

If hair has been color treated, you must take the sample test described inside to be certain of good results.

what to expect from the product. The Federal Food and Drug Act requires that the labels on cosmetics be truthful.[8] For best results, it is up to you to follow directions and to use a particular cosmetic product only for the intended use.

Certain cosmetics are meant to add color to the face. Familiar coloring products used today are lipsticks, liquid or cream foundations, and coloring for eyebrows, eyelashes, and eyelids, and brush-on tinted powders. If you are in good health, your young skin probably has an attractive natural color. Adding too much artificial color can detract from the natural beauty of your skin. If you use cosmetic colors moderately, to highlight your natural look, the results are likely to be pleasing.

Ideally, cosmetics are used to enhance a clear and clean skin. If your skin seems to be troubled often with small blemishes you might consider whether you ought to be more careful about cleanliness. Also, check up on your eating habits. Although there are many other conditions which could cause skin blemishes, the foods you eat influence the condition of your skin, just as they influence the general health of your whole body. Your body needs those four basic types of foods.

Here is one more idea to think about. Why is it that when you know you are going to be photographed you carefully comb your hair, refresh your make-up, and straighten your clothing? Photographs preserve a lasting image of you just as you appear. It is only natural to want that photographed image of yourself to be a pleasant image. But how about the images of yourself that aren't photographed—the images of you that people will keep in their minds? Will they all be pleasant ones too?

Knowing how to keep yourself well-groomed, so that you will leave a pleasant image, is more than having skills in washing and setting hair, using cosmetics, and manicuring nails. It involves knowing when and where to use these skills. Wearing hair in rollers and clips, cleaning and polishing fingernails, and applying eye make-up are all appropriate activities when they are carried on in private. But, both friends and strangers may be offended by seeing these same actions carried on in public places. A well-groomed girl keeps her grooming procedures a personal and private matter. She lets others see her *after* she is well-groomed. This is the image of herself she wants others to remember. How is your everyday image?

VII. *Social Skills That Will Help Make You Attractive*

Your behavior toward others, and with others, can add or detract from your appearance. Learning and using some basic social skills is important to your development and to your personal satisfaction. Social skills are habits of thoughtfulness which one uses in associating with other persons. "Manners," "etiquette," and "courtesy" are other terms used to describe social skills.

In addition to the personal satisfaction you receive through courteous associations with other persons, there is still another reason why social skills are important. You are growing up at a time when thousands of homemakers are employed in business

[8] For more information about cosmetics, see *Facts for Consumers—Cosmetics*, FDA Publication No. 26 (1965), Food and Drug Administration, U.S. Department of Health, Education, and Welfare, Washington, D.C.

and industry outside their homes. It is probable that, as a future homemaker, you may spend some years of your adult life as a part-time or full-time employee outside your home. Whether you choose to become a young married homemaker or remain un-married, social skills can help you find the job you want and be successful in it.

Look at some typical school situations where courtesy actions can add a pleasant touch to the day.

Sharing

Every day you share with others—laboratory equipment, or references in the library, or a table in the school cafeteria. Sharing space and equipment means that you may often need to wait patiently for your turn. When your turn comes, work rapidly; then leave the equipment as you would want to find it. Follow the library rules in the use of reference books. Before you leave your table in the school cafeteria, pause long enough to tidy the space you used. Leave laboratory equipment clean. None of these thoughtful actions takes long.

When you share work on an assigned project, remember to do just that. You are showing your social skills when you are an asset, rather than a hindrance, to a partnership. This is probably true in situations away from the classroom too. Deciding how to share the work on a project is part of the fun of working with others. Do your part with the unpleasant tasks as well as with the pleasanter ones. For instance, don't disappear when the time comes to clean up the laboratory after the project has been completed. That would show a lack of courtesy. The ability to share all responsibility in a quiet and gracious way is the mark of a courteous person.

Showing Appreciation

Did someone open the door for you when you arrived at school this morning?

Did someone pick up the pencil you dropped on the stairway?

Did the office clerk give you information you needed?

Did the library assistant find the missing magazine you needed to finish your report?

Did your best friend lend you a fountain pen so you could finish your assignment on time?

Did someone special invite you to have a malt after school?

To each one of these actions the correct response would have been, "Thank you!" Did you show your social skills?

Thoughtful gestures call for a statement of thanks in some form. An immediate thanks, spoken in a direct way, is appro-

priate for most occasions. "Thank you," or "I appreciate your help," or just "Thanks," are all suitable ways to say it.

Paid employees in public places of business who give you prompt assistance in the course of doing their work should be thanked for the help they provide. Sales clerks, elevator operators, bus drivers, and school crossing guards are a few of the persons who appreciate an acknowledgment of their services.

Sometimes a short note rather than a verbal statement is a more appropriate way to show your appreciation. Occasions which call for thank-you notes are these:

1. You have received a gift of money, clothing, books, jewelry, or some other substantial item.
2. You have been an overnight house guest.
3. You have received a special favor. For instance, a friend has given a birthday party for you. An adult friend has helped you find a part-time summer job that you wanted very much.

If you are a member of an organization which is served by adult sponsors or advisors you might want to suggest at one of your meetings that your adult helpers should be remembered with a written note at least once a year. If they do something very special for your organization, such as furnish transportation for an out-of-town trip, a note immediately following the trip would be appropriate.

Being a Successful Guest

Being a guest at a meal can be one of the most enjoyable social occasions if you know what to do.

What to wear? It is difficult to find unbreakable rules, but a dress or skirt-blouse combination is usually a wiser choice than shorts, long pants, or other casual wear. This suggestion applies whether the meal is served at the home of your hostess or in a restaurant. You show regard for your hostess and host if you come in a dress or skirted outfit. If you are invited to the home of a close friend, you could ask about the usual type of dress worn at meals. You will feel confident if you arrive appropriately dressed.

To arrive on time is an unbreakable rule. Only an emergency should keep you from being prompt. If there is a reason that will cause you to be late, it is courteous to call the hostess and tell her how long you will be delayed. If you have been invited to be a guest at a meal to be served in a restaurant, it is possible that a table reservation for a specific time has been made. If the meal is to be at the hostess's home, her plans may have to be changed because of your lateness.

When you arrive, look pleased to be there. A smile is good form in this situation. Accept the greeting of your hostess with a statement such as "It is thoughtful of you to invite me," or "I have been looking forward to coming." If you do not think "on your feet," plan ahead by recalling some interesting incidents you could add to the table conversation.

If the table setting differs from that used in your home, watch your hostess and do as she does about the tableware. Not all families follow the same pattern of table service. Do not make comments which compare the table service or the food served with that in your own home. In a restaurant it is also correct to do as your hostess does about using the tableware.

Accept the food that is served without making negative comments. Families differ in the types of foods they prefer and in the ways they prepare it. The chances are that, because they are serving a meal to company, they are trying to please you. Show that you recognize this by your positive comments. If you learn to accept a wide variety of foods now, you are more likely to be a welcomed guest later on. Expanding your ideas about family customs is one step toward maturity.

Join in the entertainment that has been planned. You may prefer to watch television, but do not mention this if you discover that the plan is to show slides.

The last requirement for being a successful guest is to remember to thank your hostess when you leave. This part will come naturally if you enjoy being a guest.

Making and Receiving Introductions

Introductions should be a good beginning. It is correct for two persons to introduce themselves to each other. Perhaps, one day, you may see a new face sitting next to you in class. Before class begins just say something like this, "My name is Alice Green and I live at 2521 West Tree Street." The new class member will probably respond in about the same way. Then you could quickly add, "I would be glad to show you around after school." These simple self-introductions would help each of you gain a new acquaintance.

How do you introduce two persons of your own age? Present a boy to a girl. To introduce Joe White to Betty Brown you could say, "Betty, this is Joe White, who transferred to our school last week." To Joe you would explain, "Betty put up this bulletin board about the Fall Festival, which you noticed." When you introduce two girls to each other, or two boys to each other, it is correct to present either one first.

48

There are times when you will want to introduce your friends to your parents. Present friends of your own age, both boys and girls, to your parents. Present the girls first:

"Mom and Dad, I want you to meet Betty Brown and Joe White. Betty and Joe are in my 9B English class."

What to say to adults after the introduction? It is enough to say, "How do you do?" until the adult takes the lead in starting the conversation.

Depending on the situation, introductions are often followed by casual conversation. Be alert to new ideas and open-minded about the viewpoints presented by other persons. It is not good taste to ask personal questions of a new acquaintance. And attempting to monopolize the conversation rates as badly as having absolutely nothing to say. You are making progress toward being an expert conversationalist when you can balance your telling and your listening.

Your social skills are a part of your appearance that shows most clearly. The examples have attempted to show that courteous actions are not attention-getting behavior. They are just doing things in the best ways possible. They should not be reserved for special occasions; they can make each day in your life a special day. And good manners grow through everyday use.

Suggested Learning Experiences

Questions and Topics for Discussion

1. What is the definition of an attractive appearance that is presented in this unit? Do you agree with this definition? Why or why not? If not, can you formulate a more accurate or complete definition?
2. Do you believe everyone has the same idea of "attractive appearance"? Support your answer with some examples.
3. How much time is reasonable to spend on grooming each day? How much time do you spend on grooming each day? What are some factors that determine how much time you spend on grooming? Are you satisfied with the results?
4. What proportion of your funds do you spend on beauty aids of all types? Are you satisfied with the results you obtain from the amount of money you spend?
5. What are ways to improve your personal appearance that are described in this unit and which cost little or nothing? Can you think of other low-cost or no-cost ways to improve your appearance?

Individual or Group Reports

6. Read and report to the class the provisions of the Federal Food, Drug, and Cosmetic Act of 1938 which pertain to cosmetics. How do consumers of cosmetics benefit from this act?
7. Compare the cost per ounce of several different brands of a cosmetic product, such as face powder, foundation cream, or cold cream. If the prices differ greatly, how might you account for these differences? Report your conclusions to the class.
8. Have the school nurse moderate a panel on health habits for teen-agers.

Individual or Group Projects

9. Plan meals for two days using the four food groups as a guide. When you include a food on your menu, place the number of the group to which it belongs beside the food you list and circle it. (See menu-planning form, page 31.)

49

10. Prepare a bulletin board or exhibit illustrating easy-to-prepare snacks chosen from foods in the four basic groups.
11. Prepare an exhibit of cosmetics which you consider to be essential for everyday use. For each product prepare a small poster or label telling the purpose of the product and how it is meant to be used.
12. Work in pairs or small groups to analyze your posture. Use a three-way mirror to observe standing and sitting postures. Or, if your classroom does not have a three-way mirror, try aligning your body with vertical and horizontal lines in bookshelves, or chalk board.
13. Observe the sitting posture and standing posture of students in several of your classes. As a result of your observations can you reach any conclusions about the posture habits of your classmates? Base your conclusions on specific examples which you observed.

Home Experiences

14. Practice the posture and coordination exercises described in this unit. Keep a record of your improvement in posture and body coordination.
15. Have a slumber party, and plan to have the group practice these exercises for entertainment.
16. Develop a plan for working toward a personal-appearance goal. (From Future Homemakers of America, *National Program of Work*. Also, see the *National Program of Work* for other ideas about personal development.)

References for Teachers

(*Available from the Superintendent of Documents, U.S. Government Printing Office, Washington, D.C. 20402.)

DAVIES, EVELYN A., *The Elementary School Child and His Posture Patterns*. Appleton-Century-Crofts, New York, 1958.

FARNHAM, MARYNIA F., "The Anxiety of Beauty," *What's New in Home Economics*, Vol. 27, No. 6 (September 1963), pp. 107–108.

*HILL, MARY M., "Nutritional Fitness of Teen-agers," *Nutrition Committee News* (July–August 1963), U.S. Department of Agriculture, Washington, D.C.

HODGES, ROBERT E., and W. A. KREHL, "Nutritional Status of Teen-age Children in Iowa," *Food and Nutrition News*, Vol. 36, No. 9 (June 1965). National Livestock and Meat Board, Chicago.

KENWAY, GENEVA, "How Your Looks Shape Your Life," *Family Circle*, Vol. 67, No. 2 (August 1965), pp. 48–49, 82, 84.

MADDOX, GAYNOR, "Teen-age Overweight Challenging Problem," *Food and Nutrition News*, Vol. 35, No. 9 (June 1964). National Livestock and Meat Board, Chicago.

RUSSELL, SALLYE SUE, "Teen-age Attitudes toward Dress," *What's New in Home Economics*, Vol. 29, No. 2 (February 1965), pp. 32, 48.

Facts for Consumers—Cosmetics, FDA Publication No. 26 (1965), Food and Drug Administration, U.S. Department of Health, Education, and Welfare, Washington, D.C.

Food for Fitness, Leaflet No. 24 (rev. 1964), prepared by Consumer and Food Economics Research Division, Agricultural Research Service, U.S. Department of Agriculture, Washington, D.C.

Future Homemakers of America—National Program of Work, for 1965–1969, Office of Education, U.S. Department of Health, Education, and Welfare, Washington, D.C.

Nutritive Value of Foods (1960), Home and Garden Bulletin No. 72, prepared by the Institute of Home Economics, Agricultural Research Service, U.S. Department of Agriculture, Washington, D.C.

Vim, A Complete Exercise Plan for Girls 12 to 18 (1964). President's Council on Physical Fitness, Washington, D.C.

UNIT FOUR

Making Choices about What to Wear

I. Is It Designed for You?

Every garment can be described in terms of its color, lines, and texture. These three design elements work together to make a garment appear the way it does. Therefore, it is not possible to choose clothing on the basis of either color, or texture, or line without some consideration for the other two. You will need to look carefully at each of these elements in order to understand why some garments appear more pleasing than others.

By observing ways design principles have been used in planning buildings, gardens, and parks, and by thoughtful application of these principles you can develop an appreciation of good design.

Why Learn about Design Principles and Design Elements?

Design principles are guides for using design elements and for understanding how design elements have been used by others in creating designs. Rhythm, balance, emphasis, and proportion are four of these guides. These guides are called design principles because they may be applied in many situations where one wishes to create an attractive design. You may be able to see pleasant results if you remember to use design principles in your activities every day. Try applying these guides to table-setting, food preparation, gardening, wrapping packages, arranging books on shelves, and putting up a bulletin board.

In this book we will consider how these principles may be applied to the design of your clothing, and to the design created by

you and your clothing. With this knowledge you will be able to analyze the design of clothing you select, and to explain why you look especially well in a particular combination of colors, lines, and textures. As a result, you will be more likely to recognize the same principles applied in other garments but perhaps in different ways. You can use this knowledge to make other clothing choices which are pleasing. Your clothing then becomes truly designed for you.

Design Principles

Proportion and scale

The principle of proportion has been applied in creating a design when the space has been divided into parts which are pleasing in size. In other words they look well together.

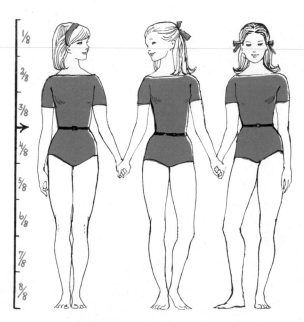

The human body is divided at the waist into two unequal parts. Ideally, the space is proportioned so that three-eighths of the total standing height is spaced from the top of the head to the waist. The remaining five-eighths of the total height is the portion from the waist to the floor. Actually, not all individuals have ideal body proportions. How monotonous our environment would be if everyone looked exactly like everyone else! If the bodice length is long in relation to the length below the waist and to total height, then we say that the person is "long-waisted." If the bodice length is short in relation to the length below the waist and to total height, we say he is "short-waisted."

An individual's height is out of proportion to his weight when he is underweight or overweight. When a person is extremely overweight or underweight his horizontal measurements are not pleasing in relation to his height, or vertical measurement. Regardless of your height, which you cannot control, your body will look well if your weight is kept in good proportion to your height. This may take some real determination on your part, but you will find this is one essential of a well-proportioned figure. Remember, too, that the principle of proportion may be applied to clothing selection to make a less than ideal figure more attractive.

Unequal divisions of space produce more interesting designs than equal divisions of space. Similarly, unequal areas of two colors are more pleasing than two equal amounts. You can apply this idea to clothing if you observe how space is divided by a two-piece outfit. Does the wearer seem to be divided into two equal parts by the outfit? Perhaps if the length of the sweater, blouse, jacket, or skirt were changed slightly the proportions would be more pleasing.

Another way in which the principle of proportion is applied is in relation to scale. We say that objects are scaled or sized "in proportion" to each other when their dimensions are consistent in size. In contrast, objects are "out of proportion" to each other when their dimensions differ greatly in scale. The design of a particular garment is in good proportion to the person wearing it if it is scaled to the size of the person. The size of collars, belts, pockets, buttons, and other details are examples of the principle of proportion applied to clothes. Equally important is the design of the fabric. Depending on its overall size, a plaid, a print, or a stripe will appear either in good proportion to the size of the wearer or it will seem to overwhelm him. Large details look best on persons with large body proportions. Small persons look best when they wear clothing that has been scaled to

smaller figures. Remember to select plaids, prints, and stripes in relation to your figure. Also, the principle of proportion may be applied in choosing hats, jewelry, purses, and other accessories. The total design created by you and your clothes is more likely to be pleasing if you select clothing which is scaled to your body proportions.

These ideas may be summarized by saying that proportion has been used well in creating a design when the space has been divided into areas that are pleasing to see, and when details in the design are consistent in scale. You can develop an appreciation for pleasing proportions in your clothing. With some practice, you will come to recognize divisions of space which look well together. If personal appearance is important to you, the principle of proportion can serve you well. See what a difference it can make.

Balance

The principle of balance has served as a guide in creating a design when the various parts of the design, color, texture, and line, have been arranged so that a feeling of rest or equilibrium results.

Balance in a design may be either formal or informal. The term "symmetrical balance" is sometimes used to describe formal balance. "Symmetrical balance" means equal balance. A design is formally balanced, or symmetrically balanced, when the design is the same on either side of the center.

Informal balance is sometimes called asymmetrical balance. Asymmetrical balance is unequal balance. This means that though each side of the design is equally interesting or important, it does not look exactly like the other side.

54

Color, texture, and line may be arranged to obtain a feeling of balance in a design. For example, when you say that a dress is "too dark" or "too light," you are saying that dark and light values are not balanced. A feeling of balance is produced when large areas of tints are equalized by small areas of either bright colors or shades. Likewise, large areas of neutrals may be balanced by small areas of bright colors. Warm colors can be used to balance cool colors. Usually smaller amounts of warm colors balance larger amounts of cool colors if they are of the same value and intensity. The principle of balance can be applied by adding a bright yellow necklace, belt, or pin to a pale yellow dress. A small area of bright color balances a large area of pale color. A gold satin collar on a dark blue velvet dress gives balance through color, and also through texture contrast. The lustrous texture of the satin collar balances the larger areas of soft but dull texture. A bright red scarf or hat accessorizing a gray coat shows how a large neutral area is balanced by a smaller area of intense color. These examples illustrate how the color and texture in accessories can add to the feeling of balance in your clothing through their colors, textures, and lines. Generally, this rule about areas may be used to achieve a pleasing balance of color: use duller, less intense colors in large areas, and bright, intense colors in small areas.

Often you will find that all one texture in an outfit is monotonous and that two or more different textures combined in an outfit make it more interesting. Contrasting textures may be used together in different amounts to produce a harmonious design. You also need to consider colors in deciding how to combine different textures to obtain balance. (See "Texture" pages 68–70.)

Lines can give balance to clothing designs, too. Some variety in line adds interest to clothing, just as different colors and textures do. Several short lines may balance one longer line. Two or more small shapes may balance a similar but larger shape. A few thin lines may balance one thick line. Vertical lines may be used to balance horizontal lines. Practice analyzing balance in your environment every day. You will soon discover how lines create balance in designs.

Emphasis

Emphasis is present in a design when your attention is attracted to a highlight in the design. It is the center of interest because it predominates over the rest of the design.

Emphasis can be created by contrasting texture, color, and line and by using unusual shape, texture, and color. Lace, a decorative fabric, immediately becomes a center of interest on a plain fabric. Fur, metallic fabrics, and vinyl-coated fabrics can make accents when used in small amounts. Scallops, fringes, and ruffles attract attention. Repetition can create emphasis. A neckline which repeats the shape of the face will accent it. One outstanding color in a print, plaid, or striped fabric may be skillfully accented by repeating the color in a belt or scarf.

Attractive lines in a particular garment may become the predominating idea in the design if they are outlined for emphasis. Or an interestingly shaped collar may serve as the central attraction on a particular dress if this is the thing you remember about it.

Usually one main emphasis in a design is enough. When several types of lines, or textures, or colors are accented in a design the result is likely to look cluttered. When several things are given equal emphasis nothing seems to be emphasized.

Analyze the design of a garment or an outfit and ask yourself some questions about emphasis. How has emphasis been created? Where is the accent located? Is attention drawn to the accented area? Is this type of emphasis becoming to me?

Which accent would be most becoming to you in this sweater-and-slacks outfit? In the first illustration (1) the colorful trim at the bottom edge of the sweater falls near the hipline. Although the collar is emphasized too, your eye is attracted first to the larger accented area at the hipline.

In a second version of the same outfit (2) the collar becomes the focal point. A center of interest high on the figure, by drawing your eye upward, tends to create an illusion of height. Emphasis at the neckline is especially advantageous to girls who want to appear taller. Quite the opposite is true for the tall girl who wants to appear shorter. She may want to make still another variation of this outfit by choosing a contrasting sweater and slacks (3). The sharp line where the two parts of the outfit meet will serve as a dividing mark to shorten the appearance of the tall figure. To create a sharp contrast either the slacks or the sweater may be accentuated by choosing vivid colors.

These ideas about emphasis may be summarized by saying that either line, or color, or texture may be used to create accent in a design. Accent can be produced either by contrast or repetition, or can be created by unusual color and texture. A design has no accent when all parts of the design are given equal emphasis. In clothing designs accents may be located so that they are becoming to the wearer.

Rhythm

A design has rhythm when the line, color, and textures have been arranged in an orderly way so that your eye moves easily from one part of the design to another. Pleasing rhythm holds a design together. It helps you see how different parts of the design are related. For example, rhythm may be created in a dress with three front panels and a contrasting inset at the neckline. The structural lines of the panels guide the eye easily to the inset, which is the point of emphasis. In other words rhythm has held the design of the dress together by helping you relate different parts.

Rhythm may be created by the repetition of lines and shapes. In clothing designs repetition of shapes may be carried out in several ways. The rounded edge of a jacket may be repeated at the neckline in rounded lapels. The shape of the lapels may be duplicated in cuffs or pocket tabs. Repetition of lines to produce rhythm may be seen in a raincoat with a front panel. The structural lines of the seams, the front opening edge, the pockets constructed in the seams are all vertical lines leading the eye upward and downward. Horizontal lines may be repeated in a tiered skirt and a rounded neckline leading the eye across. These similar lines create rhythm by relating all parts of the design.

The repetition of similar shapes helps to relate the parts of a design. In a suit or coat you may see rhythm produced by repetition of the collar shape in decorative tabs or pockets. The similar shapes help to relate the parts of the design although the two parts are of different size.

Repetition of color may also be used to create rhythm in either a dress or a two-

lines. In other words, when you wear a plaid skirt choose a blouse or shirt with straight lines. The straight lines will help relate your bodice with the straight lines in your plaid skirt.

These ideas may be summarized by saying that rhythm is an orderly arrangement of the different parts of a design which helps to relate them and hold the design together. When there is pleasing rhythm in a design your attention moves easily about the design. Rhythm may be created by repetition of line, color, and texture, and through the repetition of the same shape though in different sizes.

Design Elements

Color

Colors have characteristics just as you do. You have a name and physical features by which others can identify you and distinguish you from other persons. Colors have names and physical features too.

The term *"hue"* designates a color's name. Note the names of the twelve colors shown on the color wheel. Yellow, blue, and red are known as primary colors because from these other colors can be made; but, no other colors can be combined to form these three colors. Green, orange, and violet are known as secondary colors, or binary colors. Each secondary color is a combination of equal parts of the primary colors on either side of it. Green, for example, is made from blue and yellow in equal quantities. Violet is a mixture of red and blue. How are the other secondary colors formed?

The other hues on the color wheel are known as intermediate, or tertiary, colors. Again, as with secondary colors, each is formed from a combination of the hues on either side of it. Orange and red merge to

piece outfit. A striped shirt and slacks may be combined in a rhythmic way if the slacks carry out the predominant color of the shirt. A predominant color helps to relate the two areas and carry the eye easily from the slacks to the shirt. By using this method a tall girl could use a contrasting bodice to make her appear shorter and still achieve rhythm in the combination. Try to analyze garments or outfits to discover how colors have been repeated to create rhythm.

Plaids, stripes, and figured fabrics may add to or detract from rhythm in clothing design. A vertically-striped fabric in a dress can create rhythm by the repetition of the upward and downward lines. However if the stripes are poorly matched the rhythm will be broken at the place where the lines fail to meet. A girl who would like to achieve rhythm in vertical stripes to make her appear thinner will choose only those dresses in which stripes are perfectly matched.

You can understand how rhythm may be achieved with plaids when you remember that plaids are made up of straight form red-orange. Blue-green results from a mixture of green and blue. Note the other combinations which are needed to form the other intermediates.

Black, gray, and white are called neutrals. They are not hues, but they may be used in combination with the hues found on the color wheel to make interesting harmonies of color.

When you say, "a tint of blue" or "a shade of blue," you are describing *value* differences in blue. Value refers to the lightness or darkness of a color. A color with a large amount of white in it is called a tint. The term "pastel" is also used to describe a color of light value. A color which contains a large amount of black is called a shade. Many different tints and shades of a color can be formed by varying the amount of white or black in the color. Red becomes pink when white is

added and becomes cranberry-red when black is added. When you think of value apart from color, black is on one end of a scale and white is on the other. Study the value scale, which shows variations of lightness and darkness as we see them in clothing.

Colors with similar values usually are easy to combine. They seem to blend easily into a harmonious design. Light tints combine easily with other light tints; dark shades merge easily with other dark shades. However, some difference in value may add interest to clothing design.

Extreme values contrast. Therefore, if you prefer a contrasting appearance in the way you dress, wear widely different values together. A black skirt worn with a white blouse is an example of extreme contrast in value. Another example of contrast is a pale lilac blouse worn with a dark

Value scale 10%

middle

100%

size some features and move the eye away from others. Variety in value, if planned carefully, can add to the attractiveness of clothing.

Intensity describes the amount of color present. A particular color's intensity can be described as bright or dull. A bright hue has more color than a dull hue, though they may be equally beautiful. A bright red may be as beautiful as a dull red.

How may color intensity affect your clothing choices? Wearing bright colors may lift your spirits on a gloomy day. Vivid colors are youthful; therefore, they seem appropriate for persons of any age who have youthful characteristics. However, you may find it very tiring to wear only bright colors unless you have many changes of clothing in your wardrobe. Because bright colors are readily seen they are more likely to be remembered. Therefore, you may want to buy the garments that you plan to wear longest, such as coats, in less intense colors. Of course, this is a personal preference like so many other clothing choices.

Bright colors tend to make an area look larger than it actually is. This suggests that less intense colors would be better if you do not wish to emphasize the size of an area. Large feet may look even larger in bright green shoes. On the other hand, a bright color may add some attractive roundness to a figure that is too thin.

You may want to use bright colors in small amounts to accent larger areas of dull colors. For instance, add some youthful sparkle to a charcoal coat by wearing a bright gold hat with it. Remember, too, that because bright colors are noticed easily they will draw attention to the areas where they are placed. Therefore, locate vivid accents in areas you want to emphasize. Like the bright gold hat, a collar, a necklace, or a pin worn near the neckline

purple skirt. Strong value contrasts in clothing call attention to height and proportions. This is because the space is clearly broken up into two or more parts. On a petite figure several extreme value contrasts worn together may result in a cluttered look. Close values of one hue would be a better choice for a small figure.

It is possible to call attention to a particular part of an outfit through value contrasts. A small waist can be accented by a contrasting belt. A light collar on a dress of medium to dark value will draw attention to the face. Your accessories, such as purses and shoes, are more quickly seen when value contrast sets them apart from the rest of your clothing.

To summarize we could say that close values blend easily, but that strong contrast results when two extreme values are combined. Contrasts in values may empha-

60

will draw attention to the face and hair. You want to consider your complexion and hair coloring when you choose bright accents to be worn near your face.

We can summarize by saying that bright colors are lively and youthful in feeling. They are easily seen, and therefore they tend to increase the size of an area and to attract attention to it. If you prefer not to draw attention to large areas, bright colors can still serve you as cheerful accents in smaller areas.

A *color harmony* is a combination of colors which harmonize. A group of colors put together at random will be a collection of colors, but they will not necessarily be a color harmony. A harmonious color combination is pleasant to see, just as a harmonious combination of musical sounds is pleasant to hear. In order to make harmonious color combinations you will need some knowledge of the ways colors can be combined successfully.

Do not think of color harmonies as meaning only various combinations of the twelve colors on the color wheel at their fullest intensity and medium value. The many tints and shades of each hue make possible an endless variety of color harmonies. Different intensities of each hue can be used. Color schemes using only bright colors or only dull colors tend to be monotonous. Combinations using both bright and dull intensities are usually more interesting.

When several values and intensities of one color are harmoniously combined a *monochromatic*, or one-color, *harmony* is formed. Tints may be combined with other tints. Shades may be combined with other shades. Tints may be combined with shades. A monochromatic design may involve much contrast and variation but, regardless of the degree of contrast only one hue is varied to create the design.

An *adjacent color harmony* results when two or more colors are combined which have one hue in common. Blue and blue-green form an adjacent color harmony; so do yellow and yellow-green. As you study the color wheel you will see that adjacent color schemes are formed by combining colors next to each other on the color wheel. Adjacent color schemes are more likely to be harmonious combinations when the colors used are of the same value and intensity.

Colors directly opposite each other on the color wheel are called complements of each other. A *complementary harmony* results when two complements are used together. Each color has only one complement. Values and intensities of complementary colors can be varied in many ways to form imaginative combinations. Usually, dulled complementary colors form more pleasing combinations than complements used together at their fullest intensities. These are complementary harmonies: blue-violet and yellow-orange; blue and orange; blue-green and red-orange; green and red; yellow-green and red-violet; yellow and violet.

A *split-complementary color harmony* is a variation of a complementary color scheme. To get a split-complementary harmony, select two complementary colors; then instead of combining these two colors, combine the two colors on either side of one of the complements with the other complement.

A *triad color harmony* results when three colors equally distant on the color wheel are combined. A "triadic color scheme" is another term used in referring to this type of three-color harmony. Suitable tints or shades of the primaries—red, yellow, and blue—can be used to form a triadic color scheme. The secondary colors —violet, orange, and green—will also form

Monochromatic

Split complementary

Triad

red violet
yellow orange
blue green

Complementary

accented Neutral

a triad color harmony. If your eye is moving around the color wheel, you have already discovered that a combination of three equally distant intermediates is another source of this type of color harmony. Two combinations of intermediates are possible. The first combination includes red-violet, yellow-orange, and blue-green. The second combination which results in a triad color scheme includes blue-violet, red-orange, and yellow-green.

When a large area of one or more of the neutrals is used with a small area of a bright color, an *accented-neutral color scheme* results. A gray coat with a bright green scarf is an example of this. Also, a black-and-white-checked suit with a red scarf is an accented-neutral color scheme. Many interesting clothing combinations are possible with neutrals and vivid colors.

How *colors affect the way you feel*. Like yourself, colors have personality traits as well as physical characteristics. These personality characteristics of colors might be described as the impressions they make on individuals. Colors can cause you to feel warm or cool, gloomy or happy, excited or relaxed. Your imagination associates colors you see with your past experiences. For example, yellow, red, and orange are called warm colors. Perhaps this is so because at various times during the day, from sunrise to sunset, the sun may appear to be yellow, or red, or orange. Also, we may associate the real warmth of fire with the yellow, red, and orange that we see in the flames. Because warm colors remind us of sunlight and warmth they seem cheerful and exciting. Warm colors are easily noticed: perhaps this is why they cause an object to seem closer and larger than it actually is.

Because all of us have different past experiences, a color may also suggest different things to each of us.

Yellow may mean different things like this:

> "Yellow is the color of the sun
> The feeling of fun
> The yolk of an egg
> A duck's bill
> A canary bird
> And a daffodil."[9]

In contrast to the warm hues, blue is a cool color, and it suggests distance in both feeling and space.

> "Blue is the color of the sky
> Without a cloud
> Cool, distant, beautiful
> And proud."[10]

Green too is a cool color, especially when a small amount of blue is blended with it. It suggests quietness, coolness, and space, like this:

> "Green is the grass
> And the leaves of trees
> Green is the smell
> Of a country breeze . . .
> Green is a coolness
> You get in the shade
> Of the tall old woods
> Where the moss is made."[11]

Colors may suggest weight or lack of weight. In large amounts, black appears heavy. The same effect of heaviness may be felt in large areas of deep shades of violet, brown, red, or blue. White and the palest tints of hues suggest lightness and youth.

If you know how you want to appear, then this idea will be useful when you choose clothes for yourself.

[9] Excerpts from "What is Yellow?," "What is Blue?," and "What is Green?," copyright © 1961 by Mary Le Duc O'Neill, and from "What is Black?," copyright © 1960 by The Curtis Publishing Company, from the book, *Hailstones and Halibut Bones* by Mary O'Neill. Reprinted by permission of Doubleday & Company, Inc.
[10] *Ibid.*, p. 27.
[11] *Ibid.*, p. 51.

Black and dark shades may bring thoughts of dignity, mystery, and age. To some persons they may even seem gloomy and depressing. Black has a mysterious beauty:

> "Black is beauty
> In its deepest form,
> The darkest cloud
> In a thunderstorm."[12]

Line

How can lines be described? Lines have direction, width, and length. Direction in clothing lines can be vertical, horizontal, diagonal, or curved. Vertical lines direct the attention up and down. Continuous vertical lines suggest height and slenderness. Horizontal lines direct attention across an area and usually make the area appear wider, though the total effect, of course, depends on the width of the lines and the intensity of the colors. Curved lines tend to add softness and feminity to a design. Softly curved collars, pockets, and seam lines give a feminine feeling to a garment. In contrast to curved lines, strong diagonal

lines tend to give a dramatic appearance to a garment. Diagonal lines suggest action. Such lines look harmonious on persons with strong coloring and vivacious personalities. Otherwise, the design may appear to overpower the person.

Lines have width, as well as direction. A narrow line will give a different effect from that of a wide line in a dress design. A wide belt will accent a waistline, whereas a narrow belt may go almost unnoticed. Narrow pin stripes in a fabric may give a different feeling to a design from that given by wide, dramatic stripes, although both kinds of stripes may form vertical lines in a dress.

The length of design lines affects the total appearance of a garment. Long, vertical lines, slightly tapered at the waist, direct attention upward, giving a feeling of height. Short lines may break up a large area, but many short lines in a small area may look cluttered.

The lines in a garment contribute to good proportion in the design when the length and width of the lines are pleasing in relation to the area in which they are used. The direction of lines in a garment contributes to harmony in the design when they are consistent with the outline, or silhouette, of the garment.

The shape formed by the outer lines of your clothing is called a *silhouette*. Your silhouette is probably the most important design line in your clothing because it is this general outline of your clothes that others notice first. Your silhouette reveals structural details of your garment, such as the shape of your skirt, the location of the waistline, the style of your sleeves, and the length of your skirt. The fit of clothes, whether they are unbecomingly tight or too loose or just right, can be seen in a sil-

[12] *Ibid.,* p. 21.

houette. The silhouette encloses all other design lines in an outfit. The design lines of an outfit are harmonious when all the lines and shapes in the outfit are related to the silhouette. Study your shadow and you will be able to see the general shape of the clothes you are wearing.

The structural lines of a garment give it shape and help to form the silhouette. Seams and darts are structural lines because they help to shape the garment. These structural lines can be changed if necessary, to improve the fit and design of a garment.

Other lines are decorative only and are meant to add to the attractiveness of the garment. Of course, structural lines in a becoming design should be attractive, too. In a harmonious design decorative lines are related to the silhouette. Decorative lines can be used to accent structural lines through repetition or contrast. For example, an attractive neckline can be outlined with piping of the same color as the fabric. Or the shape of the neckline may be accented with a contrasting collar.

Decorative lines in clothing can be seen in the fabric as well as in the shapes in a garment. The lines in plaids, stripes, and figured fabrics become a part of a garment's design. These lines have direction, width, and length. You should choose appropriate design lines in the fabric as well as in the structural lines of the garment.

The lines in plaid fabrics may be accented by contrast when not all parts of the garment are cut the same way. Also stripes may be accented by contrasting direction of the line.

When analyzing the total design of a garment, look at lines in the fabric in relation to both the shape of the silhouette and the decorative lines. Straight structural lines in a garment will combine more harmoniously with the straight lines of stripes and plaids than with curved lines.

What are the best lines for you? How can you choose design lines that will accent your best features and modify the appearance of others? You can determine becoming clothing lines by analyzing your body shape and facial features.

The Shape of Your Face Can Be Accented or De-emphasized by Lines in Your Clothing

Face shapes	How to accent the shape of the face	How to modify appearance of facial shape
1. Oval	This is considered an ideal face shape. You may be interested in accenting it. Repeat the oval in the necklines you wear. Wear oval jewelry in bright colors and strong contrasts.	An oval-shaped face may be modified by wearing a contrasting neckline. These would include round, square, U- or V-shaped necklines.
2. Round	Repeat the round shape in the necklines you wear. In this case wear rounded collars, such as Peter Pan collars, or stand-ing collars that will emphasize the roundness by contrast.	If you are trying to achieve a more oval-shaped face, wear V necklines, long, pointed collars, and narrow lapels. Long necklaces, rather than choker necklaces, make the face seem longer.
3. Square	Choose square necklines which outline the squareness of your face. Accent a square face by wearing high round collars for contrast.	V- or U-shaped necklines help to soften the square line of a face. The sharp V or U shapes may be softened with either scallops or notches to break the severe lines.
4. Oblong (long, thin)	High round necklines are in such extreme contrast to an oblong face that the length of the face seems to be emphasized. Necklines that follow the same vertical line of the face, such as V necklines and pointed collars, are accents. Strong vertical lines in a dress or suit will do this also.	To modify a long thin face you want to add width to the face. This can be done with wide collars, softly rounded collars, or rolling collars. A horizontal line near the neckline can make the long face seem more oval.
5. Heart	A heart-shaped face is very slim near the jaw line. A V neckline will reflect the shape of the face.	A wide, round neckline makes the lower half of the face seem wider or more oval. Stand-away collars or ruffles also add width.
6. Long neck	If you wish to accent your long neck, choose garments that have V necklines. Blouses with narrow lapel collars or collars set off from the neck emphasize a long neck.	To make your neck seem shorter wear stand-up collars and high-neckline designs. Ascots, scarves, and necklines with horizontal emphasis conceal a long neck. Turtle-neck designs are meant for long necks. Bulky fabrics can cover a long neck.
7. Short neck	Emphasis around the neck will help to shorten it. A short neck seems shorter in choker-style necklaces, standing collars such as turtle-neck sweaters, and wide lapels.	A short neck will look longer when a garment with narrow lapels or a V neckline is worn. Some garments, especially in suits where the jacket closes with a long line and opens into a V neckline, have a lengthening effect. Collarless dresses and suits are appropriate if the back neckline is low.

Try first to select an attractive silhouette as all other lines should be related to this for a harmonious effect. Your body proportions can be emphasized by the outline of your clothing, or, on the other hand, they can be camouflaged or made less noticeable. How tall you appear to be is affected by the silhouette you create. If you want to accent tallness, choose a slim silhouette with vertical lines predominating so that your height is emphasized through repetition of the vertical lines of your figure. A silhouette with horizontal lines predominating will modify the appearance of a tall figure, making it appear shorter, by contrasting with the vertical body lines and emphasizing width.

A girl who is short in stature and plump has figure proportions which cause her to appear more horizontal than vertical. Wearing horizontal lines would only repeat the horizontal lines of her figure. Carefully chosen clothing with predominating vertical lines will tend to distract from the horizontal lines of her figure. Since silhouette reveals the fit of clothing, a chubby figure will be emphasized if clothing is fitted too closely to the body. Regardless of whether horizontal or vertical lines predominate, an attractive silhouette depends on good fit.

The shape of your face and the length of your neck can be either accented or de-emphasized by the lines and shapes you wear near your face. Note that the previous statement refers only to de-emphasizing the shape of your face. This does not mean directing attention away from the face. Your face is the most important indication of personality that you have, and it should be your center of interest. Facial shapes vary. Hereditary traits cause some individuals' faces to be designed more artistically than those of others. However, almost anyone who wants to make the ef-

67

fort can modify the appearance of a less artistically designed face through good clothing choices.

The outline shape of a face is not the only feature worth accenting. Colorful eyes, or an alert expression, or attractive teeth, or a distinctive mouth with its characteristic smile are a few other facial features that deserve to be highlighted.

Perhaps it is your goal, when you choose clothing, to accent naturally good facial lines. Or you may wish to modify the appearance of your facial contours through careful selection of the lines in your clothing. Study the chart which shows ways to accomplish either outcome. Although the chart calls attention to the shape of the face, some of the suggestions under "to accent" could emphasize other distinctive features of the face as well as shape.

Line is only one design element that can be used to either accent or de-emphasize facial shape. Color and texture also can sometimes be used in subtle ways to achieve this result. It is well to remember that few statements about the use of line can be made without some exceptions.

Texture

How can texture be described? You can see and feel texture, and sometimes you can even hear texture as it passes by. Texture refers to characteristics which are found on the surface of a fabric. The fiber from which a particular fabric is made is one reason why that fabric looks and feels the way it does. However, since manufactured fibers can be made to look and feel very much like natural fibers you will need to read the label to be sure of fiber content. Special fabric finishes and the methods by which fabrics are constructed are other factors which result in the enormous variety of textures we have available today.

Sweaters may be loopy, fuzzy, soft, hairy, furry, downy, woolly, or shaggy.

A satin bow is sleek and shiny.

Very special party dresses may be frothy, filmy, lacey, frilly, airy, or delicate.

A corduroy jacket is ribbed, ridged, or grooved. A pique blouse also is ridged and grooved.

Winter skirts may be pebbly, rough, bumpy, nubby, coarse, scratchy, or soft.

A summer dress of seersucker is crinkly and crisp; a summer dress of chambray is soft and smooth.

When you look at a particular fabric you can tell whether it is smooth or rough, shiny or dull, crisp or soft, shaggy or sleek, sheer or thick. When you handle fabrics you can feel characteristics that are present, such as the amount of crispness, or softness, or coarseness, or shagginess, or slipperiness, or thickness. Some textures have characteristic sounds. Have you ever heard a crisp fabric rustle? Taffeta ruffles rustle. A crisply starched cotton apron rustles. Crisp dry leaves rustle. Have you heard the soft swishing sound of a sleek fabric? A formal satin dress swishes. Soft gathers of silk swish. Snow in the wind swishes. Can you describe other fabric sounds you have heard?

You can learn to select textures that are becoming to the lines of your figure. Like color and line, texture in clothing cannot be considered by itself in analyzing clothing. However, there are a few guides which will help you understand effects that textures may have on your appearance. Thick, or shaggy, or fuzzy, or wrinkled textures seem to add to body size because of their own bulkiness. Also, sleek, or glossy, or shiny textures tend to increase body size because a shiny surface reflects more light than a dull surface. In contrast, smooth but not shiny textures minimize body size.

Smooth, dull fabrics reflect less light than glossy fabrics, and add little additional bulk to body size.

Textures affect the way colors look on you. Colors seem lighter and brighter in shiny textures. For instance, red in a glossy satin blouse would seem to be a brighter and more intense red than red of the same value and intensity in a fuzzy sweater. You can apply this knowledge when selecting shiny fabrics by choosing colors that are slightly less intense and in somewhat darker values than those you would choose in rough-textured fabrics. A pleasing combination of two or more textures may add interest, through variety, to your clothing. A monochromatic color scheme, particularly, would be dull indeed without some texture variations.

Decide on textures you want in your major clothing items first. You expect to wear your coats, separates, and dresses often. The textures you choose will be flattering to your figure if you stop to consider your body proportions and the ways that texture affects your figure. After you have selected major items, plan your accessories to harmonize with them. Your shoes, hats, jewelry, and purses have characteristic textures which can be seen, felt, and described. Experiment in putting together the various textures you already own. You can show your originality by creating attractive texture harmonies in the clothing you wear. Furthermore, you are learning about good design in your clothing when you attempt to apply design principles in the way you use texture, color, and line.

Whether or not particular clothing is appropriate for a specific time and place is partly determined by texture. Different textures are suitable for different situa-

tions. Delicate, airy textures are appropriate at social events with a light, airy mood. Firm, rough, coarse textures are right for school and sports events. They have a durable feeling which assures us that they are ready for action.

As the weather changes we choose fabrics to suit these conditions. In addition to providing protection against low temperatures, thick, furry, fuzzy fabrics look appropriate during cold weather. These same textures would be not only uncomfortable on a warm summer day but out of place.

These ideas may be summarized by saying that pleasing combinations of textures add interest to the design of your clothing. In addition, a particular texture is attractive on you when it is becoming to the lines of your figure. Texture, as well as color and line, helps to determine the appropriatenesss of clothing for particular occasions.

Whenever you buy clothes for yourself, consider texture as well as color. Although the color may be all right for you, the texture may be a poor choice for your characteristics. Handle the fabric carefully to feel the texture. Try on the garment to see how the texture affects your appearance and consider how you would feel about wearing it. Your decision about what to wear will improve as you study textures and how they affect you. Furthermore, you will be able to describe textures accurately and explain your preferences concerning textures as you increase your vocabulary to include terms which describe textures.

Terms Which Describe Textures[13]

airy	flexible	pebbly	shirred
bumpy	frilly	prickly	silky
coarse	furry	quilted	sleek
crinkly	fuzzy	ribbed	smooth
crisp	glossy	ridged	solid
curly	grooved	rigid	spongy
delicate	hairy	rough	stiff
dense	harsh	satiny	tough
downy	lacy	scaly	thorny
feathery	leathery	scratchy	velvety
filmy	lumpy	shaggy	wavy
fine	metallic	sheer	waxy
firm	nubby	shiny	woody
			woolly

[13] Selected from Anna Hong Rutt, *Home Furnishings,* Corrected Second Edition (John Wiley and Sons, Inc., New York, 1961), p. 13.

70

What Can Color, Line, and Texture Do for You?

What can color, line, and texture do for you? That depends on what you want them to do. Design elements may be chosen to improve the appearance of your body proportions. They can be chosen to accent your youthful personality traits. You can extend your wardrobe and improve your personal image if you make color, line, and texture work for you.

Do you want to make slim body proportions appear larger? Use this combination of color, texture, and line: a warm color—red, orange, yellow; a bright color; a shiny fabric, or a thick or bulky fabric; pleats, gathers, or layers of fabrics in a non-bulky fabric.

Do you want to de-emphasize body size, or make chubby proportions seem slimmer? Try this combination of combination of color, texture, and line: a cool color—blue, green, turquoise; less intense, grayed colors; thin but opaque fabrics and dull surfaces; garment lines neither too tight nor too loose; no excess fabric in the lines of the garment, such as large cuffs or patch pockets.

Do you like bright, warm colors but do not want to call attention to body proportions? Try these suggestions: bright, warm colors in neckline jewelry, hats, or other accessories worn near the face; dull textures in your hat and jewerly, preferably; cool colors and less intense colors for the large areas of your clothing, such as coats, dresses, and separates; dull textures and non-bulky fabrics, if you do not want to add more bulk. If you wish not to call attention to body proportions, you might use neutrals, such as gray or black, in large areas. However, personality traits, as well as your figure and coloring, need to be considered in making clothing decisions. Black sometimes seems out of place on young girls. Black suggests heaviness, dignity, and age in certain textures. It needs lively accents to make it appropriate for a person with young personality traits. Young girls are likely to appear better in black when it is used in plaids or checks rather than by itself, especially in large amounts.

Are you petite? A one-color outfit may look less cluttered than one that uses several colors. Too many different colors in a small area give a crowded appearance. Vary textures slightly to give variety to outfits. Close values would be attractive for you. Too many value contrasts tend to give the same crowded effect as too many colors.

Do you never seem to have a thing to wear? You can use color to "stretch" your wardrobe, or at least to make it appear that you have more clothes than you actually do.

If this is your goal, attempt to make your selections so that as many garments as possible harmonize with other garments. This would mean limiting your choice to a few colors, and perhaps making one color predominate in your wardrobe. Buy the garments you expect to wear most frequently in your theme color.

More attractive combinations will be possible if you choose mainly medium values rather than extremely light or extremely dark colors. Medium values combine more easily than strong values. White shoes, for instance, look best with white or with pastel colors. But shoes in gray, beige, caramel, or sand colors blend readily with both darker and lighter values.

It's fun to be fashionable, but you might try buying fad colors only in inexpensive items. Peculiar colors often go out of style in a short time.

71

When You Choose Clothing Apply Design Elements to Your Body Proportions

Figure Differences	Line and Silhouette	Color and Texture
Petite small stature good proportions	Proportion works for you when pockets, collars, belts, and other details are meant to your small size. Plaids, stripes, checks, and prints in petite proportions are meant for you. If it is well-proportioned, a two-piece garment in one color can be as attractive as a one-piece garment for you. Avoid two-piece garments which divide you in two equal parts. Small persons look submerged when covered by too much fabric. Avoid wide sleeves, layers of fabric, wide lapels and collars. A full-length coat with vertical lines will tend to give you a longer look. Wear accents high on the figure to draw the attention upward.	You can wear vivid colors like a small bright bird. Or, if you prefer, pastels may help you create a delicate appearance. Dark colors and black may appear heavy on a very small frame. Limit the number of colors in each outfit and use close values in keeping with your small size. Plan for shoes, hats, and purses the same color as your separates, dresses, and coats to give an uncluttered appearance. Wear separates of the same color or close in value. Crisp, but not heavy, textures and soft, but not bulky, textures will not overwhelm your figure.
Short, chubby	An emphasized vertical line makes short persons appear taller and slimmer. Vertical stripes, tucks, and narrow front panels will help you appear taller. Vertical seams and vertical decorative lines may draw attention upward. A figure seems shorter and heavier when divided into parts by horizontal lines or contrasting colors and fabrics. V-shaped or cowl necklines have a slimming effect. Big collars and rounded necklines appear to add pounds. Figure size is emphasized by extremely full skirts, tight belts, full sleeves, and contrasting trim on short jackets.	Dark values and dull textures tend to slenderize. Shiny textures reflect light and emphasize shape. Light, bright colors are easily noticed and emphasize shape. Medium values and subdued intensities of red, blue, green, and yellow may be more flattering for a chubby figure than light values and bright intensities. Separates of the same color will detract from size; strong contrasts will emphasize proportion and cut the vertical line of the figure. Using self-fabric belts, and skirts and jackets of the same fabric and color, will create a vertical line. Fabrics with smooth surfaces and small prints, used with a minimum of decoration, help to slenderize. Velvets, corduroy, and synthetic fur are thick fabrics that add width.
Tall, slender	You can wear large-scale plaids, prints, and stripes better than petite persons. Horizontal lines below the waistline help shorten your figure. A short, loose sweater or jacket adds a horizontal line that shortens, especially if it contrasts with your skirt. Double-breasted closings, slim skirts topped with loosely fitted blouses or bulky sweaters are flattering. Closely fitted garments with unbroken lines will emphasize your height. A dress or coat with a princess line will add to the appearance of body height by repeating vertical body lines. Downward-slanting diagonal lines, such as raglan sleeves, will detract from height.	Tall, slim figures can wear bold prints, bright colors, heavy tweeds, and plush textures better than petite girls or chubby girls. Your figure will appear shorter in boldly contrasting separates, pleated or full skirts, and long jackets. Each of these helps to create horizontal lines in your garments to modify the appearance of height and add roundness to the figure. You may add the illusion of weight to your figure through bulky mohair sweaters, ski-type sweaters, or skirts of ribbed or fuzzy fabrics. Silky fabrics, sleeveless outfits, and cinched waists accent a slim figure. Light colors and white appear to add weight; dark values in dull textures tend to slenderize.
Tall, overweight	A tall overweight girl may want to minimize her size by using a balance of horizontal and vertical lines. The T line carries the eye upward, then breaks the vertical line with a collar. The T line slenderizes with a vertical line but decreases height with a horizontal line.	Plain fabrics will minimize your size. Bulky fabrics, such as mohair, seem to add more weight to your figure. Medium values will best suit your figure. Bright colors, bold plaids or prints make the figure appear even larger. Avoid severe color contrast at hipline and waistline which will call attention to your size.

(Thick waistline)	A thick waistline can be concealed by garments that are loosely fitted, overblouses, jerkins, sweaters, and jackets. Contrasting belts or tightly fitted waistlines accent the waist. Skirts that are slightly flared tend to conceal heavy hips better than straight skirts. Gathered skirts tend to emphasize excess weight at the hipline by adding more bulk. For slenderizing effect, try V necklines; narrow, lengthwise panels; and single-breasted closings.
Average height hippy in proportion to total body size	Hip size can be minimized by skirts in dark colors and dull fabrics. An easy fit will not outline bulges. Tight fitting skirts, or bold plaid skirts, or horizontal stripes all add weight to the hipline. Shiny fabrics also draw attention to the hips. Small, delicate prints are not in proportion to the figure. Girls with large hips usually want to create good proportions between the shoulders and hips. They may use wide collars or a Y line on the bodice to draw attention away from the hips. If the bodice is bloused above the waistline it helps to proportion the figure. Skirts with an easy fit that are slightly flared help to conceal wide hips. Horizontal lines at the hips or tight, wide belts tend to make wide hips more conspicuous. Easy-fitting coat dresses may be used to hide hip bulges.
"Long waisted"— long between neck and waist in relation to other measurements	Wear close color values, or one-color outfits to avoid accenting an out-of-proportion area of the figure. Avoid strongly contrasting belts which would accent length of bodice. Double-breasted closings will add width to bodice area. A slightly raised or dropped waistline will camouflage the actual location of the waistline. If you are long waisted you want to shorten the apparent distance between your neck and waist to give balance to your figure. This can be accomplished by emphasizing the area above the bustline such as a white collar, draped neckline or colorful yoke. Strong vertical lines in the blouse, as long narrow collars, make the waist seem longer. Long overblouses, loosely fitted dresses, wide belts and garments with raised waistlines all conceal waistline problems and flatter the figure.
"Short waisted"— short between neck and waist in relation to other measurements	Separates in the same color do not call attention to your waist. A dress with a color change, a dropped belt or a decorative band at the hipline is flattering to your figure because it seems to lengthen the bodice. When the natural waistline is used, the disproportion is emphasized by textural or color differences in the bodice and skirt. If you are concerned about achieving more balanced figure proportions, you will want to wear vertical lines in the bodice to make it appear longer. Tucks down the front of a blouse, a dress with a vertical tab, or long front opening can lengthen the appearance of the torso. Loosely fitted garments, such as long sweaters, overblouses, jackets and easy fitting dresses, help to conceal your waistline. Belts, closely fitted dresses, contrasting tucked-in blouses and skirts draw attention to your short bodice. A dress fitted at the hipbone then flared makes the bodice seem more in proportion to the skirt. A shirtwaist dress with a fitted waistline will call attention to a vertical line at your waist.

II. What Should You Wear?

Each day you make choices about what to wear. On some days, depending on your activities, you may wear several different outfits during the day. Have you ever stopped to think of reasons why you make the particular choices you do about what to wear? When you were younger these decisions were probably made for you by your mother or some other family member. As you grow and mature you expect to make these routine decisions for yourself. If you are aware of reasons for your routine decisions you may be able to understand these choices.

What Determines Your Decisions about What to Wear?

The clothing you have available for use right now affects how you dress for today's activities. Not all of the clothing you own, or share, may be available for wear all of the time. A garment is not available for use while it is being washed, or cleaned, or ironed, or mended. In addition, not all of your garments may fit you well all of the time. As styles change hems must be raised or lowered. As your body proportions change in the normal process of growing, seams need to be "let out" or "taken in." Therefore, your immediate choice of what to put on today depends on the condition of the clothing you have as well as on the number of garments you own. (You will find suggestions regarding ways to keep your clothing wearable in the unit, "Learning to Take Care of Your Clothes," pages 115–150.)

Your opinions and preferences determine how you dress, too. These opinions and preferences may be very much like those of your best friends. This is only natural as best friends have ways of sharing opinions and preferences about what they do, and even about the clothes they wear. It is a comfortable feeling to know you look "right" or that your clothing "fits in" with the occasion. It is possible to blend some of your original ideas about dress into your clothing preferences which reflect opinions of your group.

Your knowledge of ways to combine clothing into attractive outfits is another condition which influences what you wear. A large assortment of clothing is not necessary to make artistic and appropriate combinations. A modest number of garments

can be stretched, through knowledge of design principles, to seem like many more. Anyone can acquire this type of knowledge. Develop your own individuality in dress by studying your characteristics and by applying the principles of design in the way you wear clothes. (See "Is It Designed for You?" pages 52–73.)

Traditions about what to wear help you to choose the appropriate costume. If there were no accepted customs about clothing to guide you, you could never be certain of how to dress for any occasion. Tradition puts some restrictions on the types of clothing you might prefer to wear at different times. If there were no traditions about clothing you would have more freedom in your choices of what to wear, but would you like it?

Your past experiences also have given you clues about how to dress. As you have observed how others have dressed for various activities you have probably arrived at some conclusions of your own about the meaning of appropriate clothing. Be a keen observer in each new situation you meet. Your conclusions about appropriate dress will expand as you have new experiences.

What Clothing Is Appropriate?

Appropriate clothing for specific occasions can be described accurately only in terms of general characteristics. It is probable that you will find some differences between communities regarding the exact types of garments which are considered proper for various occasions. Also, styles of garments considered suitable will vary somewhat from one geographic region to the next. This explains why suggestions about appropriate dress must be presented only in a very general way.

You are appropriately dressed when:
1. The characteristics of the clothing (line, texture, color, fit) are *suitable for the event or activity* for which they are worn.
2. The clothing is *suited* in design *to the age* of the person wearing it.
3. The style of the clothing is *contemporary* with the time. This does not mean high fashion or faddish, but with good current lines.
4. The choice of garments and the standards of fit are *consistent with local community traditions.*
5. You feel *comfortable* in your clothing—not only physically comfortable, but *confident about your appearance* because you know that your clothing is suitable to the particular situation.

For school

What are the general characteristics of clothing appropriate for school and most other daily activities?
1. Comfort is important in school clothing. Garments should be designed for an active schedule of walking, moving about, sitting in the classroom, and working in groups. Garments that are fitted too tightly are tiring and uncomfortable.
2. Durability is another essential characteristic of school clothing. The fabric and the construction must be lasting. Durable garments stand the strain of constant wear.
3. Opaque fabrics are more appropriate for school wear than sheer ones, and simple fabrics are more appropriate than decorative ones. Decorative fabrics, such as satin, taffeta, and laces, look out of place in school, and they are not durable.

4. School fabrics should be resistant to soiling and wrinkling. School clothing must be worn many hours without change or freshening. All garments eventually need cleaning or washing, but some garments show soil faster than others. Medium values in colors, or neutrals, are less likely to show soil than very light values. Firmly woven fabrics tend to resist soiling and wrinkling better than soft or nubby surfaces.

5. A simple design is more appropriate for school wear than an elaborate design and excess decoration.

6. Sturdy accessories look well with durable garments and, of course, wear well.

Suggestions for specific garments for school:

A simple dress	A durable coat, jacket, sweater
A casual suit of corduroy, wool blend, or seersucker	A raincoat
	Weatherproof boots
Separates—blouses, skirts, sweaters, weskets, vests, jumpers	A hat for cold weather—knit, or of furlike fabric

For dress-up

What are the general characteristics of clothing appropriate for dress-up occasions (dates, church, dining out in restaurants, being a dinner guest, plays, music programs)?

1. Fabrics for dress-up may be less durable and daintier than those selected for school wear. Decorative but opaque fabrics, such as velveteen, taffeta, and satin, are suitable for dress-up if you prefer them. Coarse, bulky fabrics may look out of place when the feeling of the occasion is dignified.

2. Sheer fabrics are inappropriate for church service.

3. Dressy accessories are of less durable material and are daintier in size than those used for everyday activities.

4. A hat is required for some religious services; it is optional in others.

5. Gloves and hosiery are appropriate for dress-up occasions even when you are not wearing a hat.

6. Gloves and hosiery should always be worn with a dressy hat.

7. Dressy flats or small heels are appropriate with decorative fabrics and hosiery.

8. When the feeling of the occasion is dignified, less intense colors are more suitable than bright colors.

76

Suggestions for specific garments for dress-up occasions:

A suit

A dressy dress of decorative fabric, or a basic dress which could be worn with dressier accessories

A jumper and blouse of dressy fabric

Suitable flats or heels

Gloves and purse to complete the outfit

A hat

For spectator sports

What are the general characteristics of clothing appropriate for spectator sports?

1. Seasonal school clothing is appropriate for most spectator sports.
2. If you prefer, bright colors could be worn. They fit into the exciting atmosphere of sporting events.
3. Casual dress which is dressier than school clothing is appropriate at college football games. For example, hosiery and small heels are worn with separates rather than flats or socks.
4. Fitted pants or Bermuda shorts may be acceptable in some communities.
5. Weather-resistant clothing is a necessity for outdoor events.

Suggestions for specific garments for spectator sports:

Separates	A warm coat or sweater for football games
A casual dress and coat	
Flats and hose	A simple dress for tennis or baseball games
A suit	

77

means of judging you than by your clothing and your actions.

6. Your destination, the length of the trip, and the purpose of your trip are guides in choosing specific garments to wear en route. Pants or other casual wear are appropriate if you are traveling with a group of friends directly to a camp or sports-resort area. Fitted trousers of any kind are inappropriate if you are going directly to a city hotel. Skirted outfits are a good choice when in doubt.

Suggestions for specific garments for travel:

An all-purpose or all-weather coat

A suit with the same characteristics as those for school wear

Separates with the same characteristics as those for school wear

A dress with matching sweater

Dressy flats, or comfortable low heels, and hosiery

A purse large enough to hold all the odds and ends you want to carry

Here are a few additional suggestions for travelers. Although hats are often considered optional, a simple hat is usually a better choice than a head scarf which may soon become wrinkled and untidy. For summer wear, a soft fabric hat is useful and easier to pack than a straw one. For winter travel choose a knit hat or one of fur or fur-like fabric. Take clothes in colors that harmonize so you can put together several outfits with a few garments. It is better management to pack a few clothes that you will be able to keep in excellent condition than to carry too many. Minimum equipment needed to care for your clothes may include a clothes brush, a lint remover, and shoe polishing equipment. For unexpected repairs pack a few spare buttons, hooks, snaps, small scissors, needle, and thread.

For travel

What are the general characteristics of clothing appropriate for travel by train, bus, or plane?

1. Versatile garments will make it possible to take fewer things.
2. Lightweight clothing is convenient to carry.
3. Clothing that is comfortable for a long time span will help make your trip a pleasant experience.
4. Wrinkle-resistant and soil-resistant fabrics will reduce to a minimum the time and expense required for cleaning and pressing while you are away from home.
5. Clothing which is conservative in design and which fits will help you introduce yourself favorably to other passengers. Strangers have no other

Suggested Learning Experiences

Review What You Have Read

1. What are design elements?
2. What are design principles? Define each of the design principles presented in this unit.
3. Why are design principles called principles?
4. What are the general characteristics of appropriate dress?
5. Appropriate dress does not mean exactly the same thing everywhere. Why is this so?

Questions and Topics for Discussion

6. Discuss the meaning of "appropriate dress" in your community. Summarize the types of outfit that would be suitable for different occasions.
7. Describe the textures of various fabrics and other materials in your classroom. Try to use words which accurately describe each texture. Try to find two or more objects in the classroom which have similar textures.
8. Is it possible for several persons to talk to each other about texture unless each has a vocabulary to describe various textures? Support your answer with examples.
9. When and where would you miss color most if all the world were black, white, and gray?

Individual or Group Projects

10. Your class may want to read all or part of the delightful book *Hailstones and Halibut Bones* by Mary O'Neill, Doubleday and Company, Inc., Garden City, New York, 1961. This small book describes colors in terms of feelings, moods, and things we remember. It is an excellent book for reading aloud. Both the words and the colorful illustrations can expand your sensitivity to colors in your environment.
11. Have a fashion review in class showing good and poor choices of clothes for different events.
12. Prepare a bulletin board showing "What Your Clothes Can Do for You." Try to illustrate one or more of the suggestions from this unit.
13. Prepare an exhibit of jewelry appropriate for school wear.
14. Plan an appropriate-clothing bulletin-board project in your school. During the school year post illustrations of appropriate clothing for the various occasions which will take place at school or in the community.
15. Survey class members to determine the sources (such as friends, movies, parents, others) which influence their choices of clothes for different situations. Report your conclusions. Which influence seems to affect clothing choices of the class members most frequently?
16. Survey parents of class members or other adults to determine sources which influence their choices of clothing. Are the influences the same as those which affect clothing choices of class members?
17. Plan a day when each class member will wear an outfit which she believes will most closely illustrate good design. Each one should be prepared to explain how one or more of the design principles have been applied in creating the design of the outfit.
18. Analyze your own body proportions, facial shape, and personal coloring. Find illustrations of clothing which show good line, texture, and color for yourself. Explain why each of your illustrations is a good choice for you in terms of design principles.
19. Give a demonstration with two or more

girls of different heights. Have each try on sweaters of different lengths to illustrate the effect of good and poor proportion in clothing. Select the most pleasing sweater length for each girl. Try to explain how the principle of proportion can be applied in choosing a sweater.

20. Give a demonstration illustrating proportion in accessories.
21. Give a demonstration illustrating the principle of emphasis in clothing and accessories.
22. Give a demonstration illustrating the principle of balance in clothing and accessories.

Individual or Group Reports

23. Plan a panel discussion on the topic "When Is Casual Too Casual?"
24. Plan a panel including a teen-ager, a wage-earning mother, a college student, and a full-time homemaker to discuss the question "What does being dressed appropriately and attractively mean to the family and its members?"

Home Experiences

25. Apply design principles to the combinations of clothing you wear.
26. Analyze the lines in the clothing you have. Would you make any different choices in future purchases?
27. Start your own file of clippings or a notebook about clothes selection. Organize the information so that it will be useful to you. Try to improve your decisions about what to wear by applying some of the suggestions.
28. If you expect to take a trip soon, plan a coordinated travel wardrobe for yourself based on the clothes you have.

Suggested Filmstrips

These three filmstrips are suitable for use with this unit. They were sponsored by the J. C. Penney Company, McCall's Patterns, and Coat's and Clark's Threads. They are available at $6.00 for the set of three from local J. C. Penney store managers or from D and A Forwarding Co., 541 West 34th St., New York 1, N.Y. A teacher's commentary booklet is included for each filmstrip.

1. Take a look at color
   How to apply design principles to choosing colors is discussed. Color harmonies are described. Intensity and value are illustrated. Some information is given on the effect of color on moods.
2. Color and You
   Personal coloring types are described with suggested color ranges for each.
3. Color as You Wear It
   Here are more applications of design principles in choosing clothes and accessories.

References for Teachers

BAER, NEIL ROLAND, "Some Directions to Art Understanding for Laymen: Lectures and Visuals in Design and Composition," unpublished M.S. thesis, Iowa State University, Ames, Iowa, 1964.

HILLHOUSE, MARION S., *Dress Selection and Design*. The Macmillan Company, New York, 1963.

O'NEILL, MARY, *Hailstones and Halibut Bones*. Doubleday & Company, Inc., Garden City, N.Y., 1961.

RUTT, ANNA HONG, *Home Furnishings*, Second Edition. John Wiley & Sons, Inc., New York, 1961.

UNIT FIVE

Making Decisions about
Buying Clothing

I. Who Should Make Decisions about Buying Clothing?

Additional garments are often needed by the various members of a family—because of change of season, or for some special occasion or some special use. This will involve a whole series of decisions that must be made, by individual members of the family or by the family group. You have probably helped make some of these decisions; possibly you have already made one or more of them by yourself.

Here are some of the decisions which must be made by family members, together or individually, when additional clothing is needed:

1. Whether they will purchase new clothing or fill the need in some other way.
2. What type of clothing should be purchased to meet the need.
3. For which family members the new clothing should be purchased.

4. How much can be spent for the garment.
5. When the garment should be purchased.
6. Where the garment should be purchased.
7. Who will make the actual selection of the clothing.
8. Which garment will be selected.

Sometimes a family may decide not to purchase certain articles of clothing new. They may decide to take care of their clothing needs in other ways. Occasionally, for example, clothing is exchanged among immediate family members, other relatives, or friends. Often attractive and useful articles of clothing may be obtained at used-clothing stores. Sometimes a favorite garment can be skillfully altered or repaired so that it may be used another season. This first decision will depend on a family's income, on their skill at repairing and altering clothing, and on each individual family member's attitude toward clothing.

Families differ, too, in the size or number of individuals for whom clothing must be provided. The clothing needed by the various individuals will differ according to their daily activities and their ages. Because school clothing is worn every day, it may need to be replaced more often than clothing for special occasions. When young children are growing rapidly some articles of their clothing are outgrown in a few months and must be replaced. Working clothes are needed by wage earners in the family. For some types of employment special clothing, such as uniforms, may have to be purchased.

Families are geographically mobile. This means that each year many families move from one part of the country to another, and because of different climatic conditions they may need different clothing. In areas where the winter season is severe families need to own clothing that gives protection from low temperatures. In parts of the South and Southwest lightweight or all-weather garments are usually enough protection.

All families have different kinds of needs which are important to them. Since clothing is only one of the many needs a family must provide for itself, it may be that not all the clothing needs of each person can be filled just as he would like. Housing, food, medical care, taxes, transportation, and recreation are a few of the other expenses which families must consider. Possibly the family income will not cover all of these and also all the new clothing that each member of the family would like. This is especially apt to be true in a large family. Decisions will have to be made as to which clothing is most necessary. Each family member must be considered.

Family income will also help to determine how much to pay for a particular garment. And not only the total amount of money the family has available to spend on clothing must be considered, but also the number of people who must be clothed on it. All types of clothing can be bought in a wide range of prices. Moreover, opinions differ about how much one should pay for an item of clothing. Families of the same size and with equal incomes may differ in how much they prefer to spend on clothing. It is a personal matter if a family prefers to buy low-cost clothing so that they will have more money for other things. Another family may prefer high-cost clothing even when it means economizing on other essentials. Our environment would be dull indeed if all families and individuals provided for their daily needs in the same way.

The decision when to buy is related to other decisions about clothing. A larger selection of clothing is usually available early in a season or several weeks before the season begins. Fall and winter clothing is shown in August. Spring clothing can be

83

bought in January and February. If a wide selection from which to choose is important, it is best to buy early in the season. At the end of each season prices on merchandise will usually be reduced. You will find that many types of seasonal clothing are sold at reduced prices following Easter, Christmas, Memorial Day, and July 4. If a reduced price is important to consider in buying, the family shopper will wait for seasonal sales.

Where to buy clothing is not always a simple decision. There are many types of retail stores where clothing may be purchased. It can be purchased in department stores, specialty clothing stores, drugstores, variety stores, supermarkets, mail-order retail stores, gift shops, used-clothing stores, and discount houses. Each type of store differs somewhat from the others.

Drugstores and supermarkets usually have for sale only a few clothing items, such as stockings and socks; and sizes, colors, and styles may be limited. Variety stores may show a broader selection of clothing than supermarkets and drugstores, but even here the selection is limited in comparison with that in specialty clothing stores and department stores. However, a specialty store may sell clothing for women and girls only, or for men or children only. Some clothing stores specialize in only one type of clothing, such as shoes or hats.

Large department stores usually display all types of clothing for all family members. There are special departments for each type of clothing. A more extensive choice of styles, colors, sizes, and quality is likely to be found in a department store than in other types of retail stores.

Used-clothing stores may have clothing for all family members in various qualities. But sizes, colors, and styles may be very limited, because it is not possible for the store manager to plan the types of garments he will have to sell; he has to take what comes.

Discount houses claim to sell certain items of clothing at lower prices than might be found in department stores. Choices of styles and sizes may be limited.

Other factors beside the clothing available are important in choosing a place to shop. If time for shopping is limited, the store must be easy to reach. A parking area near the store is a convenience for drivers. Ordering by telephone is a convenience, too, but in that case it is not possible to see the clothing or to try it on.

The actual selection of a garment in the store is more likely to be satisfactory if the person who makes the selection has some knowledge of that particular type of clothing. Ability to recognize good construction, pleasing design, and suitable materials in a garment is helpful in making a good decision. You probably now have some opportunity to choose clothing for yourself. You will find it useful to learn how to identify differences of quality between blouses, skirts, sweaters, and other clothing when you are making selections for yourself. Some suggestions about sources of information for consumers can be found in Part III, pages 89–90. Details about five types of clothing for girls can be found in Part VII, pages 98–112.

Families differ in the way they make decisions about clothing. Some families consider decision-making a group activity, each person contributing ideas and information. The value in group decision-making is that by talking and listening each one can understand better the other members in the family. In some families cer-

tain individuals are expected to make all the decisions about clothing. Sharing in the decisions may take place as ideas are suggested by other family members, but the final decision is made by one person. In still other families all decisions may be made by one person with or without hearing suggestions from other individuals in the family.

Decisions about clothing are important, but for most people clothing is not an end in itself. Rather, adequate clothing is important because it makes it possible for us to carry on daily activities comfortably and conveniently and effectively. Clothes are material goods which can aid us in reaching certain goals, such as maintaining good health, developing worthwhile friendships, and being successful in a job. Wearing clothing which makes you feel comfortable and look attractive will help you to have self-confidence. Clothes which require minimum care will free your time and energy for other accomplishments.

Here are some more ideas about decision-making in general that you may want to discuss. Throughout your life you will have opportunities to make choices alone and with others. You will be able to participate in group decisions if you have useful information to contribute to the discussion. You will have a chance to learn to listen attentively to the ideas and opinions that are presented by others, and to develop ideas of your own that you can share. You can learn to accept more than one choice or alternative.

The ability and willingness to make responsible decisions in everyday matters is a characteristic of growing up. A responsible decision-maker is concerned about the way in which his decisions will affect other persons around him. Also, he is willing to accept all the consequences of his decisions, desirable and undesirable.

If the freedom to make decisions is important to you, you will need to develop the ability to make decisions. Otherwise, you must accept decisions made for you by others.

II. Planning an Adequate Wardrobe

A plan is a blueprint or set of directions for reaching a goal. Planning is the activity or process of making the blueprint or directions. Planning is successful when the blueprint does provide help in reaching the goal. The goal must be described before it is possible to make a plan to reach it.

A plan need not be considered rigid and unchangeable once it is finished. If you want to change the goal, you will need to revise the plan. Plans for reaching some goals need never be completely finished. A plan for a successful home is never complete. It needs to be changed from time to time as goals change throughout a lifetime. The process of planning is often a continuing process.

Let us consider how to plan an adequate wardrobe. In order to plan an adequate wardrobe for yourself you must first know what this term means to you. Only then will you be able to start a plan to achieve it.

An adequate wardrobe for an individual means enough suitable clothing to make it possible for that individual to carry out his daily activities satisfactorily. In many ways this is a personal matter. You and

your friends may have differing opinions about the number of garments that each of you needs. You may find these differences in viewpoint even though your activities are similar to those of your friends. Your selection of color and design in clothing is a personal preference. Color and design, however, can help to make clothing artistically suitable for you and a pleasant experience for you to wear.

An adequate wardrobe is also a community or social concern. Many schools have guidelines indicating appropriate dress for their students. Business places which serve the public often suggest types of suitable clothing for their employees. Furthermore, respect for tradition and custom determines to some extent what is suitable to wear. For example, sports clothing is not considered to be appropriate at religious services. Concerts, plays, and other public events require clothing suitable to the dignity of the occasion.

Your wardrobe is adequate if the clothing you have makes it possible for you to carry on your daily activities. You participate in varied activities, so you may need

BLUE PRINT

skirts, jumpers, blouses, sweaters for school

shorts, slacks, jeans for play.

church and dress up dresses and suits.

suitable accessories

several types of clothing. From September to June each year you spend the largest part of your time in school. If your school has a student handbook, it will describe standards of dress for your school. These standards are meant to provide a business-like environment to benefit all students. A businesslike atmosphere will help you work well. Some acceptable types of clothing for school wear generally include skirts, jumpers, blouses, and sweaters. Casual dresses and suits of durable materials such as cor-duroy, denim, and quilted cotton are good choices for school too.

You will find that appropriate clothing for spectators at sports events is not the same in every community. Jeans, slacks, other fitted long pants, and longer shorts are acceptable at football and basketball games in some communities but not in others. In the latter case, the same type of

clothing you wear to school is probably suitable for attending sports events during the school year.

Your clothing for home wear could con-sist of various styles of slacks, shorts, and other fitted pants. Skimmer-type dresses can be both comfortable and attractive. Family attitudes toward clothing help de-termine what is appropriate at-home wear. Regardless of your choice of clothing for wearing at home, if it is neat and clean, your family will be glad you are at home. A certain way to improve the appearance of your home environment is to start with yourself.

No doubt you have some need for dress-up clothes. You may want to limit the num-ber of dresses you have during a season. Styles change, and by another season you may be ready for something new. See Part VII, "Selecting Clothing for Yourself," pages 108–112, for some ideas about choos-ing dresses.

Here are several suggestions to consider in wardrobe-planning:

1. Plan to buy garments that you will use. Do you have clothing you don't know where or when to wear? Buy-ing more clothes does not mean that your wardrobe will become more adequate. Think about the intended use of each garment before you buy it. Start your plan by describing uses you have for clothing now.

2. Plan for several garments that can be worn together, or that can be com-bined in various ways. Start with clothing you already have. Plan the color and style of several purchases at the same time although you may buy them at different times. For in-stance, if you buy a coat in the fall, plan a skirt and blouse that can be added later in the semester. If you plan only in terms of single gar-

ments that you think you need or would like, you may soon have a collection of unrelated items. Your clothing is more likely to combine well if you plan for it to combine.

3. Plan to buy colors that will permit as many combinations as possible. Like many other persons, you probably add garments to your wardrobe gradually. You will need to follow a color plan for several years to develop a color-coordinated wardrobe, that is, one in which the colors can be used together. Discovering colors you like can be one of the most pleasing parts of wardrobe-planning and clothing selection. (See pages 58–64.) Colors that harmonize well will permit you to make better use of all the clothing you have. If you select more solid colors than stripes, plaids, or figured designs you can combine more items. After you have made some decisions about colors, you can carry a color list when you shop to remind you of your plan. For example, carry a list of your skirt colors. Include jumpers, too. Use this reminder where you shop for blouses and sweaters. This guide will help you build combinations and avoid collecting odd, unmatched articles. Samples of the fabrics of clothing that you already have will help you match or coordinate new garments with them.

4. If you can sew, you could plan to make some simple garments which would increase the use of other garments. Blouses can be made from fabrics which coordinate with ready-to-wear skirts which you have purchased. A dress constructed from a simple pattern could be combined with a matching sweater.

5. Plan accessories you need when you plan other additions to your wardrobe. Purses, costume jewelry, headwear, and other accessories will look right if they are planned as part of the total design of an outfit. Follow your color plan when you choose these things. If you consider the shape and size of accessories they can be beautiful as well as useful.

6. Plan better care for the clothing you already have. This will maintain the appearance of your clothing and perhaps increase the number of wearings you can get from it. Your appearance will be improved by a garment which is clean and pressed. A plan to care for clothing is part of an over-all plan for a wardrobe.

A plan for an adequate wardrobe is never completely finished. It changes as ideas and goals about clothing change.

88

III. How Do Consumers Learn about Clothing?

If you believe it is important to develop skill in purchasing clothing, you will need some knowledge of ready-to-wear clothing. You will need to learn about fibers, fabrics, and fabric finishes. Also, you will need to know how various garments are constructed so that you can recognize good-quality construction.

Several sources of information about ready-to-wear clothing are available to consumers. However, not all of these information sources are equally useful, and not all may be available to you.

Advertisements

Clothing advertisements in magazines and newspapers sometimes contain useful information. Of course, because their purpose is to encourage people to buy, advertisements are planned to give a favorable impression of particular places to shop or of certain garments that are for sale. In spite of this, illustrations of clothing in advertisements may help you form an idea about the appearance of a garment you expect to buy. Also advertisements will give you information about prices, and about fabrics, colors, and sizes available.

Labels

Labels on ready-to-wear garments are a source of useful information only if you understand the meaning of the various terms used on these labels. Parts IV, V, VI, and VII, pages 90–112, will help you understand these terms. Generally, clothing labels include certain types of information: Size; Fabric description; Name of each fi-ber and percentage of each fiber; Kinds of finish used, if any; Care instructions; and Brand name or trademark name.

Pamphlets and Publications from Government Agencies

Inexpensive pamphlets and booklets can be ordered from the Superintendent of Documents, United States Government Printing Office, Washington, D.C. Pamphlets obtained from this source are prepared by specialists in government agencies. Lists of pamphlets about topics such as buying clothing, caring for clothing, and sewing can be requested.

89

Your County Extension Home Economist will be able to supply useful booklets which give facts about buying clothing. She can suggest booklets which have been prepared by clothing specialists who are employed by the Agricultural Extension Service in your state.

Publications from Other Sources

Consumer Reports and *Consumers' Research Bulletin* are two magazines that you may be able to find among the periodicals in your school library. Reports in these magazines describe products of interest to consumers. Frequently, reports about clothing are included.

Clothing manufacturers provide pamphlets describing their products as a part of their advertising. A booklet that is provided free by a manufacturer to tell you about his products may emphasize desirable features of the clothing and overlook less desirable features.

Several large retail organizations that have stores in many cities throughout the country have what they call consumer information services or consumer education services. One of the services provided to consumers is printed information describing new types of clothing found in their stores.

Newspapers publish many good articles about current developments in clothing design, care of clothing, and new fibers and fabrics.

Fashion magazines can be more than a source of entertainment. If you read these periodicals for information, you will discover many ideas that you can use.

IV. Fibers

Fibers are threadlike strands which can be spun into yarns. These yarns are then made into fabrics by weaving, felting, knitting, and other processes. As you learn to understand the various fibers you can better understand the fabrics which they become.

Fibers can be separated into two types: those which are formed by natural processes, and those which are developed in laboratories by experimental procedures.

Natural Fibers

The main natural fibers that are used in clothing are cotton, wool, linen, and silk. These fibers are formed by natural processes carried on in plant and animal life.

The four common natural fibers can be further subdivided into fibers from animal sources and fibers from plant sources. Wool is the fibrous coat of sheep and goats, which can be clipped from the animals. Hairs of some of these animals are used. Wool is sometimes mixed with hair from llama, alpaca, and angora, and from camels to make cloth. Silk fibers are the filaments produced by silkworms as they make their cocoons, one stage in the life cycle of the silkworm. Familiar fibers found in plants are cotton and linen. Cotton fibers are formed in the seed pods of the cotton plant as it ripens. Linen fibers are formed in the stalk of the flax plant.

The fabrics in your clothing will have the characteristics of the fibers from which they are made. You should expect a blouse which is labeled "100% cotton fabric" to show the traits of cotton. When two or more fibers are used in making a fabric, it will have some traits of each fiber. A fabric of 65 per cent polyester and 35 per cent cotton is frequently found in washable blouses and dresses.

Each fiber has individual characteristics which make it more suitable for certain uses than other fibers. Cotton fabrics are comfortable to wear, can be washed easily, and are low to moderate in cost. Cotton is a good choice for garments that need to be washed often. Because of their low-to-moderate cost it may be possible to own several cotton garments. Linen fabric is comfortable and can be washed easily, but it is usually more expensive than cotton.

Study the chart on page 93, which compares the characteristics of natural fibers and summarizes differences in clothing made from these fibers. (See also the discussion of fabric finishes, pages 122–125.)

Manufactured Fibers

Manufactured fibers are synthesized, that is, formed from raw materials through planned manufacturing processes carried out in factories.[14]

One way to begin understanding manufactured fibers is to learn their names. You will need to know fiber names before you can recognize a particular fiber when it is described orally or on a printed page. You will be able to ask questions accurately and expect accurate answers only if you use correct terms when asking questions. You will be able to tell another person about fibers only when you know what to call them. Learning the correct name of something helps you to learn more about it.

Manufactured fibers can be recognized by their trademark names, by their generic names, or by both. A *generic name* is a name used to identify a group of fibers which have similar characteristics.

These are generic names, that is, names of groups of fibers with similar characteristics:

acetate (including triacetate)	olefin
	polyester
acrylic	rayon
azlon	rubber
glass	saran
modacrylic	spandex
metallic	vinal
nylon	vinyon
nytril	

Not all of these manufactured fibers are used for clothing. Those commonly used in clothing are acetate and triacetate, acrylic, olefin, modacrylic, nylon, rayon, polyester, and spandex. Rubber and metallic fibers are used for clothing only to a limited extent: rubber for lingerie and waistbands of sportswear, metallic fibers combined with other fibers for interesting fabrics.

The Textile Fiber Products Identification Act of 1958 requires that the fiber content of fabrics be identified on an attached tag or label. This labeling law, which went into effect in 1960, refers to manufactured fibers and to natural fibers except wool. The generic name[15] and percentage of each fiber which consists of more than 5 per cent of the fabric must be listed. Percentage refers to weight of the fiber in the fabric. Let's consider two examples: a ready-to-wear dress may be labeled "100% Dacron polyester" to indicate that the fabric contains only one fiber; the fiber content of "100% nylon exclusive of ornamentation" is on the label of a packable robe. Fibers must be listed in descending order on the label beginning with the fiber consisting of the largest percentage of the fabric. A fab-

[14] Rayon and acetate are made from wood pulp and cotton linters, but many other manufactured fibers are produced directly from chemicals.

[15] "Cotton," "silk," "wool," and "linen" are generic names for natural fibers.

ric which is a blend of two or more fibers might be labeled like this:

74% Celanese acetate

26% cotton

If a fiber consists of less than 5 per cent of a fabric, the fiber name and percentage may be listed only if the fiber affects the characteristics of the fabric. An example of this case may appear on a label as:

97% acetate

3% spandex—for elasticity

A fiber may not be mentioned by name or percentage if it is 5 per cent or less, by weight, of the fabric, and if it does not affect the characteristics of the fabric. The terms "other fiber" or "other fibers" are used on labels to indicate the presence of such fibers. An example of this is a pair of knit gloves marked, "98% Creslan acrylic, 2% other fibers."

Two other provisions of the Textile Fiber Products Identification Act require certain additional facts on fabric labels. These two types of information might be of interest to the consumer. First, the manufacturer must be identified. Second, imported products must be labeled telling the country where they were processed or manufactured.

In addition to generic names, trademark names are usually found on labels attached to ready-to-wear clothing and on fabrics sold by the yard. A trademark name identifies an individual fiber which belongs to a generic group of fibers. Unlike a generic name, it is not required to be on a label. Trademark names are given to individual fibers by manufacturers to name their own products. These trademark names, or trademarks or brandnames, are registered with the United States Patent Office. At the present time there are hundreds of trademark names for fibers in use.[16] Examples of common trademark names are Kodel, Dacron, Lycra, Cantrece, and Avisco.

A trademark name is usually capitalized when it is used on labels or in advertisements in order to identify a fiber produced by a particular manufacturer. A generic name appearing on the same label or in the same advertisement will probably not be capitalized.

Study the chart on page 94, which shows both generic names of manufactured fibers and a few examples of trademark names. Then look for fiber names on the labels next time you go shopping.

Besides learning the names of some manufactured fibers you will need to understand how these fibers compare and contrast with natural fibers. You can ex-

[16] *Changing Times,* November, 1960, p. 14, referred to 700 trade names for fibers. Of course, not all have clothing uses.

Natural Fibers in the Clothing You Wear

Fiber Name (and Source)	Fiber Characteristics	Typical Clothing Uses	How These Fibers Affect Clothing Characteristics
Cotton (cotton plant)	Strong, durable Mildews Absorbs moisture well Does not spring back into shape	Blouses Dresses Skirts Underwear Socks Sportswear Housecoats	An all-cotton garment will: be comfortable in warm weather wrinkle easily without special finish wash easily, if color-fast need to be ironed at high temperature unless it has wrinkle-resistant finish be durable; withstand wear burn readily mildew if stored damp be inexpensive to more expensive
Linen (flax plant)	Strong, durable Mildews Absorbs moisture well Is expensive to produce	Blouses Dresses Skirts Suits	An all-linen garment will: be comfortable in warm weather wrinkle easily without special finish wash easily if color-fast need to be ironed at high temperature unless it has wrinkle-resistant finish be very durable; withstand wear burn readily mildew if stored damp be expensive
Wool (sheep)	Warm Durable Returns to original shape quickly Absorbs moisture	Knit garments Sweaters Gloves Skirts Coats Sportswear for cool weather Socks Suits	An all-wool garment will: be warmer than cotton, linen, or silk resist wrinkling absorb odors be durable; withstand wear need protection against insects (moths) need careful handling if washed need to be pressed at low temperature be moderately priced to expensive
Silk (cocoon of silkworm)	Smooth, lustrous Strong Expensive to produce	Blouses Dresses	An all-silk garment will: feel luxurious need ironing at low temperature show water spots unless it has special finish probably need to be dry-cleaned, unless carefully handled in washing be expensive

Manufactured Fibers Used in Clothing Generic Names and Trademark Names

Generic Name	Trademark Name	Combined names as they appear on labels or in advertisements (look for both)
acrylic	Orlon Acrilan Creslan Zefran	Orlon acrylic Acrilan acrylic Creslan acrylic Zefran acrylic
polyester	Dacron Kodel Fortrel Vycron	Dacron polyester Kodel polyester Fortrel polyester Vycron polyester
olefin	Vectra	Vectra olefin
spandex	Lycra Blue C Vyrene	Lycra spandex Blue C spandex Vyrene spandex
nylon	Antron Nylon 66 Enka Chemstrand Caprolan	Antron nylon Nylon 66 nylon Enka nylon Chemstrand nylon Caprolan nylon
modacrylic	Dynel Verel	Dynel modacrylic Verel modacrylic
rayon	Zantrel polynosic Avril Corval Enka	Zantrel polynosic rayon Avril rayon Corval rayon Enka rayon
acetate—regular	Avisco Chromspun Estron	Avisco acetate Chromspun acetate Estron acetate
triacetate	Arnel	Arnel triacetate

pect clothing to have characteristics like the fibers from which they are made. Here are some reasons why knowledge of these fibers is important:

1. Clothing made from natural fibers and that made from manufactured fibers may look much alike in the store.

2. Manufactured fibers and natural fibers will affect a garment differently in the care it will need, in the way it will withstand wear, in the way it feels, and in how much it will cost.

3. Types of clothing formerly made from natural fibers only are now made of manufactured fibers too.

4. Some additional types of existing manufactured fibers are developed in laboratories each year.
5. Some new uses of manufactured fibers in clothing are developed each year.

Man-made fibers used in clothing have some general characteristics which affect clothes care. They do not absorb water, therefore they seem to resist becoming wet. Fabrics dry rapidly because water clings only to the outside of the fibers.

Besides being water-resistant these man-made fibers are heat-sensitive. This means that the fibers are affected by high temperatures. A moderate to low ironing temperature is needed. A warm, rather than hot, washing temperature is preferable. An exception to heat-sensitivity is triacetate, a type of acetate. Furthermore, man-made fibers do not shrink and they are wrinkle-resistant.

Look for labels which tell you how to care for garments. (See "Learning to Take Care of Your Clothes," pages 126–129, for information about complete care labels. For more details about fibers in clothing, see also "Selecting Clothing for Yourself," pages 98–112.)

We can summarize by saying that in order to understand information about fibers on labels and in advertisements we must know: (1) the characteristics of natural fibers; (2) the generic names of manufactured fibers; (3) the general characteristics of the basic fiber groups.

V. Fabrics

The term "fabric" refers to finished cloth which is either made into ready-to-wear garments in factories or sold by the yard.

"Broadcloth," "chambray," "sailcloth," and "denim" are names of a few typical fabrics you may recognize.

Many women and girls have had experience in buying fabrics by the yard. Perhaps you have helped someone to select fabrics or have chosen some for yourself. You also choose fabric each time you buy ready-to-wear clothing. In this case the designer and the manufacturer decide which fabrics will be used.

You are more likely to be satisfied with the fabrics you choose if you learn how to recognize differences in them and know what to expect of them.

Fabrics are commonly made by weaving and knitting. Fabrics are also made by felting and bonding, though few fabrics of this type are used for clothing. Felting is the process of matting wool fibers together by the use of heat, moisture, and pressure. Wool felt is used for hats and purses, and is sold by the yard. Bonding is another process that uses heat and pressure to bind together certain fibers—fibers other than wool. Orlon, Dacron and nylon are used in making bonded fabrics. Pellon, used in linings and interfacings, is an example of a bonded fabric.

The term "bonded" has another meaning when it is used to describe fabrics. It may refer to fabrics made of two or more layers of cloth. A bonded fabric may be made by permanently attaching an outer fabric to a lining material by a heat process. For instance, a stretchy material might be sealed to a firm lining material to prevent it from stretching. Do not confuse the two meanings for the word. (Read more about bonded fabrics in "Learning to Take Care of Your Clothes," page 122.)

Woven Fabrics

Looms are the machines used in the weaving process. Warp yarns, which are threaded on the loom, are crossed over and under at right angles by filling yarns. The product resulting is a woven fabric.

At one time weaving cloth on hand-operated looms was a skill homemakers needed. They wove the cloth at home and later sewed it, by hand, into clothing.

In our country today weaving on hand-operated looms is still carried on as a business in a few places. The products from this hand-loomed process are usually very expensive because many hours of labor are needed to produce an article—a blanket, a bedspread, or even a scarf. Churchill Weavers of Berea, Kentucky, is a weaving industry in which hand-operated looms are still used.

Today the usual way to produce woven fabrics is through large-scale factory methods using power-operated looms. Such methods tend to make fabrics less costly.

Grainline

A characteristic common to all woven fabrics is grainline. Every woven fabric has a lengthwise grainline and a crosswise grainline. Lengthwise grainline refers to the warp yarns, which are also called lengthwise yarns. Crosswise grainline refers to the woof, or weft, yarns. These are also called crosswise yarns, or filling yarns. Sometimes in a description of grainline the word "thread" is used instead of "yarns." A garment which has been cut exactly "with the grainline," or parallel with the threads, tends to hold its shape well. In other words, garments cut with the grainline will stretch less than garments which were not cut with the grainline. They will hang correctly.

One sign of quality in both a ready-to-wear garment and in one sewed at home is that it was cut on the grainline. Then the garment will not have unwanted folds and it will hang correctly. Grainline is important in your clothing vocabulary.

Three Basic Weaves

There are three basic weaves which you can learn to recognize when you buy ready-to-wear clothing and when you buy fabric by the yard. They are plain, twill, and satin. Fabrics produced by these weaves differ in the way they look and in the way they withstand wear. Usually a beginner at sewing can best learn about grainline by using a fabric of plain weave for the first project. Grainline can be seen more easily in a plainweave fabric than in the others. Compare these three weaves by studying the chart on page 98.

Knit Fabrics

The use of knit fabrics for clothing is increasing every year. Many types of ready-to-wear knits are available. Sweaters have long been an example of a popular type of knitwear. But the list also includes pajamas and robes, slips and other underwear, hosiery, dresses, suits, swimwear, coats, jumpers, shorts and slacks, gloves, and hats. It is possible to dress from head to foot in knits—except for shoes!

Knit fabrics have different characteristics from woven fabrics. They wrinkle less, and they do not show wrinkles as woven fabrics do. They stretch easily. Knits are comfortable to wear because they adjust easily to the shape of the body.

If you look at a knit fabric closely, perhaps magnified, you will see that it is not made in the same way as a woven fabric. *Knitting* is the process of interlooping one or more yarns to make fabric. Warp knits and filling knits are the two basic types of knit fabrics. In filling, or weft, knitting the yarns are interlooped across the fabric. Filling knitting is done with one yarn. Nylon hosiery is an example of filling knit. In warp knitting the looped yarns run in a

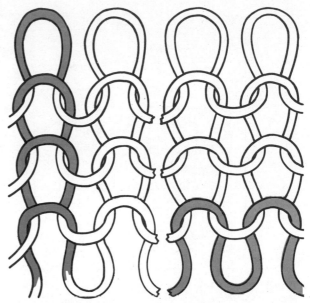

vertical direction. More than one yarn is used in warp knitting. Usually, warp knits are tighter and less stretchy than weft knits. Jersey is an example of warp knit.

A *course* is a row of loops running crosswise in knitted fabrics. This corresponds to the filling yarn in woven fabrics. A *wale* is a row of loops running lengthwise in the fabric. This corresponds to the warp yarn in woven fabrics.

You may find the term "bonded knit" used on labels and in advertisements. A *bonded knit* is a knitted fabric permanently sealed to a lining material. The lining cuts down on stretching when stretchiness is not preferred. This gives a better shape to the garment. A dress of bonded knit fabric will stretch less and fit better than an unlined knit. Bonded knit fabric can be bought by the yard if you want to sew it yourself. Labels on yard goods and on ready-made knits will tell you the fiber content. Look on the labels for exact care instructions also.

Examine several knit articles and compare the amount of stretch lengthwise and crosswise; compare differences in stretch between knit and woven fabrics.

Weave	A Microscopic Look at the Weave	Fabric Names	Characteristics of These Fabrics	Typical Clothing Uses
Plain		seersucker broadcloth sailcloth gingham Indian head chambray poplin oxford cloth duck organdy shantung percale	A wide variety of fabrics Organdy is sheer and fragile; sailcloth and duck are sturdy.	sportswear blouses sleepwear dresses skirts housecoats
Twill		denim gabardine ticking serge	Diagonal design on the surface Very strong and durable	sportswear casual dresses skirts
Satin		satin sateen	Smooth, sometimes shiny appearance Threads snag easily Not durable; will not withstand wear as well as a plain or twill weave	Satin: formal bridal gowns and evening gowns Sateen: dressy and casual dresses and blouses sportswear (but is not durable)

VI. Selecting Clothing for Yourself

When you select ready-to-wear clothing you think about the way it fits you, about the color, the style or design, and the price. The way the garment was put together is important to consider too. The quality of work used in assembling and finishing the garment will affect the way it fits and the way it will withstand wear. Knowledge of the clothing you intend to buy will help you get exactly what you want.

For example, durability may not be essential in all types of clothes, but an informed consumer will recognize durable construction when it is essential.

Five types of ready-to-wear garments are described for you in this section: shorts and other casual wear, skirts, sweaters, blouses, and dresses. Useful information will be given about each of these types of garments on the following subjects:

1. Style and design
2. Sizing and fit
3. Construction details which indicate good quality.
4. Factors which affect durability
5. Factors which affect cost
6. Factors which affect care

Casual Wear for Play

A good fit is necessary for comfort and an attractive appearance. Before you shop for shorts and longer pants, measure your waist and hipline to find out your size. What if your measurements do not correspond to the sizing chart? It is then better to choose the size that fits you at the hipline rather than the one that fits your waistline since it is usually easier to make alterations at a waistline than at the hipline.

Not all manufacturers of ready-to-wear garments follow exactly the same sizing procedure. Therefore, a Size 9 Junior may fit you well in one brand but not in another. Here is one manufacturer's sizes for junior and misses sizes.

Occasionally it is possible to find shorts or long pants in proportioned sizes. The terms "proportioned sizes" and "custom sizes" are used by manufacturers to describe sizes scaled for figures of different heights. The purpose of such sizing is to aid the buyer in choosing the garment that is most likely to fit her. "Tiny," "typical," and "tall," or "short," "medium," and "tall" are terms used to designate sizes that are satisfactory for persons of different heights with typical proportions. Purchase proportioned sizes by the size that would indicate the best length for you as "9 short," "9 medium," or "9 tall."

The way shorts and longer pants are designed can affect the fit and comfort. Since you expect to move, stretch, and sit in these garments you need plenty of ease. The

Tiny	fits figures 5 ft. 2 in. and under
Typical	fits figures 5 ft. 3 in. to 5 ft. 6
Tall	fits figures 5 ft. 7 in. and over

amount of ease allowed is part of the design of a garment. Sports pants designed with no waistband are likely to give a smoother appearance at the waistline.

Stretch pants are made from woven fabrics which expand in wearing more than other woven fabrics. Garments made of stretch fabrics are meant to be comfortable as well as trim looking. Correctly fitted stretch pants will return to their original shape after each wearing. Study the labels on stretch pants before you buy to find out if any special care in washing is suggested. If you buy stretch pants which are too small, or if you do not give them the required care, they will soon become *stretched* pants, with more sag than shape.

If your appearance is important to you, you will want to consider the length of the tailored pants you select. The best length for your sports pants depends on your total height and the length of your legs. You can find the best proportion between you and the pants by carefully trying on several lengths and looking at yourself, both front and back, in a full-length mirror.

The total appearance created by shorts and longer pants on you is also affected by the distance around you, especially at the hipline. If your shape is not designed to fit neatly and trimly into pants then none of the various styles will improve the appearance of your figure. Rather, shorts and longer pants may accent your figure in an unattractive way.

[17] From Sears' Fall and Winter Catalog, 1964, p. 81.

Pants Measurement Chart
Juniors' and Misses' Sizes[17]

Size	7 8	9–10	11–12	13–14	15–16
Waist	23½	24½	25½	27	28½
Hips	32½	34	36	38	40

If tailored pants do not help you to make a good appearance, there are some alternative choices for you. A culotte skirt, a tennis dress, or a short shift with shorts underneath can show your figure attractively. They will not restrict you in active sports and they are comfortable. The designers who first created these styles probably were aware that not all girls are shaped perfectly. They must have known, too, that most girls enjoy wearing attractive casual clothes regardless of their shape.

For winter in cold climates a one-color pants suit is a good choice for sportswear. A one-color outfit with a longer jacket can give a smooth look to an imperfect shape. A one color suit will not outline figure proportions as readily as two or more contrasting colors. Another color principle may be applied; bright colors attract attention, dull intensities blend and recede.

Styles in Ready-to-wear Shorts and Longer Pants.

Long length

jeans	capri pants
anklers	stretch pants
jump suits	with stirrup
ski pants	pants suits
	ranch pants

Knee-length or slightly longer
kneecapper pants
pedal pushers
cabin-boy pants or deck pants
Dutch-boy pants

Above the knee
short shorts
Nassau shorts
Jamaica shorts
Bermuda shorts
walking shorts

Other sport outfits
    culotte skirts   skirt over shorts
tennis dresses (shorts with short skirt)
short shift or skimmer over shorts

100

You expect sportswear to be durable, wrinkle-resistant, and washable. Fabrics which withstand active wear well are denim, stretch denim, duck, sailcloth, stretch sailcloth, cotton twill, and tarpon cloth. Other fabrics which are attractive in sportswear, but which are less sturdy, are cotton sateen, poplin, gingham, terry cloth, and cotton knit.

Sportswear of cotton knit will be very wrinkle-resistant. Many other fabrics now have special finishes which make them wrinkle-resistant. Labels on garments will tell you about this.

Think about the time and effort that will be needed to care for the shorts or pants you select. Sportswear will be easy to keep clean if it can be washed by machine with other family clothing. Be sure bright colors are color-fast or they may have to be washed separately. Garments made of stretch fabrics may need some special care in washing. How much time are you willing to give to the care of garments which need special attention?

Durability doesn't always affect the purchase price, but maintenance should be considered in the cost of the garment. Regardless of the purchase price a garment is not economical if it is costly in time and money to maintain in wearable condition. Maintenance includes the expense required to keep the article clean, repaired, and altered, as needed. You can expect minimum repairs if you consider durability when you are shopping for sportswear. Take time to look at the quality of the zipper and buttons and to inspect the strength of the buttonholes and seams. Firm fabric might be expected to withstand wear better than one which appears to have few threads per square inch.

Skirts

Skirts have no place to go without blouses, sweaters, vests, weskets, and jackets. Therefore, you have chosen a skirt wisely if it will combine well with several other separates.

It may be easier for you to find separates than one-piece dresses that fit you well. The advantage of buying separates is that, if necessary, you can select different sizes in blouses and skirts. A one-piece dress is the same size all over, but you may not be. If you are still growing in several directions, at different rates, you will like separates.

Like the shape of any clothes you wear, the shapes of skirts are important to your appearance.

A slim and well-proportioned figure looks well in a sheath skirt or a straight skirt. The skirt must have enough ease through the hipline to fit well and to allow for comfort in sitting. Special care should be taken in choosing the size because this style is difficult to alter. (See diagram for checking fit in a sheath skirt, page 103.)

Do you need a different size?

Would a different style be more attractive?

Gathered skirts and skirts with unstitched pleats appear bulky and full at the waist. If you want to look larger in that area, these styles would be good choices. Girls with tiny waists, and tall, slender girls look well in these skirts. If you think you are already somewhat bulky at the waistline you may want to consider other designs. A skirt without a waistband will reduce bulk at the waistline.

If both appearance and comfort are important to you, slightly flared and A-line skirts are good choices. The slight fullness makes these styles comfortable for walking, for sitting in the classroom, and for going to the movies.

Sizing of ready-to-wear skirts is not the same in all brands. Usually waist size is used in finding your correct skirt size.

If your hip measure differs from your waist size much more than the two measurements differ in the chart above, you may be able to buy a better fit if you use your hip measure as the guide in finding size.

Although not every store may have these, skirts, as well as pants, can sometimes be purchased in proportioned sizes. (See page 99.) Similar to proportional sizes in short and long pants, "proportion" is used to describe some special skirt sizes. Various terms are used in sizing systems to describe differences in length. For example, skirts of a particular style which are marked "8 short," "8 average," and "8 tall" might be expected to be similar in waist and hip measure but they would vary in length in order to provide more accurate fit.

Sheath Skirt

Good Fit	Poor Fit
1. Waistband smooth	1. Waistband wrinkles or rolls
2. Smooth below the waistband	2. Wrinkles below the waistband
3. Hipline free of bulges at side, front and back; stays in place; adequate ease	3. Hipline has strained appearance; cups under at hipline back, front, or side; bulges visible; not enough ease
4. Side seams at right angles to the floor	4. Side seams pull to front or back
5. Hem parallel to the floor	5. Hem is uneven
6. Length attractive; current style	6. Length is too long? too short?
7. Feels comfortable when seated	7. Uncomfortable when seated

Good or poor fitting shows readily on a straight skirt. Consider the side and back views as well as the front. Alterations may be needed more in one area than another and for comfort as well as appearance. A skirt that is fitted too closely to the body will not only be uncomfortable but is likely to stretch. A skirt with side seams and center front and center back seams is easier to adjust than a skirt with a center back seam only.

In addition to style and size there are other details which affect the way skirts look and fit. Sheath skirts and A-line skirts will keep their shapes better if they are lined. A lining is best when made of firm fabric that will not stretch. If the skirt is washable the lining should be washable also. A generous hem will permit the skirt to be lengthened if necessary. Ready-to-wear skirts that are made well will be cut on the grainline of the fabric. Skirts which

103

identify wool which has been made into cloth, used by a consumer, then reprocessed into another product. Furthermore, the percentage of wool, reprocessed wool, or re-used wool in a garment must be stated in the label.

The exact quality of a wool fabric cannot be determined from the label. The label will tell you only whether the wool fibers are new, reprocessed, or re-used and the percentage of each. But there are good and poor qualities of re-used wool as well as good and poor qualities of new wool. The term "re-used wool" will probably indicate that the fibers have been weakened by use and reprocessing.

Probably only an expert could tell by examining a skirt whether it contained new, reprocessed, or re-used wool. A skirt containing a large amount of re-used wool might feel harsher than one of new wool. But this would depend on the quality of each type of wool. If a skirt containing re-used wool is priced low as compared to a skirt of new wool, it may be a good bargain. Actually, it might be the best choice, particularly if you did not expect to wear the skirt for many years.

have been cut off-grain will appear odd if they are made of plaids, stripes, or figured fabrics. An off-grain skirt will not hang evenly on your body and it may not stay in place. Seam edges will not stretch and ravel if they are finished in some way.

You may find some unfamiliar terms on labels attached to wool skirts, sweaters, and other wool garments.

The Wool Products Labeling Act of 1939 is another federal labeling law intended to aid consumers.[18] This law, effective since 1941, regulates information on labels attached to wool garments. For instance, certain terms must be used correctly. The term "wool" may be used only to refer to wool which has never before been made into fabric. "Reprocessed wool" refers to wool which has been made into cloth before but never used by a consumer before being reprocessed. "Re-used wool" must be used to

Sweaters

Like weaving, knitting is a process for making fabric. Sweaters are still knit by hand at home, and many women and girls find knitting a pleasant recreation. If you have observed hand knitting, you have an idea of how knit fabric is produced. If the home knitter were paid for every hour of her hand work to produce a sweater, the cost of the product would be too much for many consumers. A considerable amount

[18] The Textile Fiber Products Identification Act, also a federal labeling law, is described on pages 91–92.

of skill developed through practice is needed to knit a wearable sweater by hand.

Large quantities of knit fabric can be produced by machines in factories. This large-scale production makes low-cost and moderate-cost sweaters, as well as other knit garments, available.

Manufactured fibers can be processed so they look very much like animal fibers. Therefore the major differences to consider are cost, comfort, and the care required.

Two basic sweater designs are the cardigan and the slip-on. The common feature of all cardigan sweaters is that they open down the entire length of the center front. Variations of cardigans include those which are designed to be closed by buttons or zipper, and others with no front closure.

A slip-on sweater has no front opening. As the name suggests, it must be slipped on over the head. This type of sweater is also called a pullover.

Sweater sizes are based on bust measure. In this manufacturer's sizing chart for

Cardigan. Full length opening down the front

Slip-on. No front opening

sweaters you can note how bust measurement is related to sweater size. For example, Size 30 corresponds with the bust measure of 27–28 inches.

If your bust measure is 30, then Size 32 is the sweater size recommended. Not all manufacturers use the same sizing system. Therefore, in different brands, you will find some differences in the fit of a Size 32 sweater.

[19] From Sears' Fall and Winter Catalog, 1966, p. 261.
[20] Ibid., p. 230.

Junior Sweater Measurement Chart[19]

Size	34	36	38	40
Bust (inches)	31–32	33–34	35–36	37–38

Petite Junior and Junior Measurement Chart[20]

Petite Junior sizes: for shorter than average young figure (5 feet 1½ inches and under without shoes); garments are proportionately shorter in total length than regular Juniors'.

Junior sizes: for the young figure of average height (5 feet 2 inches to 5 feet 6 inches without shoes); small to medium frame more defined waistline, higher bosom, slightly shorter from shoulder to waist than Misses' sizes.

Size	3 or 3P	5 or 5P	7 or 7P	9 or 9P	11 or 11P	13 or 13P	15
Bust (in.)	29½–30	30½–31	31½–32	32½–33½	34 –35	35½–36½	37 –38
Waist (in.)	20 –20½	21 –21½	22 –22½	23 –24	24½–25½	26 –27	27½–28½
Hips (in.)	31½–32	32½–33	33½–34	34½–35	35½–36½	37 –38	38½–39½

The diagram above points out eight places on a sweater where fit is important.[21]

1. Neckline—fits snug and comfortable; lies smooth and flat.
2. Shoulder seams well set—don't sag.
3. Armholes—comfortable—don't bind.
4. Sleeves—set neatly in armholes—don't pull on shoulders—have ample width through upper arm. If long—should come to the wrist, have slight ease to keep them from working up.
5. Fit through body should have ease, slight fullness, no strain.
6. Front opening—should stay neatly closed. No gapping between buttonholes.
7. Line around lower edge even.
8. Rib knit at lower edges and wrists should fit neatly.

A sweater that looks stretched when you have it on is too small. Your clothes should not only make you look good, but help you to feel comfortable as well.

Sweaters are available in both natural fibers and manufactured fibers. The fiber you choose will affect the cost, care, and comfort of the sweater. The chart shows some differences.

[21] From Penney's *Fashion and Fabric*, Fall and Winter, 1964.
[22] Cashmere refers to hair of the Kashmir or Tibetan goat. It may be combined with wool to make cashmere sweaters.

Comparison of Sweaters—Wool, Cashmere[22] and Manufactured Fibers

Fiber	Care needed	Other characteristics
Wool	Hand-wash carefully and block, or dry-clean. Protect from moths. Needs airing; absorbs odors	Very warm, good choice for cool weather Moderate cost to expensive
Cashmere*	Dry-clean Needs airing; absorbs odors Protect from moths	Expensive, considered luxurious Soft; lightweight Very warm
Acrylic Orlon Acrilan Creslan Zefran	Machine-wash if water temperature can be controlled Or hand-wash, low to moderate temperature Some can be tumble-dried if temperature can be controlled Does not absorb odors	Less expensive than wool and cashmere Good choice for year-round wear Some may resemble cashmere in softness
Nylon Antron	Is easily hand-washed Use low water temperature Does not absorb odors	Not so warm as wool, but good year-round wear Less expensive than wool and cashmere

Blouses

Blouses can expand a wardrobe if they are selected carefully. They are appropriate apparel every day of the week for school, play, work, and dress-up.

This simple Bermuda-collar blouse looks well with a gored skirt or slacks

This overblouse is suitable for combining with an A-line skirt or a sheath skirt or shorts. The simple design and solid-color fabric make it suitable in several combinations.

The overblouse with lace and the tuck-in blouse with sleeve ruffles and lace will look best combined with dressy skirts. Either would look mismatched with a denim skirt of sportswear.

Details such as lace or ruffles or unusual necklines, or sheer fabrics may limit the uses of a blouse.

Blouse sizes are based on bust measurement.

107

Front

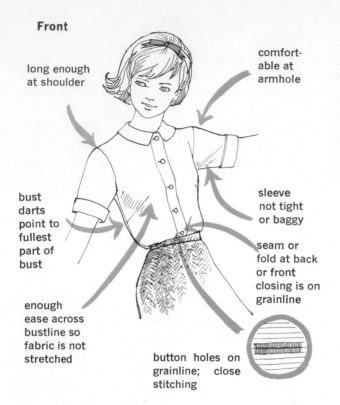

long enough at shoulder

comfort-able at armhole

bust darts point to fullest part of bust

sleeve not tight or baggy

seam or fold at back or front closing is on grainline

enough ease across bustline so fabric is not stretched

button holes on grainline; close stitching

Back

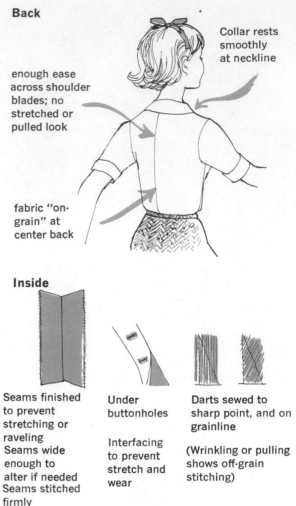

enough ease across shoulder blades; no stretched or pulled look

Collar rests smoothly at neckline

fabric "on-grain" at center back

Inside

Seams finished to prevent stretching or raveling
Seams wide enough to alter if needed
Seams stitched firmly

Under buttonholes

Interfacing to prevent stretch and wear

Darts sewed to sharp point, and on grainline

(Wrinkling or pulling shows off-grain stitching)

There are certain signs that will show whether or not a blouse fits well.

In addition to design and fit, other features are important in blouse selection. A wrinkle-resistant fabric finish will help you maintain a neat appearance all day. Color-fast colors will not need to be washed separately. Plaids look best when they are matched or combined to form a pleasing design. Pockets and yokes may be cut purposely on the bias of the fabric as a part of the design.

Dresses

Certain kinds of dresses look all right almost anywhere. Other kinds of dresses are designed for special occasions, such as parties, concerts, plays, or church. The best use of a dress is determined by (1) its style or design, and (2) the fabrics and other materials from which it is made.

If you wish a dress to have several uses, it should have simple lines and be made of an opaque fabric. The design should follow current fashion yet not be extreme in style. Fabrics for a versatile summer dress might be broadcloth, pique, or chambray. Some winter fabrics which are suitable for many occasions are knits or jerseys, corduroys, and lightweight flannels of wool or manufactured fibers. A dress made from any of these fabrics would look well with dressy shoes and purse, and would look equally well with flats and a school purse. A versatile dress with the characteristics mentioned above could be worn often in a short period of time. It would be appropriate for church, for informal school parties, for concerts and plays. Later, combined with different accessories, it could provide a suitable outfit for school wear, for shopping, and for club meetings.

A dress of unusual design, made of sheer fabric or non-durable fabric, is appropriate for special occasions. Organdy and chiffon are sheer fabrics which look well at dress-up events in summer. Other fabrics for special occasions are taffeta, faille, satin, velvet, and velveteen. These fabrics are suitable for dresses to be worn at parties, concerts, and plays, and if the design is simple, at church. Large ruffles, many tiers of fabric, very low necklines, and other extreme designs are appropriate in a party atmosphere, but for church a dress designed with simple lines would be more appropriate than one of extreme style.

One of the problems in learning to buy ready-to-wear dresses is understanding sizes. Sizes of ready-made dresses and some other types of garments for girls and women are based on body measurements. *Subteen, teen, junior,* and *miss* are four terms used to describe body types or figure types. Differences between these types are these:

1. Differences in body height
2. Differences in bust, waist, and hip measurements
3. Differences in length of body from waist to neck

Subteen sizes are meant to fit young figures, about 4′ 10″ to 5′ 1″ tall, with only slight development in the bust and hips. Subteen sizes may range from 8S to 14S.

Teen describes sizes for girls who are taller and longer-waisted (longer from waist to neck) than the *subteen* figure. *Teen* sizes may range from 10T to 16T. Both *teen* sizes and *junior* sizes fit girls who are about 5′ 2″ to 5′ 5″ tall.

You will find *juniors* sized in uneven numbers from 7 to 19. They are planned for figures slightly more developed than *teen*. *Junior-petite* sizes will fit shorter girls who need junior sizes. *Junior-petite* sizes may include sizes 3 to 13 and they are usually designated as 3P, 5P, 7P and so on in order to set them apart from regular *juniors*.

Misses sizes are designed for girls whose figures are fuller and slightly taller than those who can wear *junior* sizes. *Misses* are even-numbered sizes ranging from either size 6 or 8 to size 18 or 20. *Petite-miss* sizes are available in some brands. These sizes give a better fit for shorter girls, about 5′ 3″ or less, who would otherwise wear regular *misses* sizes.

Not all manufacturers use the same sizing system. In other words, not all manufacturers base their sizing systems on similar body measurements. For this reason you will find that a particular size is not exactly the same in all brands. For example, not all dresses marked size 9 will fit you in exactly the same way. In spite of differences between brands, an awareness of body types or figure types will help you to understand sizing of ready-to-wear dresses. When you shop for a dress, remember that there are sizes for different figure types.

The best fit for an individual also depends on the style of the dress. A dress with a straight skirt may fit very differently from a dress with a pleated skirt although both are marked the same size. The length of the body from neck to waist needs to be considered in selecting a dress with a waistline seam. This seam will fall exactly at the wearer's waist if the dress fits her well. A shift or skimmer dress without a waistline seam may have a more casual fit. The hip measurement is important in a dropped-waistline style.

Size	6	8	10	12	14	16	18	20
Bust	31–31½	32–32½	33–34	34½–35½	36–37	37½–38½	39–40½	41–42½
Waist	22–22½	23–23½	24–25	25½–26½	27–28	28½–29½	30–31½	32–33½
Hip	33–33½	34–34½	35–35½	36–37	37½–38½	39–40	40½–42	42½–44

Juniors[23]

Size	3	5	7	9	11	13	15	17
Bust	29½–30	30½–31	31½–32	32½–33½	34–35	35½–36½	37–38	38½–39½
Waist	20–20½	21–21½	22–22½	23–24	24½–25½	26–27	27½–28½	29–30
Hip	31½–32	32½–33	33½–34	34½–35	35½–36½	37–38	38½–39½	40–41

This is one manufacturer's sizing system for junior and misses dress sizes. Correct size within the figure type may be selected by studying the bust, waist, and hip measurements.

Your measurements may show that you need a different dress size at the hipline from that indicated by the bustline. You may have difficulty finding a one-piece dress which fits you well. For a ready-to-wear dress, it is best to buy the size in which the bodice, or upper half, of the dress fits. Much sewing skill is needed to make good alterations at the shoulder and bustline. If alterations are done at the store this will add to the cost of the dress.

A-line skimmer styles, or two-piece dresses, may fit you best and require little alteration. A skimmer has a less definite waistline than other styles. It does not fit so closely to the body as other styles. Poor body proportions are not accented as they would be in other styles. The unbroken line is flattering to the natural lines of the body.

A two-piece dress also has advantages in fitting. Only skirt alterations will be needed if you buy the size in which the bodice fits well. If your size and shape change, each half can be altered separately as needed.

Easy alterations would aid in keeping the dress wearable over a longer period of time.

A two-piece dress has another advantage. Either piece may be combined with other separates to make additional outfits. For example, the dress skirt might be worn with a sweater instead of the regular bodice. The color, fabric texture, and the style of the dress as well as the separates you have will determine whether extra combinations are possible. For example, either piece of a two-piece dress in a plain color and of a cotton or a knit might easily combine with other separates. A two-piece dress is economical because it has many uses and can be worn frequently.

A dress fits well because of the construction details which cause it to fit well. Study the diagram, on page 111, which shows the details that add up to good fit. You can learn to look for these details in dresses when you shop.

Construction details affect not only the appearance of a dress, but also the wear you can expect from it and the care it will need. These are details you can learn to notice *inside* a dress:

[23] From the chart, "Size Yourself Up." Sears, Consumer Information Division, Chicago, Illinois 60607.

1. seams sewed straight, free of bulges and puckers, wide enough for alteration
2. seams finished to prevent raveling and stretching
3. darts sewed to a sharp point; no ripples or pulling along the dart edge
4. no holes punched at the point of the dart, making it impossible for the dart to be shortened
5. a waistline stay tape to prevent stretch at the waistline
6. interfacing to reinforce buttonholes and so increase wear
7. interfacing to give shape to collars and collarless necklines
8. Hem of even width; wide enough to lengthen dress if needed

These details are important on the *outside:*

9. zipper placket which is smooth; no puckers
10. buttonholes stitched on grainline; close stitches will increase wear

11. dress cut on the grainline; no pulling or wrinkles caused by off-grain fabric

Fit is Important for Appearance and Comfort

Bodice	Skirt
1. Neckline fits smoothly and is comfortable	1. Skirt hangs smoothly at the hipline; has enough ease; no wrinkles; does not cup under at the hipline front or back
2. Shoulder length is comfortable	2. Hem is parallel to the floor
3. Armhole does not bind	3. Length is attractive for body height and leg length; it is current style
4. Bust darts are directed toward the fullest part of bust	4. The skirt is comfortable when seated
5. Enough ease across the bustline; no pull or stretch	
6. Enough ease across the shoulder blades	
7. Sleeves are comfortable; not tight, not baggy	
8. Waistline is located at the waist	
9. Belt stays smooth; does not roll	

VII. Improving Your Choices

You will select clothing for yourself throughout your lifetime. Therefore, it is worthwhile to learn how to make the process of buying clothing a satisfying experience. Being satisfied with the clothing you buy is the reward you can expect for developing your shopping ability. Like many other mental skills, the ability to choose wisely when shopping is developed gradually through years of practice. Even then, an experienced shopper occasionally makes what she considers a "poor buy."

These three procedures can help you develop your shopping ability:

1. Examine your clothing and accessories to discover why some of these purchases were satisfactory and others were unsatisfactory.
2. Collect information about the type of clothing you choose for yourself.
3. Practice using this information the next time you shop for a garment.

Considering Your Clothing and Accessories

By thinking carefully about your clothing and the accessories which you have found pleasing it is possible to discover the exact features which made them pleasing. For example, consider the purse you carry to school. Do you like it because the color combines well with your school clothing? Does it have an attractive shape? Do you feel comfortable with it because it holds adequately all the things you want to carry? The characteristics of a well-liked item are the bases for making another satisfactory choice.

By noting carefully the features of a garment you have not found pleasing you may be able to realize mistakes that you want to avoid in future purchases. Do you have a blouse you do not like? Why is it unsatisfactory? Is it uncomfortable to wear? Is

112

the color not quite as becoming to your complexion as you thought it would be? Does it wrinkle easily, making you feel untidy when you wear it? You are more likely to avoid mistakes in the future if you realize the mistakes that you have made in the past.

Suggestions about sources of information were described on pages 89–90.

Information about the clothing you buy can be useful in making a final selection among several garments. Remember that knowledge can help you only if you make use of it during actual buying trips to the store.

Shopping-Experience Inventory

1. During the last twelve months how many of the following items of clothing did you purchase by yourself *with no suggestions or advice* from anyone? Write the number in the blank in front of the garment.
   _____coats_____
   _____sweaters_____
   _____raincoats_____
   _____skirts, summer_____
   _____skirts, winter_____
   _____blouses_____
   _____dresses_____
   _____shorts, other sportswear_____
   _____socks_____
   _____hosiery_____
   _____underwear_____
   _____purses_____
   _____gloves_____
   _____scarves_____
   _____other items (list these)_____

2. If you paid for any of the items purchased (Question 1) from your earnings, allowance, or gifts of money, write the total number of those things you paid for in the blanks following the items.

3. Do you ever buy clothing which you pay for from earnings, allowances, or gifts, taking suggestions or advice from other people? Place an X in blanks preceding the people who help you.
   _____your mother
   _____your sister
   _____other relatives
   _____friends
   _____sales clerks
   Any comments or explanations:

Suggested Learning Experiences

Review What You Have Read

1. Explain the meaning of each of these terms:

fiber	knitting
natural fiber	bonded
manufactured fiber	(2 meanings)
generic name	bonded knit fabric
trademark name	warp yarn
weaving	filling yarn

Questions for Discussion

2. In what ways do individuals in a family share in making decisions about buying clothing?

3. What are different types of stores that might sell clothing? How do they differ?

4. What are sources of information about ready-to-wear clothes? Why are not all sources of information about ready-to-wear clothing equally helpful?

5. What procedures were suggested that could help you improve your shopping ability?

6. How did you decide on the last skirt, sweater, or blouse you purchased? Why did you select the one you did?

7. Where do you obtain information about the clothes you select for yourself? What do you think consumers should know about the clothes they buy?

An Individual Project

8. Collect information about a type of garment or accessory you expect to purchase soon, such as socks, slips, sweater, or blouse.

Laboratory Activities

9. Examine samples of the three basic weaves with a magnifying lens. Explain how they differ in appearance.
   What are other characteristics of fabrics made by each of these basic weaves?
10. Examine samples of knit fabrics with a magnifying lens.
   After studying close-up views of knits, can you explain how "interlooping" yarns differ from weaving yarns.

Observing Demonstrations

11. Observe a demonstration of the weaving process on a hand loom. You will be better able to understand weaving as a method for making cloth.
   You may know someone who weaves on a small portable loom as a hobby.
12. Observe demonstrations on how to check fit in (a) skirts, (b) blouses (c) sweaters, (d) dresses.

Observing an Illustrated Talk

13. How can you tell whether or not a ready-made skirt might be altered? Observe an illustrated talk by your teacher or a resource person on this subject.

Preparing a Bulletin Board or Exhibit

14. Prepare a bulletin board comparing skirt shapes—(a) straight or sheath skirt (b) A-line (c) gathered or unstitched pleats.
15. Prepare a bulletin board illustrating knit clothing. How many examples of knits can you find?

References and Sources of Material for Teachers

COLES, JESSIE V., *Consumers Look at Labels*. Council on Consumer Information, Colorado State College, Greeley, Colorado, 1964.

LABARTHE, JULES, *Textiles: Origins to Use*. The Macmillan Company, New York, 1964.

RYAN, MARY SHAW, *Clothing: A Study in Human Behavior*. Holt, Rinehart and Winston, Inc., New York, 1966. Part III, "Social-Psychological Aspects of Clothing Related to the Age of the Wearer."

TATE, MILDRED THUROW, and ORIS GLISSON, *Family Clothing*. John Wiley & Sons, Inc., New York, 1961. Chapter 12, "The Teenager."

Textile Handbook, Third Edition. American Home Economics Association, Washington, D.C., 1966.

Sources of Information about Fibers and Fabrics

International Silk Association, Inc., Education Department, 185 Madison Avenue, New York, N.Y. 10016.

Man-Made Fiber Producers Association, Inc., 350 Fifth Avenue, New York, N.Y. 10001. Three booklets—free: *Index of Educational Materials on Man-Made Fibers; Man-Made Fibers: A Summary of Origins, Characteristics, and Uses*, 1964; *Man-Made Fiber Industry Fact Book*, 1965.

National Cotton Council of America, P.O. Box 12285, Memphis, Tenn. 38112. Catalogue of educational materials on cotton and cotton products.

Scalamandré Silks, Inc., 973 Third Avenue, New York, N.Y. 10022. *The History of Silk* by John Kent Tilton (a small booklet).

Wool Education Center, 520 Railway Exchange Building, 909 Seventeenth Street, Denver, Colorado 80202.

UNIT SIX

Learning to Take Care
of Your Clothes

I. What Is Your Share in Family Clothes Care?

Clothing is one of the major needs of families and individuals. Keeping clothes clean and otherwise wearable involves time, effort, space, and some money. This unit is planned to help you consider ways in which you might share in this home-making responsibility. General information is provided for you about some of the major clothes-care tasks. Facts and ideas about storing, as well as about washing, ironing, and pressing clothes are included. Also there is a section on labels that you will want to study carefully. It is important to learn to recognize good labels and to use them as guides in clothes care. When you finish this unit you should be able to summarize the several general factors which determine the best care for a specific garment.

Already, as a young teen, you have probably assumed at least partial responsibility for your own clothes. Have you thought of the care of your clothes as part of that responsibility? For instance, have you ever thought of storage as a type of clothes care needed every day? Do you practice good habits of hanging up your clothes and storing the articles you wear every day? If so, you know that this is good use of your time. The few minutes you spend in hanging up clothes immediately may save many minutes of pressing later.

Perhaps you do not have as much room for clothes storage as you think you need. Furthermore, the storage place may not be where you prefer it to be. This is not an unusual situation. Many girls must share storage space in the home with other family members. Remember this is a part of living in a family group. One positive way to deal with your storage situation is to make the best use possible of the space you do have. (See "Storage for Clothes," pages 144–148, for ideas on how to do this.)

Do you have a share in the task of keeping family clothes washed, ironed, and pressed? If you can press some of your own clothing satisfactorily, you are contributing. Or your responsibility may be even greater. Do you willingly spend time each week ironing some clothing worn by other family members, as well as your own?

Do you hand-wash some of your own clothes? Perhaps you assist with the family washing either occasionally or regularly. Are you ready to ask, "What is there to learn about washing clothes?"

Here are a few questions you may want to investigate:

Does the way clothes are washed make any difference in their appearance?

How should different fabrics be washed?

What is the best water temperature to use?

What products are available for washing clothes? How are they meant to be used?

How do fabric finishes affect washing and ironing?

The following pages will help you answer these questions.

Usually, girls enjoy working with clothes and the fabrics from which they are made. Your experiences in washing, ironing, and pressing clothes is one way for you to learn more about fabrics and fibers.

Use the checklist on page 117 to find out what you actually do now about sharing in family clothes care.

What Is My Share in Family Clothes Care?

For my share in clothes care I:	At least once a week or more often	Sometimes— less often than once a week	Not at all
—hand-wash some of my own clothes			
—hand-wash clothes for other family members			
—sort my own clothes for machine washing			
—sort family clothes for machine washing			
—iron some of my own clothes			
—iron all my own clothes			
—press some of my own clothes			
—press all my own clothes			
—press or iron some clothes for other family members			
—fold family clothes after machine washing			
—help with family washing at a coin-operated laundry			
—hang up my own clothes; have general responsibility for storage			
—brush and air my own clothes when necessary			
—deliver clothing for dry-cleaning or pick up clothes at the dry-cleaner's			
—deliver shoes for repairs or pick up shoes from the repair shop			

117

II. What Factors Determine Care for Specific Garments?

Wisely selected clothes will not make you well-dressed unless you give them adequate care. In order to maintain their appearance and usefulness, your clothes must be given continuous care. Your clothes are serviceable when they are clean and free of undesirable odors, stains, and excessive wrinkles.

What does clothes care actually mean? Systematic clothes care usually includes a number of separate processes. Minimum ordinary care may include washing; either ironing or pressing; airing; brushing; and suitable storing of clothes not being worn. Some types of clothes may require occasional dry-cleaning and stain removal. Repairs and occasional alterations might also be considered a part of regular clothes care. (Repairs and alterations are treated in Unit 8, page 231.)

In order to obtain maximum use from your clothes, you need to know how to give them the type of care they need. Good clothes-care procedures will maintain the original shape, color, size, and texture of each article of clothing. Poor clothes-care procedures can result in shrinkage, faded colors, stretched shapes, and changed textures. Any of these results may cause a garment to be unwearable.

The most satisfactory care for a particular garment is not determined by any one thing. Usually a combination of several characteristics of a garment determines the care it needs. The fiber content, the fabric, the fabric finish, the design, and construction detail of the garment must be considered. Information about each one of these characteristics will help you understand the care directions attached to a specific garment. With enough information about each of these factors perhaps you could make some decisions about caring for garments to maintain the original color, texture, size, and shape when exact directions are not available.

118

How Does Fiber Content Affect Care?

One way in which fibers differ is in the way they react to water. Many synthetic fibers commonly used in clothing do not absorb water. Fabrics made of these fibers seem to resist becoming wet. Soil clings only to the surface of the fibers. When they are washed, water can clean the outside of these fibers but it cannot penetrate inside. Therefore, water seems actually to run off the fabrics. That is why they dry rapidly. Examples of such quick-drying fibers are: nylon, acrylics, modacrylics, polyesters, spandex, acetate and triacetate. You have noticed how nylon hosiery dries rapidly. The same is true of Dacron polyester blouses. The quick-drying fibers are sometimes blended with other fibers which do absorb water. In that case drying may not be so rapid.

Although synthetic fibers do not absorb water, they may absorb oils. An oily spot, once in the fiber, is difficult to remove. An oil stain is likely to be permanent.

Because these quick-drying fibers do not absorb water, clothes made from them are difficult to dampen for ironing. To overcome this disadvantage they can be ironed before they are completely dry after washing.

These man-made fibers are heat sensitive, that is, they tend to be damaged by high ironing temperatures and by washing in very hot water. Fabrics of synthetic fibers can be satisfactorily ironed only at low temperatures. Some do not require ironing at all when not blended with another fiber. (See the sections on "Pressing and Ironing," pages 142–146 and on "Keeping Clothes Clean," pages 131–141.)

In contrast to these synthetic fibers, the natural fibers soak up water readily. Cotton, linen, silk, and wool are all very absorbent. Cotton and linen can be cleaned easily by machine washing, and dried either by machine tumble drying or line drying. Both of these fibers are useful for clothing. Cotton is more popular perhaps because of its low cost. In addition to clothing, many household articles which require washing often are made of cotton. Sheets, bath towels, dish towels, wash cloths, table cloths, place mats, and curtains are household articles commonly made from cotton.

Neither cotton nor linen fibers are weakened when they are wet. Actually both are stronger when they are wet than when they are dry. Because of their strength both cotton and linen will withstand frequent machine washing and drying probably better than any other fibers. Of course, when you compare the durability of particular garments you must also consider the fabric, special finishes, and the construction of the garment.

Neither linen nor cotton fibers have much resiliency. This means that wrinkles will not "hang out" of linen or cotton fabrics. Ironing is necessary after washing. A touch-up pressing may be required between wearings.

Wool garments can be washed more satisfactorily than formerly, since shrink-resistant finishes have now been developed. Also, nylon is sometimes blended with wool to make a more stable or shrink-resistant fabric.

Wool fibers become weakened when they are wet. Therefore, careful handling is required in washing wool garments. Read the care labels on clothes you buy. These labels may suggest either hand washing or machine washing. Hand washing involves less agitation, or action, than machine washing. If a wool garment is machine-washed, a short washing cycle is best. This will cause less strain on the wet fabric. For the same reason do not wring a wet wool garment; squeeze the water out of it.

Excess heat is harmful to the strength and appearance of wool fibers. Water at a low temperature, or even cool water, is suitable for washing wool fabrics. If the garment is to be machine-dried, use a low or no-heat temperature setting.

Wool absorbs water easily. The individual wool fibers can hold water inside of them. Because of the great amount of water it can absorb, a wet wool garment will feel very heavy. Wool takes much longer to dry than cotton or linen or any of the synthetic fibers.

Use a low to moderate pressing temperature. When wool is too dry while being pressed it becomes brittle and feels harsh. Keep it moist as you press. Add moisture to wool fabric by using a steam iron or a damp pressing cloth.

Silk can be washed, but it may become very limp from washing. Like wool, silk fibers are weakened by water. Silk must be handled carefully. The appearance of a fine silk garment might be maintained better by sending it to a dry-cleaner. Also, a dry-cleaner can treat silk fabrics to give them an attractive, crisp appearance.

Press silk at a moderately low temperature, about the same as that used for wool.

How Does Fabric Construction Affect Care?

The looseness or firmness of the weave of the fabric of a garment affects the care of the garment. Good clothes-care procedures will help maintain the original size and shape of the garment. A closely woven fabric will withstand more handling without stretching than a loosely woven one will. When there are too few yarns per square inch they tend to pull apart easily. Such fabrics need careful handling in hanging up, washing, drying, and pressing.

Woven stretch garments are still a rather recent development, but the amount of information about their proper care is increasing. Watch for labels that give specific care directions. A good-quality stretch garment should return to its original size

120

and shape after wearing. Allow an article to rest between wearings. Stretch yarns need time to recover. Fiber content should be considered in caring for stretch fabrics. For instance, if the article is cotton, wash it like cotton. Stretch denim is an example of a cotton stretch fabric.

Knit clothes are "easy care" clothes. They require little or no ironing. They can be folded and stored flat in a drawer, thus saving closet space. Fiber content, as well as fabric construction, is important in the care of knits. This is true of woven stretch garments also.

As an illustration of how the care of knit fabrics depends on the fiber content, let's compare an Orlon acrylic sweater with a wool sweater. The Orlon acrylic sweater could be safely machine-washed at low water temperature, if the added trim could withstand machine-washing action. Ma-

chine drying at low temperature is not only possible, but sometimes recommended, for Orlon acrylic sweaters. The tumbling action fluffs the sweater into soft texture. Acrylic fibers will retain their original shape and the sweater will not stretch. It will dry quickly because the fibers do not absorb water.

In contrast, gentle hand washing would be better laundry procedure for an all-wool sweater. Wool differs from manufactured fibers in absorbency. Wool fibers can absorb and hold a great amount of water. The sweater will become very heavy when completely wet. If washing-machine agitation is added to this weight the sweater will stretch. Gentle squeezing and drying on a flat surface are recommended rather than tumble-drying. Because of the difference in absorbency, the wool sweater will take much longer to dry than the Orlon acrylic

sweater. Wool is resilient. This means that it will return to its original shape if no excess stretching has occurred.

Bonded fabrics are another recent clothing development. If you remember that "bonded" means attached, then it is easy to understand the special characteristic of all bonded fabrics. An outer fabric is permanently attached to a lining material by a heat process. These fabrics have some firmness, or body, yet they are flexible. Tricot, a soft knit material, is one type of lining used. Also, taffeta and other smooth backings are used.

Care of bonded fabrics depends on the fiber content of both the lining and the outer material. Washing and pressing temperatures must be suited to the most sensitive fiber in the combination. A cotton lace might be attached to an acetate taffeta lining. The acetate requires a lower temperature than the cotton. Pressing the cotton fabric at usual cotton temperature may damage the acetate. The open construction of lace will not protect the lining. When you shop, look for the fiber content of both the lining and the outside fabric.

Pile fabrics, such as corduroy, velvet, and velveteen, require some special care. Tiny vertical yarns produce the characteristic appearance of pile fabrics. Pile fabrics are sometimes called napped fabrics. You can learn how to maintain the soft, deep textures of these fabrics. The fiber content must be considered as well as the fabric construction.

Care suggestions for pile fabrics, woven stretch fabrics, knits, and bonded fabrics are included in later parts of this unit. (See "Keeping Clothes Clean," pages 131–146, and "Storage for Clothes," pages 146–148.)

How Do Special Fabric Finishes Affect Care?

Fabric finishes are treatments or processes used to improve fabrics in various ways. Less desirable characteristics of fibers can often be controlled by special finishes. For example, cotton and linen fibers tend to wrinkle easily. Furthermore, they shrink when washed in hot water. Cotton, linen, and wool fabrics can be made both wrinkle-resistant and shrink-resistant. Cotton, though it is naturally very absorbent, can be made water-repellent. Wool can be made moth-resistant. As a result clothing made from specially treated fabrics may serve you better than those which have not been treated. Finishes improve the appearance of fabrics and affect the care they need.

Finishes are permanent, durable, temporary, or renewable. A permanent finish lasts the life of the garment. A durable finish lasts through several launderings or dry cleanings, but has a tendency to gradually lose some of its effectiveness. A temporary finish lasts until the fabric is washed or dry cleaned. A renewable finish is temporary but can be replaced.

Finishes can be grouped into several types according to the ways they affect fabrics:

    crease-and-wrinkle-resistant
    permanent-press or durable-press
    minimum-care, or wash-and-wear
    shrink-resistant, or shrinkage-control
    moth-resistant
    mildew-resistant
    stain-and-spot-resistant
    water-repellent
    waterproof
    crisp finish

The type of finish describes what the particular finish can be expected to do. Also, finishes have brand names or trademark names, just as man-made fibers have brand names. Fabric manufacturers use their own trademark names to identify their fabric finishes. For instance, Koratron, Dan-Press, Burmi-Press, Penn-Prest, Never-Press are a few of the brand names for permanent-press finishes.

A useful clothing label will include the type of fabric finish. However the type of fabric finish is not always named, nor is a clear description of the finish always included on the label. For this reason, you will find that it is helpful to recognize trademark names of some of the commonly used fabric finishes. Frequently, garments will have several labels and hang tags attached. The information on these labels probably includes the fiber generic name or names; the fiber trademark name or names; the fabric trademark name; and the trademark names of finishes. You will want to understand terms which identify finishes, fibers, and fabrics, or the labels will be of no value to you when you go shopping.

In the chart on the next page you will find information concerning names of fabric finishes, trademarks which will help you identify particular finishes on garments, purposes and qualities of fabric

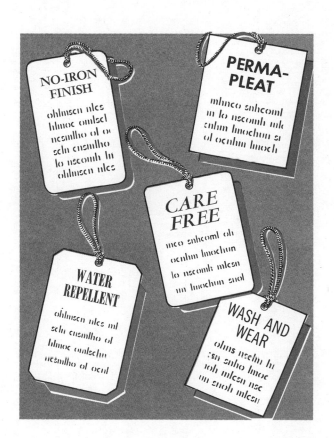

Do You Know Your Fabric Finishes?

Type of special fabric finish	Trade-mark name on label	What it means	What it tells you about clothes care
1. Crease- and wrinkle-resistant	Wrinkle-Shed—permanent crease-resistance for cottons. Tebilized—crease-resistance for linens, spun rayon, cottons. Everglaze—(designates fabric on label)	A permanent-crease—or wrinkle-resistant finish on the fabric should last as long as the garment. The fabric should resist wrinkling.	Wrinkles tend to flatten upon hanging. Sometimes, a disadvantage is that fabrics will not take a press causing garment edges to appear unpressed. Cotton fabrics will be damaged by chlorine bleaches.
2. Permanent-press	Koratron Never-Press Super-Crease Sharp-Shape Dan-Press Burmi-Press Presslokt Penn-Prest Conepress	Used mainly on garments of cotton and cotton blends. Assembled garment has been given permanent press. It differs from other wrinkle-resistant finishes because the garment is treated after it is partly assembled or totally assembled. Other finishes are applied to yard goods.	The garment should hold original shape, pleats, and creases. No ironing should be needed. Stains are difficult to remove. Do not use chlorine bleach. Use washing temperature suited to most sensitive fiber in a blend.
3. Minimum-Care or Wash-and-Wear	These are finishes for cottons: Sanforized-Plus Everglaze Ban Care Minicare Perma-Pressed	Minimum-care means that the garment requires little ironing. A wash-and-wear finish should give the fabric a wearable appearance without any ironing.	The label should tell you the best way to wash a minimum-care or wash-and-wear fabric. Wash-and-wear cottons can usually be washed in hot water (120°F.—150°F.) and dried in a drier at high temperatures (160°F.—180°F.). See further directions below. Remove from drier before completely dry to prevent wrinkles from setting. Drip-dry. Wringing causes wrinkles. Chlorine bleach damages the finish. Touch up with warm iron if needed.
4. Shrink-resistant, or shrinkage control	Sanforized—used on cottons or linens Lanaset Dylanized "Bancora" Kroy® Process Sanforlan used on wool Sanforset—used on rayons	Shrinkage controlled to less than 1%. The wool garment is machine washable under conditions described on the label.	Cottons can be laundered repeatedly without excess shrinkage. Garment size will not change due to shrinkage. Remember that the fiber is wool even though it has been made shrink-resistant. For pressing and washing it should be treated like wool.
5. Moth-resistant	Used on wool: Woolgard Mitan Moth Snub	Wool given a moth resistant finish is resistant to damage by moths.	Garments will have resistance to moth damage. Read label regarding dry cleaning or washing care needed to maintain the finish.

	Trade names	Description	Care
6. Mildew-resistant	Fresh-tex is a finish which includes mildew-resistance.	Mildew resistance is useful on cottons, linens, and rayon in moist, humid climates. Damage from mildew and mold is prevented.	Mildew damage is less likely, but reasonable care in storing clothes is still necessary.
7. Stain and spot-resistant	Syl-mer Unisec Hydro-Pruf Zepel—resists oil as well as water-borne stains.	Some finishes make fabric resistant to water-borne stains, or oily-type stains, or both. Finish used may be same as water-repellent finish. (see below)	Although fabric resists staining, stains may be difficult to remove. For stain removal directions see chart p. 00. Fabrics with water-repellent finishes will be difficult to dampen. If ironing is needed, either use a steam iron, or iron before completely dry.
8. Water-repellent	Cravenette Hydro-Pruf Zelan Zepel—resists both water and oil-borne stains.	Fabrics are resistant to water, but are not waterproof.	Some water-repellent finishes must be renewed when the garment is dry-cleaned. Zelan and Zepel are durable to washing and dry cleaning.
9. Waterproof	Reevair	The fabric actually sheds water.	Dry-cleaning is not suggested, as the fabric may stiffen.
10. Crisp finish	Bellmanized Salerized Fresh-tex	Gives starchy appearance. Applied to sheer cottons, such as organdy, lawn, batiste. Also used on sheer rayon and nylon fabrics.	Fabrics stay crisp through wear, laundering and dry cleaning. No need to starch.

finishes, and necessary care for specially treated garments.

Knowing what to expect from a garment which has a specific fabric finish will enable you to choose your clothes carefully for specific purposes. You will also avoid damaging the finish or the garment itself if you know and follow the basic rules for cleaning a garment with a particular finish. You might be very disappointed if you used a chlorine bleach with a permanent-press dress and the dress lost all of its permanent-press qualities.

Fabrics which have been given crease-and-wrinkle-resistant finishes should resist excess creasing and wrinkling. A permanent finish of this type will last as long as the garment. Cottons, linens, and rayons can be given crease-and-wrinkle-resistant finishes. Without this treatment these fabrics tend to wrinkle easily.

Minimum-care or wash-and-wear finishes also mean that a cotton fabric so treated requires little ironing. A wash-and-wear fabric finish gives a garment a wearable appearance with little or no ironing. Wash-and-wear garments can be drip-dried to avoid wrinkling during the drying process. Wringing or squeezing the fabric adds wrinkles, so that a touch-up pressing with a warm iron may be needed.

When choosing wash-and-wear cottons, select fabrics which have a soft feel. These will repel wrinkles more easily than fabrics which are stiff. Remember, too, that wrinkles show less in printed fabrics than they do in solid-color materials.

Before purchasing a garment with a wash-and-wear tag, test it by grasping a small part of the material in your hand. See whether the fabric is wrinkled when you release the material.

Permanent-press is another wrinkle-resistant finish. It differs from other finishes of this type in that the garments are treated after being partially or totally assembled.

125

Other wrinkle-resistant finishes are applied to yard goods, which may then be either manufactured into garments or sold as yard goods. Permanent-press garments hold their original shapes, pleats, and creases. No ironing should be needed. Extra care should be taken when washing permanent-press clothes. These garments should be turned inside out before being laundered. This will help to prevent discoloration along crease lines in garments such as slacks.

Special shrinkage-control finishes have been developed for the plant fibers, cotton and linen. This is an especially important fabric finish because of the many types of wearing apparel made of cotton. Cotton is an inexpensive, durable fiber. Shrink resistance makes it possible to wash cotton clothing in hot water as often as necessary.

Wool also can be made shrink-resistant. Wool is another natural fiber that tends to shrink easily without special treatment. However, even with a shrinkage-control finish, reasonable care in water temperature and in pressing is still required.

Different shrinkage-control processes are used on different fabrics depending on the fiber. Cotton and linen, wool and rayon each requires a different treatment.

Wool garments can be treated with various moth-proof finishes. These finishes make the wool fibers resistant to damage by clothes moths. These insects lay their eggs on unprotected wool clothes. The larvae hatched from the eggs eat the fibers. Wool is a relatively expensive fiber. This type of protection can prevent damage to costly garments. Read the labels on ready-to-wear garments regarding the cleaning or washing care needed to maintain the finish of wool garments.

A mildew-resistant finish is useful on cottons, linens, and rayons in most humid

climates—the kind of climate in which mildew grows best. Sometimes the dark spots caused by mildew and mold can be washed out or bleached out. If not, the stains left behind may make the garment unwearable. Synthetic fibers are not damaged by mildew growth.

Stain-and-spot-resistant finishes make fabrics resistant to either watery stains or oily-type stains or both. A stain-and-spot-resistant finish may also be called a water-repellent finish.

Water-repellent finishes make fabrics resistant to water but not waterproof. However, a water-repellent finish is useful on fabrics which would otherwise absorb water readily. Without special treatment cotton, linen, and wool are very absorbent.

Stain-and-spot-resistant finishes which give resistance to oily stains are particularly useful for synthetic fibers. These fibers resist water, but they absorb oily materials readily. Some brands of water-repellent finishes do not withstand dry cleaning and must be renewed each time the garment is cleaned. Other brands are durable to both washing and dry cleaning. Fabrics with water-repellent finishes will be difficult to dampen. If ironing is needed, either use a steam iron, or iron before completely dry.

A waterproof finish causes a fabric actually to shed water. This type of finish is useful in rain wear. Dry cleaning is not suggested as the fabric may stiffen. Read the label for specific care directions for specific garments.

A crisp finish gives a starchy appearance to sheer cottons, such as organdy, lawn, and batiste. Delicate nylon fabric and rayons can also be given a fresh, crisp feel. Crisp finishes will withstand laundering and dry cleaning. There is no need to starch sheer blouses and party dresses which have this finish.

Fabric finishes improve the appearance of clothing and reduce the care they require. However, like most conveniences, they are not always perfect. Clothing may be slightly uncomfortable because of finishes which have been applied. For instance, a water-repellent finish may close the pores, or tiny holes, in the fabric, making it impossible for perspiration to evaporate. Therefore, you may seem uncomfortably warm in a water-repellent garment because of unevaporated perspiration on the skin.

It is important to find out whether or not the finish is durable. Some finishes last as long as the clothes are wearable. They are considered durable finishes. Others become less effective after many washings. Others do not withstand even one dry cleaning, and must be renewed after each cleaning.

Cottons treated with permanent-press finishes are believed to be weakened slightly. Minimum-care or wash-and-wear finishes also cause cotton to lose a small amount of its natural strength.

How Does Garment Construction Affect Care?

Specific construction details will affect the care that a garment needs. For example, consider applied trims, seams, and seam finishes.

If you are buying a dress do you examine the seams? Are they durable? The exact number of stitches will vary with the fabric. A weak seam is the result of too few stitches per inch for that particular fabric. If the seam is weak, the dress may need repairs after a few washings.

Have plain seams been finished? Finished seams are a good construction feature. This is true especially if the dress is to be machine-washed often. Raveled seam allowances cause a shaggy appearance inside, and the seams become weaker as the seam allowances disappear in ravelings.

Can all parts of the dress be washed in the same manner? Look at the attached trims. Buttons, laces, bows, and ribbons should be washable at the same water temperature as the rest of the dress. If not, such trims may determine the type of care for the entire dress. Read labels carefully to find out whether all parts of the dress can be treated the same way. Then you will know the care the dress requires.

III. Labels and Hang Tags

Some information concerning how to care for your ready-to-wear garments may be available on garment labels. Newer labels may include "Sure Care Symbols."[24] These symbols, used by some manufacturers, are specially designed to help consumers. The correct care methods for the particular garment so labeled are described in symbols.

Think of a symbol as a short way to deliver a message. For example, this symbol on a road sign tells you that the road ahead curves to the left. The Sure Care Symbols on clothing labels have exact meanings also. However, they will have no meaning for you unless you understand each symbol. Picture symbols are only one type of symbol used to explain correct care. Letters and combinations of letters also give specific directions. In addition, water temperatures are included with washing instructions. Each symbol stands for a different instruction. Several symbols together on a label mean several different instructions for complete care of the garment.

The pictures, letters, and numbers give you these directions concerning the garment:

1. Whether to wash or dry-clean
2. Whether to wash by hand or machine
3. Recommended wash temperature
4. Recommended drying methods
5. Whether or not to iron
6. Recommended ironing temperature

As you study the symbols you can better understand how each one suggests a certain action. Getting to know the symbols is like learning a code.

For example, this symbol tells you that you may wash the garment by machine or hand. You can easily recognize the symbol as resembling an automatic washer.

When the suggested water temperature is added to the symbol you have an additional help on how to proceed in washing the garment.

When the capital letters *TD* are included you know that the article can be tumble-dried if you prefer.

Are you beginning to see how much help these three exact directions give you? How much clearer these directions are than just "washable" on the label! This combination of symbols on a label tells you that the garment can be machine-washed in hot water with any soap or detergent and, if you prefer, tumble-dried. Hand washing would also be satisfactory.

The following letter symbols give facts about the correct washing method:

DD —drip dry
SD —spin dry
DF —dry flat
LD —hang on line to dry
DR —dry rapidly (for example, remove excess moisture between towels)

Still other guides for washing clothes are included in the system of symbols. A message about bleach is carried by these signs:

B —use bleach carefully
B̸ —do not use bleach

24 Sure Care Symbols for labeling textiles and textile products were developed and promoted by the National Retail Merchants Association, 100 West 31st Street, New York.

Wash by hand

Do not wash

This symbol tells you that a garment may be dry-cleaned satisfactorily. It represents the type of machine used in the commercial dry-cleaning process.

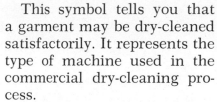

Throughout the system of symbols an X over another sign means that the particular method is not recommended. The example above illustrates this. When you see the "hand" sign you know that hand washing is recommended, but when the hand is crossed out it means "Do not wash."

Recommended wash temperatures range from hot to cold. Sometimes it is helpful to know when an article should be washed separately. Each of the following figures has exact meanings for you about washing:

160°—hot water with any soap or detergent
120°—medium hot water with any soap or detergent
105°—warm water with mild soap or mild detergent
CW —use cold water; it lessens the danger of staining and shrinkage
WS —wash separately; it lessens the danger of staining and shrinkage

But you need to know more than the best way to wash the garment. A complete care label will tell you whether the garment should be ironed. Furthermore, correct ironing temperature for the fiber will be included. It is easy to associate an iron with ironing. Letters added to the sole plate of the iron tell you the correct temperature to use:

H —hot iron
M —medium-hot iron
C —cool iron
S —steaming iron
L —little or no ironing

Remember to look for care labels when you buy. They may have a special message for you in the form of Sure Care Symbols. Will you be able to decode the message?

Test your understanding of the Sure Care Symbols below. Study each label, then explain the care directions given on each.

1. A green skirt of 85% wool—15% nylon blend has this care label:

2. A white blouse, 65% polyester—35% cotton, has this care label:

3. A white, 100% cotton blouse has this care label attached:

4. A blue, 100% polyester housecoat with nylon lace trim has this label:

129

Sure Care Symbols[25]

Follow these symbols to WASH or DRY-CLEAN and IRON your clothes or home furnishings with satisfactory results. Look for the labels with these simple guides to happier washdays.

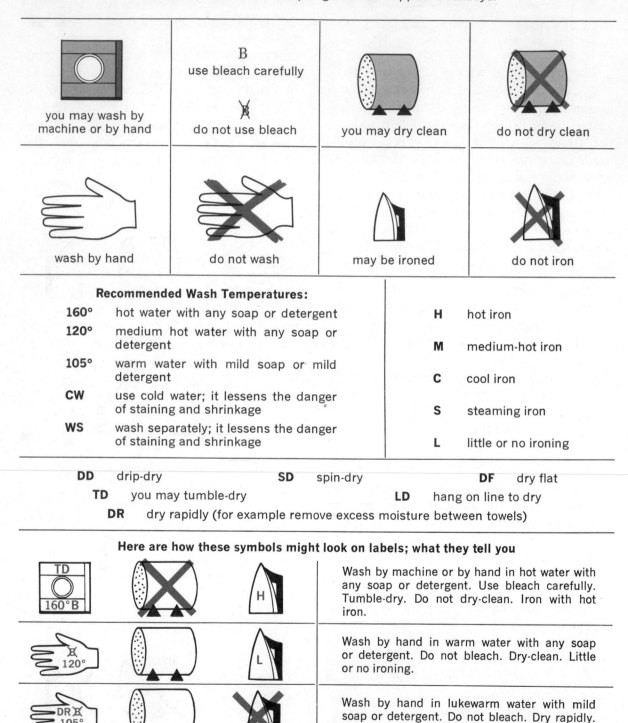

you may wash by machine or by hand

B
use bleach carefully

do not use bleach

you may dry clean

do not dry clean

wash by hand

do not wash

may be ironed

do not iron

Recommended Wash Temperatures:

160°	hot water with any soap or detergent
120°	medium hot water with any soap or detergent
105°	warm water with mild soap or mild detergent
CW	use cold water; it lessens the danger of staining and shrinkage
WS	wash separately; it lessens the danger of staining and shrinkage

H	hot iron
M	medium-hot iron
C	cool iron
S	steaming iron
L	little or no ironing

DD	drip-dry	SD	spin-dry	DF	dry flat
TD	you may tumble-dry		LD	hang on line to dry
DR	dry rapidly (for example remove excess moisture between towels)				

Here are how these symbols might look on labels; what they tell you

Wash by machine or by hand in hot water with any soap or detergent. Use bleach carefully. Tumble-dry. Do not dry-clean. Iron with hot iron.

Wash by hand in warm water with any soap or detergent. Do not bleach. Dry-clean. Little or no ironing.

Wash by hand in lukewarm water with mild soap or detergent. Do not bleach. Dry rapidly. Dry-clean. Do not iron.

[25] Committee on Public Relations, National Retail Merchants Association, 100 West 31st Street, New York, N.Y.

Sure Care Symbols may also be found on care labels attached to some fabric products used in the home. Sheets, pillowcases, and bedspreads are examples of such products.

Clothes-care labels which do not include Sure Care Symbols may provide enough written directions. Complete written directions will include the types of information already mentioned: whether to wash or dry-clean; whether to wash by hand or machine; recommended wash temperature; recommended drying method; whether or not to iron, and recommended ironing temperature.

Does this care label give you enough directions?

IV. Keeping Clothes Clean – Washing; Ironing; Pressing

Washing Clothes

Do you know your washing aids?

Have you ever taken a thoughtful look at the vast assortment of washing products in your local market? Have you counted the many cardboard boxes, glass bottles, and plastic containers of various sizes and shapes?

Both *soaps and syndets* are used for keeping clothes clean. "Syndet" is a shortened term derived from the two words "synthetic detergent." "Detergent," "synthetic detergent," and "syndet" are all useful words to know. "Detergent" may mean either soap or non-soap products. "Synthetic detergent," and "syndet" refer only to non-soap products.

Soap is manufactured from fat and lye. It makes suds more easily and performs best in cleaning clothes if used in heated, soft water. Soap may suds very little, if at all, in extremely hard water. Instead, it combines with dissolved minerals in the water to form a scum in the water and on the clothes.

Syndets are clothes-washing products too, but they are not manufactured from the same type of raw materials as soap. Syndets dissolve and make suds more readily than soap in either cold water or hard water or both. They do not leave a scum behind in the basin or tub or washing machine when washing is done in hard water the way soap does.

Whether water is hard or soft determines to a great extent whether soap or syndet will clean clothes effectively. Syndets are used more extensively than soaps in this country. Perhaps this is so because in a large area of the United States only hard water is available. Hard water refers to water which has minerals dissolved in it. Calcium and magnesium are hard-water minerals. Water hardness is measured and described as grains of mineral per gallon.

131

Different degrees of water hardness are recognized. Different descriptions of water hardness may vary slightly, but the following will explain what is meant by differences in water hardness. Water with 0–3 grains per gallon is considered soft; with 3–7 grains, as moderately hard; with 7–10 grains, as hard; and with more than 10.5 to 30 grains, as very hard. The water-hardness map, on page 134, shows areas where different degrees of water hardness are located.

Clothes-washing problems caused by hard water can be solved by removing the dissolved minerals from the water. Water softeners, like other mechanical aids, can be installed in homes. The principle applied in these water-softening devices is to remove the hardness minerals by chemical reaction. The hard water flows into a tank where it filters through softening materials. The water, which is then free of minerals,

flows into the household water system. Eventually the materials which remove the water minerals become saturated. They are then renewed or recharged, and the process is continued.

Another method of dealing with water hardness is to add water-softening products directly to the wash water. Powdered water softeners can be added to the hard water at the time it is used. The minerals are not removed but their effect on soap is lessened. Soap can then dissolve in the water more easily, and make suds. The amount of water softener required depends on the hardness of the water. When hard water is used without some type of water-softening treatment, syndets are more satisfactory for cleaning clothes than soaps.

Do you have an interest in science and in finding out how knowledge can be used to overcome everyday problems? Perhaps you would like to investigate further the problem of water hardness in the United States. How extensive is water hardness? How can its causes be explained? What problems (other than those connected with washing clothes) are caused by water hardness? What are water-softening methods for home use? for industry?

Bleaches are used to maintain the original white appearance of white fabrics. Also, some stains can be removed from clothing with the aid of bleaches.

There are two general groups of bleaches: chlorine bleaches and non-chlorine bleaches. Each type affects fibers and fabric finishes differently. The best way for you to find out whether a particular brand of bleach belongs to one group or the other is to read the product description on the container. If you see the word "chlorine" in the description, you can be reasonably sure that it is a chlorine-type bleach. If the description says definitely that the product is not a chlorine bleach, or that it

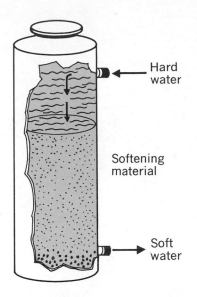

Hard water

Softening material

Soft water

does not contain chlorine, or if the word "chlorine" is not included in the list of ingredients, you know that the product is a non-chlorine bleach. Chlorine bleaches are recommended for washing white cottons and linens which do not have crease- and wrinkle-resistant finishes. Chlorine bleaches are not recommended for washing fabrics of synthetic fibers, wool, silk, and fabrics with crease- and wrinkle-resistant finishes. When a chlorine-type bleach is used in very hard water it may cause brown stains on the clothing. Non-chlorine bleaches are milder than chlorine bleaches in their action on fibers and fabric finishes. They are considered safe for clothing when a chlorine-type bleach is not recommended.

Bleaches can be purchased in several forms—powder, liquid, and tablets. Directions on the various products tell correct amounts to use. Bleaches are added to the washing water and removed with the rinse. A liquid bleach should be dispersed in the wash water before the clothes are added; otherwise it should be diluted well before adding. Powders and tablets should be dis-

solved in the water. The bleach solution should be thoroughly removed from the clothes by rinsing before the washing process is completed. If bleach is left in the fabric, the fibers may be weakened.

Fabric softeners give clothes a soft, pliable, and, sometimes, a fluffy feel. Fabric softeners are useful in treating clothes that have been washed often in hard water with syndets. These conditions tend to make fibers somewhat stiff and harsh. The softening liquid is added to the final rinse, so that it actually remains in the fabric. Fabric softeners soften the fabrics; they do not soften hard water.

Clothes that are soft and pliable wrinkle less, and therefore they are easier to iron. Clothes that are meant to be soft and pliable look and feel better when they are kept in that condition, as hosiery, sweaters, underclothes, nightwear, and some types of blouses. Some household articles also, such as towels and fluffy rugs, may be kept in better condition by adding a softener to the rinse when washing them.

Fabric softeners reduce static electricity in garments made of synthetic fibers. Does your all-Dacron blouse cling? Does your nylon slip snap when you take it off? That's static electricity. Try using a fabric softener the next time you wash them.

Starch gives crispness and body to limp fabrics. For instance, by the use of starch limp cottons can be made smooth, fresh-looking, and slightly stiff. Of course, cottons with a special crisp fabric finish do not require starching to have this appearance. And clothes with wrinkle-resistant finishes have a smooth, somewhat crisp appearance without the help of starch.

In spite of modern fabric finishes there are still ready-made clothes on the market that will look well only if they are given "body" or crispness by starching during the laundry process.

133

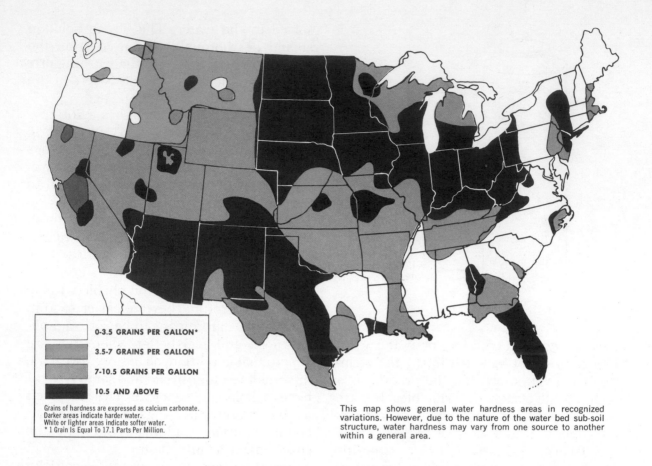

0-3.5 GRAINS PER GALLON*

3.5-7 GRAINS PER GALLON

7-10.5 GRAINS PER GALLON

10.5 AND ABOVE

Grains of hardness are expressed as calcium carbonate.
Darker areas indicate harder water.
White or lighter areas indicate softer water.
* 1 Grain Is Equal To 17.1 Parts Per Million.

This map shows general water hardness areas in recognized variations. However, due to the nature of the water bed sub-soil structure, water hardness may vary from one source to another within a general area.

Besides making fabrics crisp, starching also provides them with some resistance to soiling. Dirt particles cannot cling to a smooth, slick surface so easily as to a rough surface.

Starching products are sold in powdered or in concentrated liquid form. Water is added to the powder or the concentrated liquid according to directions. The solution is then added to the final rinse water.

Spray starches in pressurized cans are also manufactured. This product is applied to the clothes after they have been washed, and then either dried or partially dried. It is sprayed on to the clothes as they are ironed. This product is convenient for stiffening small areas when other parts of the garment are to be left untreated. For example, by using a spray starch a collar might be given some crispness but the remainder of the garment left untreated.

Some general guides

Water temperature for washing may be given on clothing labels as part of the washing directions. If you understand the terms used to describe washing temperature, you will be able to follow washing directions accurately. Typical words which describe water temperature are "hot," "medium," "warm," "cool," and "cold." What temperature is water when it is warm? or medium hot? or hot? Generally these terms do not refer to one specific degree of warmth. Rather, each term means a range of several degrees of temperature.

134

On "Your Guide to Wash-Water Temperatures," (page 136), for example, 140°F to 160°F is described as very hot water. Medium-hot water is approximately 120°F, but may be a few degrees more or less than 120°F. Warm water centers around 100°F. Warm water feels more comfortable to your hands than hot or medium-hot water. You will be able to hand-wash clothes at 100°F or slightly warmer. Cold water covers a wide range, from 80°F to 60°F and cooler. Cold-water washing is sometimes recommended for particular garments. Syndets dissolve and suds in cold water as well as in warmer water.

You will find that some knowledge of these various washing temperatures will be helpful. You will be able to understand better both specific washing directions and general guides for washing clothes. Remember that the best washing temperature for a particular garment depends on more than fiber content. The fabric, fabric finishes, and construction details must also be considered. (Read about sorting clothes, pages 136–138.)

Washable garments look better and wear longer if they are washed at the proper water temperature. For best results consideration should be given to water temperature whether clothes are to be washed by hand or machine-washed. Water that is too hot affects colors and can cause some types of fibers to shrink. Water that is too cool will not clean heavily soiled clothing. Remember that correct water temperature is an important detail in the process of washing clothes. Clothes are basic human needs and it is good management to keep them attractive and useful. The ability to give proper care to clothing is a homemaking skill worth developing.

A good label on a washable garment will provide complete washing directions including the best water temperature to use. Not all care labels are equally helpful. Some labels give only partial directions and some give no directions at all.

These labels illustrate the type of washing directions you might find on a label. Which label provides the most complete guide?

Your Guide to Wash-Water Temperatures[26]

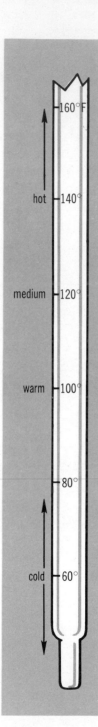

Very hot; water fills only from "hot" line of water heater, with temperature control set for "hot." Provides most soil removal and sanitizing; ideal for white cottons and linens, heavily soiled articles of wash-fast colors. Wrinkles man-made fabrics; may cause some colors to run.

Hot, mixed with some cold water. Fills automatically on "medium" water control. Lightly soiled loads usually wash clean. Provides no sanitizing; somewhat superior to warm water in soil removal.

Temperature of "warm" setting in automatics. Suitable for silk and washable woolens, comfortable for hand-washing. Provides no sanitizing; protects colors. Wrinkles man-made fabrics less than hot water.

Temperature of unheated water supply. For lightly soiled or thoroughly pretreated laundry. Use plenty of liquid detergent, a cold-water detergent, or a granular detergent dissolved in hot water before adding. Gives least cleaning, no sanitizing, minimum wrinkling of man-made fabrics; may not remove wear wrinkles.

Why sort clothes? For best results in washing clothes clean and in maintaining the original appearance of clothes some sorting is necessary. Sorting is necessary for several reasons:

1. To separate clothes which should be washed at *different water temperatures*
2. To separate clothes which require machine washing for *different lengths of time*
3. To separate clothes which require *hand washing* from those which can withstand *machine washing*

Satisfactory water temperature is determined by fiber content and fabric finishes, and by whether the clothes are white or colored. White cottons and linens without crease- and wrinkle-resistant finishes can be safely washed in very hot water. Cottons and linens with crease-and-wrinkle-resistant finishes should be washed at a more moderate water temperature than that used for untreated cottons and linens. When fabrics with crease-and-wrinkle-resistant finishes are dried in an automatic dryer, a cool rinse is recommended. This procedure is to prevent wrinkles from forming. Colored cottons and linens should be washed in warm, rather than hot, water. The dye might be affected by extremely hot water.

Generally, warm water is recommended for washing most synthetic fibers used in clothing. This includes acetate and triacetate, rayon, spandex, nylon, olefin, polyes-

[26] From *Home Laundering: the Equipment and the Job*, Home and Garden Bulletin No. 101. (1964), p. 11, U.S. Department of Agriculture, Washington, D.C. Available from the Superintendent of Documents, U.S. Government Printing Office, Washington, D.C. 20402. Price, 15¢.

Dust and dirt particles cannot penetrate into synthetic fibers. Therefore these fibers can be easily cleaned. When these fibers are machine-washed, a short period of agitation is enough. Fabric finishes reduce the required machine-washing time. Wrinkle-resistant or minimum-care finishes cause cotton and linen to resist soiling. Therefore, a short washing cycle is enough for clothes with this type of finish.

Clothes can be sorted into those which require handwashing and those which can withstand machine washing. For best results, those which require hand washing should always be washed by hand. The second group may be washed either by hand or by machine. Clothing labels tell you whether machine or hand washing is advisable.

Fabric construction is one factor which determines whether hand or machine washing would be more suitable. Knits, particularly wool knits, need gentle hand washing to keep their shapes. However, the label on a specific garment may suggest a brief soaking in the washing machine but with no agitation. Pleats, ruffles, and other similar construction details require careful hand washing, too. Hand washing is also most satisfactory for delicate and sheer fabrics. Organdy, batiste, lace, and net might easily be torn by the turning and spinning action of a washing machine and automatic dryer. Moreover, since such garments do not tend to become heavily soiled, they would not need vigorous washing action.

Usually, white clothes which require the same water temperature and washing time are combined for machine washing. Colored clothes, which might "run" or lose dye, should be washed separately; otherwise the dye from the colored clothes may affect the white clothes that have been washed with them. White nylon has the

ter, and modacrylic. However, care labels on specific articles may direct otherwise. When no exact washing temperature is suggested it is safe to use warm water for synthetics.

Wool and silk should be washed in warm water. Hot water causes wool to shrink and to become harsh. It also causes silk to shrink and may make it limp.

If a fabric consists of a fiber blend, the most sensitive fiber should be considered in deciding on water temperature for washing. For example, you have a blouse of white cotton and polyester with a crease-and-wrinkle-resistant finish. Which is the more delicate fiber? What water temperature would you use for washing and what water temperature would you use for rinsing?

Clothes to be machine-washed can be sorted according to the length of washing time required. Heavily soiled clothes need a longer washing period than slightly soiled ones. The clothes you wear for active work and play will tend to soil more than others.

peculiar characteristics of taking dye colors from colored clothes. This is why a white nylon garment may appear slightly tinted after being washed with colored articles.

Stains caused by food or other materials are a special clothes-cleaning problem. It may be possible to remove some spots from washable clothes by following usual washing procedures. Rubbing the spot with detergent before washing may be enough special treatment to remove it. But many stains require more elaborate treatment.

There are many guides for removing specific stains. It is difficult to remember exact directions for removing a particular stain from a specific fabric without using such a guide. And even if you are using a guide, it is always a good idea to try out a stain-removal procedure on a fabric sample before you use it on the garment itself. In attempting to remove a stain—especially an unknown stain—there is always some risk of damaging the fabric. If the stain has been in the garment for some time, or if a heavily soiled spot has been pressed over, it may be very difficult, if not impossible, to remove it. If the garment is an expensive one and you do not want to risk damaging it, it may be wise to go to the expense of getting an expert dry-cleaner to remove a bad stain.

Until you gain a good knowledge of fabrics limit your attempts at stain removal to inexpensive washable items. Some stains in washable garments can be adequately treated with just detergent and hot water.

Using a dry-cleaning fluid at home requires reasonable caution. If you use any type of dry-cleaning solvent handle it with care following directions exactly. If you do not understand the directions, or if it is not possible for you to follow the directions it would be best not to use the product. Check carefully first.

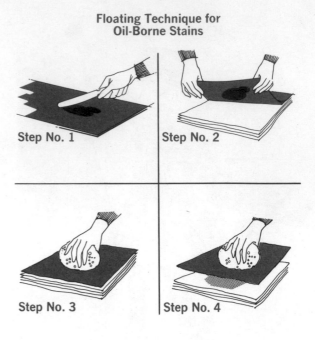

Floating Technique for Oil-Borne Stains

Step No. 1

Step No. 2

Step No. 3

Step No. 4

Stain-resistant fabric finishes are of some help in preventing stains on clothes. (See the chart "Do You Know Your Fabric Finishes?" pages 124–125. Moreover, many man-made fibers do not absorb water readily, and may, therefore, resist watery stains to some extent. However, oily stains may be very difficult to remove from man-made fibers.

The following chart summarizes suggestions on how to remove some common stains. Notice that a particular stain is treated differently depending on whether or not the fabric is washable. This shows the need to consider the fabric as well as the type of stain.

Some of the procedures involve several steps. Stain removal requires patience. When you stop to consider the problems involved in removing stains from fabrics you can understand why it is worth the effort to avoid staining your clothes if it is possible. You will save time and expense as well as your clothes.

138

Washable Fabrics	Dry-cleanable Fabrics
Blood Soak in lukewarm water and detergent. If yellow stain remains, apply laundry bleach.	Treat with cold water to which table salt has been added (1 ounce per quart of water). Salt helps prevent color bleeding. Rinse and blot with towel.
Candle Wax Remove surface wax with dull knife. Place towel under stain, wet thoroughly several times with cleaning fluid. Dry and launder in heavy suds. Use laundry bleach if color of candle remains.	Remove surface wax with dull knife. Sponge with cleaning fluid.
Chewing Gum Remove gum from surface with dull knife. Soak affected areas in cleaning fluid.	Same as for washable fabrics.
Chocolate or Coffee Rinse in lukewarm water. If brown stain remains, apply laundry bleach.	If color-fast, sponge with lukewarm water.
Deodorants Cream, stick, or spray variety: Wash in solution of detergent and warm water.	Sponge with dry-cleaning solvent.
Fruit and Berry Wash in detergent. Apply white vinegar. Rinse thoroughly. If stain remains, use laundry bleach.	Apply liquid detergent to affected areas. Rinse locally.
Grass Wash in detergent. Bleach last traces with laundry bleach.	Apply same procedure locally if color will withstand treatment.
Grease and Tar Place towel under stain. Pour cleaning fluid through stained area.	Same as for washable fabrics.
Hair Coloring (temporary) Sponge with vinegar; rinse. Apply thick solution of detergent and warm water; rinse. Add ammonia to second detergent solution; rinse. Apply a sodium perborate bleach.	Take to dry-cleaner. Identify stain.
Hair Dye Wash in solution of detergent and warm water with vinegar added. Bleach with laundry bleach.	Take to dry-cleaner. Identify stain.
Hair Sprays Wash in solution of detergent and hot water, rinse in clear water. Sprays with shellac base: Sponge with alcohol solution (1 part alcohol, 2 parts water); wash in solution of detergent and hot water and rinse.	Take to dry-cleaner. Identify stain.
Hand Lotions with Silicone Base Wash in solution of detergent and hot water. Rinse.	Sponge with dry-cleaning solvent.

[27] Textile Handbook, Third Edition, revised, 1966 American Home Economics Association.

Washable Fabrics	Dry-Cleanable Fabrics
Home Permanents Wash immediately in solution of detergent and hot water (chemicals bleach dyes in fabric). Rinse.	Take to dry-cleaner. Identify stain.
Ink Pour water through stained area; repeat if bleeding of ink continues. If stain does not bleed, dry the treated area and then wet with water. Apply detergent and white vinegar. Rinse. A patented rust remover is also useful on ink stains and may be tried either alone or in combination with above treatment. Rinse thoroughly. Apply household ammonia. Rinse. Bleach remaining traces with laundry bleach.	Take to dry-cleaner.
Ball-Point Pen Ink Place blotter under fabric. Drip home dry-cleaning solvent through spot. Soak in solution of detergent and warm water. Rinse in cold water. Use mild bleach, but test fabric first.	Take to dry-cleaner and inform him that the ink stain is of the ball-point ink variety.
Lipstick Turn garment inside out and place stained area over absorbent towel. Pour cleaning fluid slowly through stained area until bleeding stops. Dry. Launder in hot, soapy water.	Same as for washable fabric. Apply cleaning fluid treatment only.
Lipstick and Rouge, Permanent Type Soften spot with undiluted liquid detergent. Wash in solution of detergent and warm water.	Take to dry-cleaner. Identify stain.
Liquid Shoe Polish Wash in solution of detergent and warm water, sponge with denatured alcohol solution or sprinkle sodium perborate bleach powder on moistened stain to bleach.	Take to dry-cleaner. Identify stain.
Mercurochrome, Merthiolate, Metaphen Launder in detergent solution. Apply household ammonia. Rinse. Repeat if stain does not come out. Bleach any remaining traces.	Take to dry-cleaner.
Mildew Launder and use chlorine bleach if color and fabric permit. Rinse thoroughly.	Take to dry-cleaner.
Milk, Cream, and Ice Cream Soak in lukewarm water and detergent. Rinse and launder in usual manner.	Sponge with cleaning fluid. If stain remains, sponge lightly with water if color is fast.
Mud Allow to dry. Brush lightly, using stiff bristle brush; launder.	Dry and brush.

Washable Fabrics	Dry-Cleanable Fabrics
Makeup, Liquid Wash in thick solution of detergent and hot water, then rinse in suitable bleach water.	Sponge with dry-cleaning solvent.
Makeup, Pancake Sponge with home dry-cleaning solvent. Wash in solution of detergent and warm water and rinse.	Sponge with dry-cleaning solvent.
Paint Sponge with cleaning fluid as soon as possible.	Same as for washable fabric.
Water Emulsion Paints, Spray Paints Wash in solution of detergent and warm water while paint is wet, or sponge cold-water paint with water. If paint is dry, soften with Vaseline, soak in equal parts of ammonia, water, and turpentine, then rinse in turpentine and wash in solution of detergent and warm water. In all cases, test fabric first. Hardened paint is almost impossible to remove.	Take to dry-cleaner. Identify stain.
Perspiration Launder.	Sponge with water, if possible.
Perfume or Cologne Wash immediately in solution of detergent and hot water—don't let stain age. Bleach with sodium perborate or suitable commercial bleach.	Take to dry-cleaner. Identify stain.
Perfume, Solid Stretch fabric over bowl. Drop warm alcohol from eye dropper over spot. Rinse. Wash out in solution of detergent and warm water. Do not use alcohol on acetate as it will affect dye and dissolve fabric.	Take to dry-cleaner. Identify stain.
Plastic Glues and Lacquers Check labels to determine base. **Nitrocellulose base:** wash in solution of detergent and hot water; apply banana oil, then dry-cleaning solvent. **Resin base:** wash in solution of detergent and hot water, then acetone (test fabrics first), then use dry-cleaning solvent.	Take to dry-cleaner. Identify stain.
Rust Apply patented rust remover as manufacturer directs.	Same as for washable fabrics.
Sun-Tan Lotions Sponge with dry-cleaning solvent. Wash in solution of detergent and warm water with vinegar added (approximately ½ cup to one gallon). For lotions containing tannic acid; drop warm glycerine from eye dropper and let stand on fabric for one or two hours. Rinse.	Take to dry-cleaner. Identify stain.
Tea Rinse in lukewarm water. If brown stain remains, use laundry bleach.	Sponge with water, if possible.
Water Spots Launder.	Wipe very lightly with damp cloth.

Ironing and Pressing

It is quite probable that the time will come when ironing and pressing will no longer be a necessary part of clothes care. Irons and ironing boards may someday be mainly historical items, like butter churns, spinning wheels, and candle molds. Each year textile experts continue to improve our fibers and fabrics. Already we have man-made fibers which resist wrinkling. Fabrics made from these fibers require little or no ironing. Natural fibers can be treated with special finishes so that they resist wrinkling. Permanent-press finishes are used to "shape-set" ready-made garments before they leave the factory. This means that the shape and fit of permanent-press-treated garments are fixed. Such garments might be expected never to need ironing as long as they are wearable. However, it will be helpful to have some general guides for pressing and ironing.

The terms "ironing" and "pressing" are sometimes wrongly used as if they meant the same thing. Actually, they should be used to refer to two different processes.

Ironing refers to the process of removing wrinkles from damp, washable clothing. Heat and pressure from an iron are combined with moisture in the clothing to smooth it. Wrinkles are flattened and the original appearance of the clothing is restored. Moisture in the clothing is removed during the ironing process. Ironing usually is done with a gliding motion.

Pressing is also a process for removing wrinkles from clothing, but the fabric is smoothed by *adding* moisture, as well as by using heat and pressure. A steam iron may be used, or a dry iron and a damp pressing cloth. Instead of sliding the iron on the fabric the iron is placed on the fabric, then lifted. Wool clothing and clothing with wool-like texture are always pressed, not ironed. Also, washable clothing is sometimes pressed between wearings, although it may be ironed after washing.

Using a steam-dry iron

Get acquainted with a steam-dry iron. It is a helpful tool in clothes care. Learn how to use it and how to care for it. If you have constructed a garment for yourself, perhaps you have already learned to operate a steam iron. If not, why not learn now?

Steam-dry Iron Parts Identified

filler opening

handle shaped to fit hand

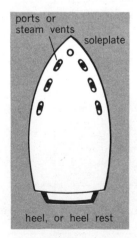

ports or steam vents

soleplate

heel, or heel rest

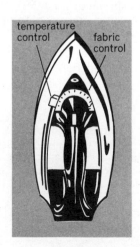

temperature control

fabric control

142

Empty Iron After Using

Empty the iron immediately after ironing is completed. Do not let it stand with water in it.

Store Iron on Heel Rest

Cool iron before storing. Wrap cord loosely. Do not store in the carton or on the sole plate.

Keep Sole Plate Clean

If materials stick to sole plate, cool iron, wipe with damp cloth. If hard to remove, use a household cleanser on a damp cloth.

All steam-dry irons, regardless of the particular brand, have some common features. There is an opening for pouring in water (the direction book will tell you how much). Steam vents in the sole plate (the area that heats) allow the steam to come out and dampen the fabric. A temperature control regulates the temperature of the sole plate. The heel rest is at the bottom and back of the iron. (Store the iron on the heel rest when it is not in use.)

Proper care will keep an iron in the best condition. Empty the water immediately after you have finished using the iron. Distilled water is recommended to avoid clogging the iron with mineral deposits, which are usually present in water.

Use the correct temperature for each fiber. This will protect both the clothes and the iron. For example, most man-made fibers are heat-sensitive; they become soft and melt at high temperatures. The fabric, of course, will then be damaged and particles will stick to the sole plate. Also, if you iron starched cotton at a high temperature, starch may stick to the sole plate and scorch. If particles become stuck to the sole plate, use a soft, dampened cloth to wipe it. If this method does not clean it sufficiently, polish the sole plate with a powdered household cleaner.

One large manufacturer of small appliances offers these additional suggestions for cleaning the sole plate of an iron:

1. "If fabric or starch sticks to the sole plate, it may be removed with a fine-grade (00) steel wool. Avoid getting soap into the steam vents.

2. "To remove synthetic fabric from the sole plate, heat the iron to the lowest setting until the residue softens somewhat. Scrape off as much as possible with a thin piece of wood. (Wooden kitchen spatula is fine.) Then use fine steel wool (Grade 00) to completely remove the rest."[29]

[28] Illustrations and care suggestions from "Instructions for Your New Hoover Spray/Steam and Dry Iron," Model 4400, The Hoover Company, North Canton, Ohio.
[29] Care directions from bulletin, *The Spray, Steam, Dry Iron*, supplied by Wathena Shine, Home Economics Department, Portable Appliance Division, Westinghouse Electric Corporation, Mansfield, Ohio.

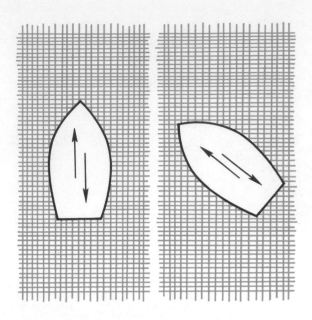

Some general guides

Some general guides for pressing and ironing may be applied to many types of garments. First, *press or iron with the grainline* to avoid stretching the fabric. Fabrics stretch when the interwoven yarns are pulled apart from each other. Also, a garment will lose its original shape as yarns are pulled out of line with each other. Whether you handle fabrics to sew them or to keep clothes wearable, the same idea applies. (See diagrams above.)

Second, when you press or iron a garment *use the best temperature for the fiber content.* Complete directions for care on a ready-to-wear article will tell the appropriate ironing temperature. When you buy fabrics for sewing, look for this information on the end of the bolt or on a separate attached label. If such information is not available, you will need to rely on your knowledge of fibers. Also, the fabric guide on the iron will show the temperature settings for the different fibers. The natural plant fibers, cotton and linen, can be ironed safely at highest temperature setting. A

temperature range of 400°F to 450°F is suitable. The natural animal fibers, silk and wool, require a medium setting of 300°F. The man-made fibers, which are manufactured from chemicals, should be ironed at low temperature settings. They are damaged easily by excess heat.

This group of heat-sensitive fibers includes nylon, polyester, acrylic, spandex, and acetate. Triacetate belongs in the acetate group but has different characteristics. It can be ironed at a higher temperature, of 425°F. Rayon is a man-made fiber, but it can be ironed at a higher temperature than the heat-sensitive fibers mentioned above.

Fabrics of fiber blends need some consideration, too. Again, remember to look on the care label for the exact ironing temperature recommended. If this is not given, use the lowest temperature required for any of the fibers in the fabric. For instance, iron a polyester and cotton blend at the temperature suitable for the polyester.

Bonded fabrics resist wrinkling. This is one of their advantages. Little or no pressing will be necessary between wearings. If pressing is necessary, the pressing temperature must be suited to the fibers. It is possible with bonded fabrics to use two different pressing temperatures satisfactorily. You can press the outside fabric from the outside using the temperature suited to its fiber content. Then you can press the lining from the inside using the best temperature for its fiber content. There are exceptions to this procedure. If the outside fabric is either lace or a loosely woven material it will not protect the lining fabric. In this case the most sensitive fiber in the combination should determine the pressing temperature.

To maintain the original shape of a garment use these techniques carefully as you press. Be sure to press with the grainline.

144

Remember that this prevents unnecessary stretch. Press darts over a pressing ham to maintain the rounded area. For a smooth outside appearance, press long seams open. Lumps or rough places along seam lines detract from an otherwise good appearance. When pressing seams open in an unlined garment, slip a strip of paper under the edge of the seam. This will prevent the outline of the seam from showing on the outside and your garment will have a smooth appearance.

"Touch-up ironing" means that only a few places in the garment are ironed. Wash-and-wear garments generally resist wrinkling during washing but seam, collar, or buttonhole areas may need a small amount of attention.

Good pressing and ironing is done in such a way as to *preserve the original texture* of the fabric. A dull, non-shiny fabric can become shiny because of poor pressing. A dark fabric will develop a shine rather quickly this way. On the other hand, shiny fabrics may be pressed so that they lose their luster. A napped fabric with a deep, rich texture may become flattened by careless handling.

There are two easy ways to prevent shiny areas from developing on dull fabrics. Press the garments from the inside; or press them on the outside using a dampened pressing cloth. A firm, lint-free, absorbent piece of cotton cloth makes a satisfactory pressing cloth. Several layers of cheese cloth are also suitable. For pressing wool use also a piece of wool fabric directly over the wool garment. Cover the wool pressing cloth with a dampened cotton cloth. Wet the cotton cloth, then wring it out until it feels damp but not wet. An unwanted shiny appearance will develop on a wool garment when it is pressed dry. Wool needs moisture and a moderately low temperature.

It should not be necessary to press wool garments frequently. Wool is wrinkle-resistant and resilient. Resiliency is the ability of the fiber to "bounce back" to its original shape after being crushed or bent. Allow wool clothes to hang a few days between wearings and wrinkles will hang out. If the garments are hung in a damp, warm bathroom the wrinkles will hang out more quickly. By this means the attractive texture of a wool garment can be maintained with minimum pressing.

A fabric with a shiny surface can be ironed on the outside purposely to keep the surface lustrous.

Napped fabrics, such as corduroy, velvet, and velveteen will continue to appear to have depth if they are given proper care. Although they will become flattened in wearing, the nap can be raised. The objective in caring for napped fabrics is to raise the napped texture, not to flatten it. An iron should not be placed directly on a napped fabric. Steam and moisture alone are enough. Pressure is not necessary; it is actually damaging. Steam the fabric on the outside, holding the steam iron close to it but not on it. Or steam it from the wrong side by running the steam iron lightly over the surface. Avoid lowering the iron on to the fabric. A dry iron and a damp press cloth can be used instead of a steam iron. Brushing will also raise the nap.

Characteristics of a well-pressed garment

Pressing can add to a garment's attractiveness. How will you know when you have pressed carefully? There are some signs that indicate a job well done:

1. The garment is free of wrinkles. No new wrinkles were added in the attempt to remove those already in the garment.

2. The original texture has been preserved. Luster, dullness, and napped texture have been retained as before pressing, by using a different method for each.
3. The original shape of the garment has been maintained. The garment has not stretched from pressing. Rounded areas were pressed over a rounded surface.
4. No outline of inside details shows on the outside. Darts, facings, hems are not outlined on the outside.
5. Inside, long seams have been pressed open if they were pressed open originally.

V. Storage for Clothes

Guides to Good Storage

Here are suggestions to start you thinking about some guides to good storage:[30]

1. Each item might well be stored as near as possible to the place where it will be put on.
2. All items used together should be stored together.
3. Stored items should be easy to locate at a glance.
4. Like articles should be stored or grouped together.
5. All items used regularly should be stored within an area of easy reach.
6. All items should be easy to grasp at the point of storage.
7. All items should be easily removable without having to remove other items first.
8. Heavy equipment should be stored at or near floor level.
9. All space should be utilized for utmost efficiency.

Can You Apply These Guides to Solve Clothes-Care Problems?

Conserve your time and energy

How can you benefit from applying the guides on this page to good storage? Good clothes storage benefits you in several ways. First, it conserves your time and energy. The way your clothing and accessories are arranged affects the effort and time you spend dressing every day. Second, a good storage plan helps you make the best use of limited space. Third, good storage protects clothes colors, shapes, and fabrics, so that your clothes remain useful longer.

Getting ready for school can, if your clothes are stored efficiently, become a systematic process rather than a frantic race with the clock. You can dress in less time

[30] The nine principles of storage are taken from Penney's *Fashions and Fabrics*, Fall and Winter, 1963, pp. 20–21.

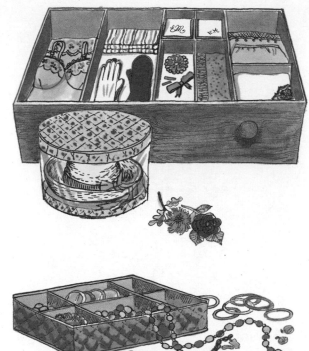

when like articles are stored together, when items are stored near where they are put on, when the articles you need can be easily located at a glance, and when the items you need are easy to reach. When these storage principles have been followed, you can quickly locate the belt, jewelry, and shoes that you need at the moment. Time is often wasted in aimless searching for poorly arranged clothing. Moreover, small articles are easily misplaced when there is no storage plan. Are you tired before you start the day because you needlessly waste much time and energy getting dressed?

Use all space efficiently

If you plan exactly how you will use your storage space, you are more likely to use all the space available to you and to use it efficiently. Perhaps some of these suggestions will help you.

If it is mainly separates that are to be hung in a closet they could be hung on two rods, one above the other, thus using half as much space as with one rod. This arrangement makes it possible to hang blouses and jackets apart from skirts. Different-weight fabrics can be protected from crushing against each other. Freshly ironed blouses can be protected from wrinkling due to crowding. The remaining space could be used for another kind of storage, such as a chest of drawers.

Make a plan for space above and below the hanging rods, if any. An upper hanging rod is convenient only if it is low enough to be reached easily. Therefore, there may be enough space above it to add a shelf. This would provide ideal storage for articles that are used only occasionally or for seasonal clothes. An overhead shelf would keep these things separate from things used every day.

147

Cotton, rayon, linen, and wool can be damaged by mildew. Mildew is a fungus or mold. When conditions are right, it can grow directly on clothes, causing damage in the form of stains and odor. Usually a damp, warm environment and stale air encourage mildew to grow. You may have encountered the odor of mildew in a house that has been closed for a long time.

Fabrics that can be damaged by mildew should be stored clean, dry, and in a dry storage area. This is a good practice for clothes in daily use as well as for seasonal clothing. Freely circulating air in a well-ventilated closet will discourage mildew growth.

The area under the lower hanging clothes might be used for another shelf, a movable shoe rack, or a foot locker.

Protect fibers, fabrics, and shapes

Clothes remain wearable longer when fibers, fabrics, and shapes are protected. This is another way you benefit from a good storage plan. Seasonal clothing, when it is not being worn, might be stored in specially designed, zippered clothes bags. Also, individual garments can be covered by plastic bags of the type used by dry-cleaners. Use scotch tape or masking tape to close the top and bottom. Wool garments can be protected from moth damage this way. The larvae (the worm stage) of the clothes moth, feed on wool and other animal hair. The adult moth, which is a flying insect, lays eggs directly on clothes. The hatched eggs become the larvae which cause damage by eating the wool fibers. This is why wool garments should be stored in tightly sealed bags. Dry-cleaning wool garments before they are to be stored for a long period will remove moth eggs which may already be on the fabric.

148

The odor on clothes caused by mildew might be removed by washing the clothes, if they are washable. However, mildew stains may be more difficult to remove.

Some types of clothes collect odors easily and need to be aired between washings or dry-cleanings. All wool and wool-blend fabrics tend to retain odors more than others. Your wool jacket, coat, skirts, and sweaters are typical garments which may require frequent airing. Cotton garments may acquire a stale odor if they hang for a long time in an unventilated room.

Ideally, garments should be aired outside in clean, fresh air, but outdoor airing is not always practical. In some city areas

where there are concentrations of smoke and car-exhaust fumes, hanging clothes outside may leave new odors in the clothes rather than airing away the old ones. Moreover, when there is dust and soot in the air the clothes may become soiled from being hung outdoors.

One possible substitute for outside airing is to circulate air around clothes indoors with an electric fan. Hang the articles on a clothes rack and direct the fan so that air freely circulates around them. Or air out the entire closet, or other storage space, in the same way.

Another way to deal with odors on clothes is to use a vacuum cleaner on them. The upholstery attachment can be used on clothing fabrics in the same way as on furniture upholstery fabrics. Vacuum-cleaning the clothes will pull loose dust from the surface as well as agitate the air in and around the fabric.

Sometimes dryers are used to freshen clothes. If this is done, it is important to use the no-heat setting, especially when freshening woolens. The no-heat setting is usually the last 5 to 7 minutes of the drying cycle.

149

Garment shapes, as well as fibers and fabrics, should be considered in storing garments. Knit garments stretch easily when they are not handled carefully. Hanging causes knits to stretch unnecessarily. Therefore, knit clothes, such as sweaters and jersey blouses, should be folded and stored flat. Woven stretch fabrics could be stored the same way. This is true of sportswear which you might ordinarily store flat anyway. Other garments of stretch fabrics can be hung just as you would other clothes. After each wearing, a garment of woven stretch fabric requires some time to "recover," or return to its original shape before being worn again.

Heavy clothes and loosely woven fabrics need some special consideration to preserve their shape. A heavy garment, such as a winter coat, might best be hung on a wide wooden hanger or a padded hanger. A wire hanger may not support it evenly over the shoulders. If the coat is to be stored several months, a wire hanger is likely to leave a ridge in the fabric across the shoulders.

Loosely woven fabrics need firm support, too. Hang skirts evenly, attaching both the front and back of the waistband to the hanger. Check hems to see that they hang evenly all around. Button a jacket so that the front does not sag down.

WHEN NOTHING ELSE WORKS

TRY READING THE DIRECTIONS

When nothing else works

In this unit some aids to good clothes care have been described for you. Information has been included about clothes-care labels, products, and equipment. Products are useful, equipment can serve you, and labels help—only if you follow directions!

Suggested Learning Experiences

Review What You Have Read

1. Discuss the meaning of the term "clothes care." Make a list of all the daily and weekly activities which might be considered clothes care. Make a separate list of those activities you consider necessary for adequate clothes care. What does "adequate clothes care" mean?

2. How does good storage affect the appearance of a garment?

Individual or Group Projects

3. Work in small groups or individually to examine clothing labels and the garments to which they are (or were) attached. New garments might be loaned

150

by class members or stores. Garments that have received some wear might also be examined if their labels can also be supplied. After examining the labels and the garment, try to answer these questions: Does the label provide a clear explanation of the care required by the garment? If not, what information is missing?

4. Ask a local clothing-store manager whether the store sells articles with permanent labels which include the Sure Care Symbols. This will tell the store manager that you are aware of this type of labeling. Invite the store manager to explain to the class how Sure Care Symbols on labels can help consumers. A committee might interview a store manager concerning this topic if a classroom talk cannot be arranged.

5. Prepare an exhibit of washing products, including soaps, syndets, bleaches, and fabric softeners. Group similar types of products in your exhibit. Write a definition of each type of product (soap, syndet, bleach, fabric softener). For each group of products in the exhibit prepare labels which define the products and explain the correct use.

6. Work in groups to collect a variety of clothing labels that state the trade names of fabric finishes. For ideas consult the chart "Do You Know Your Fabric Finishes?" pages 124–125. The labels might be grouped together according to the type of finish. Have a contest to see which group can collect labels with all the trademarks listed on the chart.

7. Be creative. Design your own care tag, using the Sure Care Symbols. Use an article you know how to care for properly. Design a hang tag on lightweight cardboard. Or use white percale and a laundry marking pencil. The tag may then be sewed into the garment.

8. Demonstrate the correct way to use a steam iron.

9. Can you think of some original ideas for storing clothes?

Individual or Group Reports

10. Give an oral report explaining the differences between water-repellent and waterproof finishes. Point out the advantages and disadvantages of each of these two types of fabric finishes. You might show two all-weather coats with different finishes, and demonstrate the effectiveness of each coat in keeping the wearer dry. You might find out the price of renewing a water-repellent finish.

Home Experiences

11. Plan a home experience. Study the ways you store your clothes at home. Can you improve your own clothes storage by applying one or more of the nine storage principles described in this unit?

References for Teachers

(*Available from the Superintendent of Documents, U.S. Government Printing Office, Washington, D.C. 20402.)

COLES, JESSIE V., *Consumers Look at Labels*, Council on Consumer Information, Colorado State College, Greeley, Colorado, 1964.

"Colors in Laundering," *Home Laundry Management Efficiency: A Report on the 15th National Home Laundry Conference, 1961*, pp. 58–60, American Home Laundry Manufacturers' Association, Chicago.

"Cotton Wash and Wear," *Home Laundry Efficiency: A Report on the 15th National Home Laundry Conference, 1961*, pp. 49–52, American Home Laundry Manufacturers' Association, Chicago.

DUNHOFF, NANCY, "Profile of Permanent Press," *Practical Forecast*, Vol. 2, No. 1 (September 1965), pp 94–95, 134, 136.

FLYNN, P. J., "Maintenance and Care of Textiles," *Fashions and Fabrics*, Spring/Summer, 1966, p. 13, J. C. Penney Company, New York.

151

*Home Laundering: The Equipment and the Job, Home and Garden Bulletin No. 101 (1964), U.S. Department of Agriculture, Washington, D.C.

"How to Keep Nylon and Dacron White," du Pont Textile Fibers Technical Information (December 1961), E. I. du Pont de Nemours and Co., Wilmington, Delaware.

*LYLE, DOROTHY SIEGERT, "Drycleaning," in Consumers All, the Yearbook of Agriculture, 1965, pp. 382–385, U.S. Department of Agriculture, Washington, D.C.

Maytag Encyclopedia of Home Laundry, The. Maytag Company, Popular Library, New York, 1965.

*McNEIL, ETHEL, "Laundry Hygiene," in Consumers All, the Yearbook of Agriculture, 1965, pp. 371–373, U.S. Department of Agriculture, Washington, D.C.

MEIGHAN, MARY, "Interrelation of Laundry Equipment, Textiles, and Laundry Aids," What's New in Home Economics, Vol. 28, No. 7 (October 1964), pp. 68–69.

"Natural and Synthetic Fibers, Fabrics, and Finishes in Modern Home Laundry," Home Laundry '65—Update for Excellence, A Report on the 18th National Home Laundry Conference, 1964, pp. 6–19, American Home Laundry Manufacturers' Association, Chicago.

"New Stretch Fabrics and Fibers," Home Laundry Management Efficiency: A Report on the 15th National Home Laundry Conference, 1961, pp. 61–62, American Home Laundry Manufacturers' Association, Chicago.

"New Trends in Laundry and Products, Usage, and Purchasing," Home Laundry '65 —Update for Excellence, A Report on the 18th National Home Laundry Conference, 1964, pp. 42–54, American Home Laundry Manufacturers' Association, Chicago. "Bleaches," pp. 42–44; "Detergents," pp. 45–50; "Fabric Softeners," pp. 51–52; "New Trends in Starch," pp. 53–54.

"Permanent Press—No-Iron Finish," Consumers Newsletter, Fall, 1965. J. C. Penney Company, New York.

*RICHARDSON, FLORENCE M., "Removing Stains," in Consumers All, the Yearbook of Agriculture, 1965, pp. 373–376, U.S. Department of Agriculture, Washington, D.C.

*ROBERTS, S. HELEN, "Stretch Fabrics," in Consumers All, the Yearbook of Agriculture, 1965, pp. 352–355, U.S. Department of Agriculture, Washington, D.C.

"Stain Removal Chart," Textile Handbook, Third Edition, pp. 87–89, American Home Economics Association, 1966.

"Stain-Resistant Fabrics—Are They Really?" Changing Times, Vol. 19, No. 6 (June 1965), pp. 27–28.

STERLING, MRS. ANNE, A Handbook on Fabric Care. American Institute of Laundering, Joliet, Illinois, 1961.

STRAWN, BERNICE, "The Know-How of Laundry Products," Practical Forecast, Vol. 9, No. 2 (October 1963), pp. 60–61, 68, 82.

"Stretch—A New Concept of Woven Fabrics," What's New in Home Economics, Vol. 28, No. 6 (September 1964), pp. 54–57, 62–63, 66–67, 70–71, 75.

*WALSH, MARY L., "Soaps and Syndets," in Consumers All, the Yearbook of Agriculture, 1965, pp. 368–370, U.S. Department of Agriculture, Washington, D.C.

Sources of Material for Teachers

American Home Laundry Manufacturers' Association, 20 North Wacker Drive, Chicago, Ill. 60606.

Home Economist, National Cotton Council of America, Box 12285, Memphis, Tenn. 38112. Available on loan is a Fabric Finishes Kit illustrating different finishes which may be applied to cotton.

National Institute of Drycleaning, 909 Burlington Avenue, Silver Spring, Md. 20910, Bulletin service.

Mrs. Anne Sterling, Director of Consumer Information, American Institute of Laundering, Joliet, Ill. 60434.

UNIT SEVEN

Learning as you Sew

I. Why Learn to Sew?

You find satisfaction from your everyday activities because of the things you are able to do. There is real pleasure in riding a bicycle; playing a musical instrument; singing; tennis; swimming; modern dance; painting; ballet; participating in team sports; weaving; sewing! There is a special kind of satisfaction in being able to do something well and there is adventure in finding and using new ideas. A sharp imagination needs to work through skilled hands. Your good ideas about clothing will remain in the idea stage until your hands give these ideas form and shape. Learning a worthwhile skill is learning to control your abilities so that you produce something both useful and beautiful.

With some how-to-do-it ability you can increase your wardrobe and enjoy yourself at the same time. Wouldn't you like to sew a skirt to match your favorite sweater? If you use flattering colors and styles, it will give you pleasure to wear the clothes you make. You can feel proud of doing things as well as knowing about them.

Also, knowing how clothing is put together can make you a smart shopper. As you learn about good fit in clothes you sew, you will be better able to judge fit when you buy. A smart shopper is a good judge of both quality and design. A knowledge of clothing construction is an understanding of details that make up good quality and good design.

You can use sewing skills to give a personal look to the clothes you buy. Improving both design and fit in ready-to-wear clothes can be as much fun as making clothes. You may want to add or remove decorative trim so that the style is right for you. A common alteration which many girls can do themselves is adjusting skirt lengths.

Another important use for your sewing ability is to maintain your clothes in wear-

able condition. No garment looks as well as it should when it has tears, missing pieces, or rips. Ideas for using your sewing skills to take care of clothing repairs are presented in Unit 8, pages 243–246.

A knowledge of clothing construction may start you on the road toward a vocation. Various occupations require some knowledge of textiles and clothing. Furthermore, new occupations are being developed constantly. Perhaps in your lifetime you will find ways to use new information about textiles and clothing in an occupation that is not yet known. Your study of clothing and fabrics is an opportunity for you to explore your interests in this area. (For more ideas about vocations related to textiles and clothing see Unit 9, page 249.)

II. How Can You Develop Sewing Skill?

Skill in sewing is the ability to use many different sewing techniques well. Like many other skills, it must be developed through continuous practice over a long period of time. You can begin to develop your skill by constructing garments requiring the use of basic sewing techniques. A series of sewing projects for beginners, ranging from fairly simple ones to more difficult ones, is suggested in this unit. This series outlines clothing construction experiences to guide the development of your skills. It includes many individual sewing techniques that you may learn through several well-chosen projects. This group of projects is suggested as a guide to your study of clothing construction over a period of several years. You and your teacher should decide where it is best for you to begin. Make a plan for learning that fits the time available.

There are several stages in learning each separate sewing technique. First, you must see all the steps in the particular technique. There are several possible ways for you to see these steps. Your teacher may demonstrate for you each part of a technique in its proper order. Or you may be shown the technique in a film, filmstrip, or slides. Samples of each step may be posted on a bulletin board or exhibit center for you to study. Also, you may study the illustrations which can be found in your textbook or in other references. As you view demonstrations, films, slides, samples, and illustrations, make notes that will help you as you work on your projects.

After you have seen a particular technique demonstrated or illustrated, you are ready to try the procedure yourself with guidance from your teacher. Think carefully about the procedure, and ask questions about your work. Review your notes, and study illustrations and samples again as often as necessary. Now is the time to make sure that you understand the procedure and that you are doing it correctly. Your first garment may take much longer to complete than later projects, but remember that you are learning the basic skills as you sew.

There is another step in learning a skill. It is important that you learn and use the vocabulary which describes materials, equipment, and procedures. Understanding new terms will help you to follow both oral and written directions. And only if you know the correct words will you be able to ask meaningful questions about your work.

The last stage in learning a sewing technique is continued practice. You may want to plan some home projects which require the use of the technique on different garments from those you completed at school. Skill is the result of practice.

III. Equipment for Sewing

Small Equipment

Equipment for measuring

There are many useful tools for measuring when you sew. At different times you may need to use a tape measure, a transparent ruler, a yardstick, a hem marker, and a small 6-inch or 4-inch gauge. A tape measure may be used on either flat or rounded surfaces, and should always be used for body measurements. Either a ruler or a yardstick is necessary for drawing straight lines and checking parallel lines, as well as for measuring. When you are ready to mark a hem, you will need either a yardstick or a hem marker. A few inches, or even a fraction of an inch, may be measured with a small gauge.

Measuring accurately is a basic procedure when you sew. Your success depends upon your understanding of the various lengths and widths used frequently in clothing construction. A common seam allowance is ⅝ inch wide. Can you recognize a ⅝-inch width? How does it differ from ½ inch? Fabrics can be purchased in different widths, including 36 inches, 45 inches, and 54 inches. Which should you buy? Will this make a difference in your pattern layout? Your pattern guide may direct you to stitch ¼ inch from an edge. Can you measure ¼ inch accurately? These examples show the importance of accurate measurements. The ability to measure accurately is a basic skill you will use every day you sew.

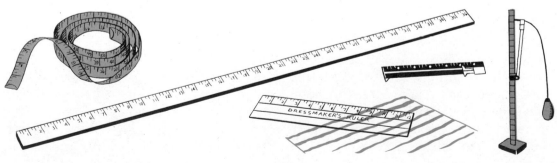

156

You will test your measuring ability when you:

choose the correct pattern for yourself

check the fit of your pattern against your measurements

alter your pattern, if necessary

match pattern grainline marks with fabric grainline

stay-stitch

mark adequate seam allowances

turn edges for edge-stitching

make buttonholes

plan a hem width

attach a waistband

sew a zipper placket

As you sew, watch for the many ways you need to use your measuring equipment.

Cutting tools

Shears and scissors are not the same thing and are designed to do different cutting jobs. Shears have longer blades than scissors, and a handle with one part larger than the other so that it fits the hand comfortably for cutting out garments. Scissors are smaller than shears, have a handle with both parts the same size, and are used for cutting threads, for clipping, and for trimming.

Marking tools

Marking tools include tracing wheels, dressmakers' carbon paper, chalk, and an ordinary writing pencil. Carbon paper, available in several colors, and a tracing wheel may be used to transfer pattern markings to fabric.

Pressing equipment

Good pressing equipment is important to good sewing. Make the ironing board and iron one of your regular stations as

Useful Measurements in Clothing Construction and Various Ways of Expressing Them

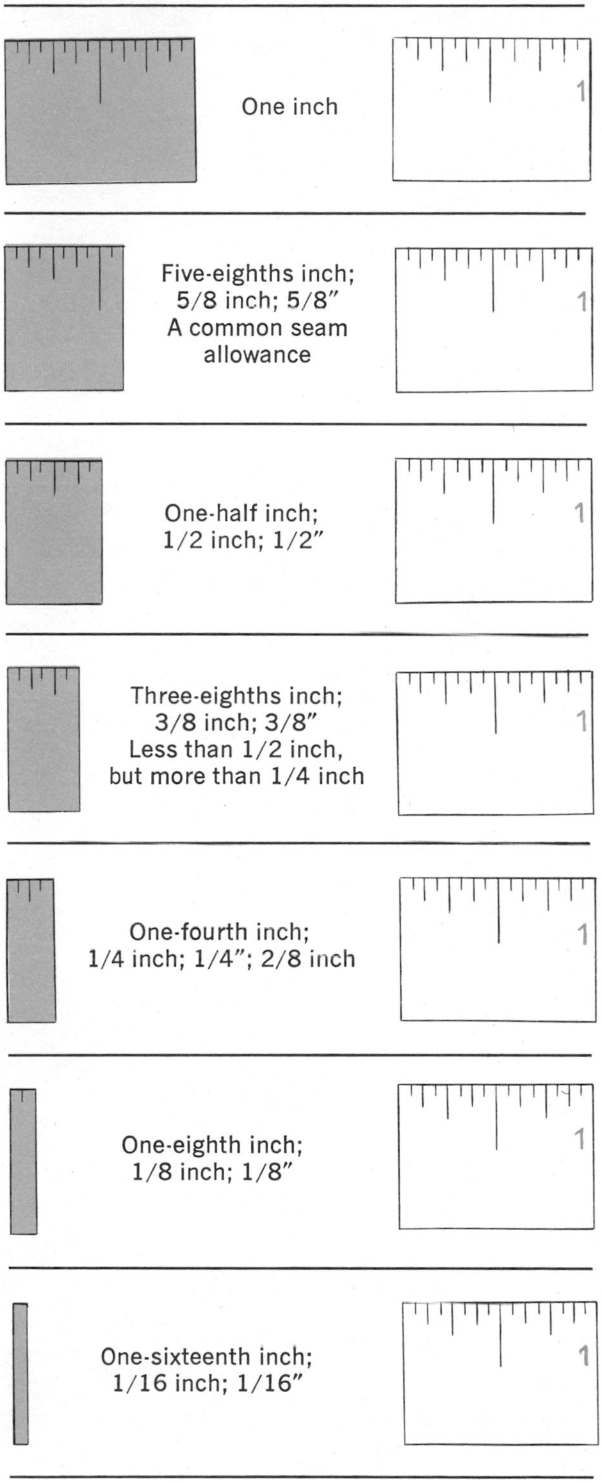

One inch

Five-eighths inch; 5/8 inch; 5/8″ A common seam allowance

One-half inch; 1/2 inch; 1/2″

Three-eighths inch; 3/8 inch; 3/8″ Less than 1/2 inch, but more than 1/4 inch

One-fourth inch; 1/4 inch; 1/4″; 2/8 inch

One-eighth inch; 1/8 inch; 1/8″

One-sixteenth inch; 1/16 inch; 1/16″

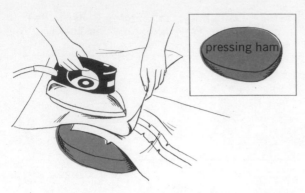

pressing ham

A thimble

An essential piece of small equipment for hand sewing is a thimble. A thimble protects your finger as you push your needle through your fabric. Choose one which fits your middle finger comfortably. Learn to use the side of the thimble rather than the end.

You may share the use of some small equipment in your home economics department. However, for convenience you will probably want to purchase some small items, and if you develop a genuine interest in sewing clothes for yourself, it may be worthwhile for you gradually to purchase your own shears, scissors, and other equipment that you will want to use often. Quality equipment is a sound investment for the girl who sews often. You will find that sewing is easier and more pleasant when you use the correct equipment.

you sew. Learn to use a tailor's cushion, sometimes called a pressing ham. This is a firm cushion for pressing rounded seams and corners which might lose their shapes on a flat ironing surface. (See illustration of a pressing ham, above.) A point presser, as its name indicates, is used to press points, as in collars. Sleeve boards are small ironing boards which simplify the task of pressing any small rounded area, but mainly sleeves.

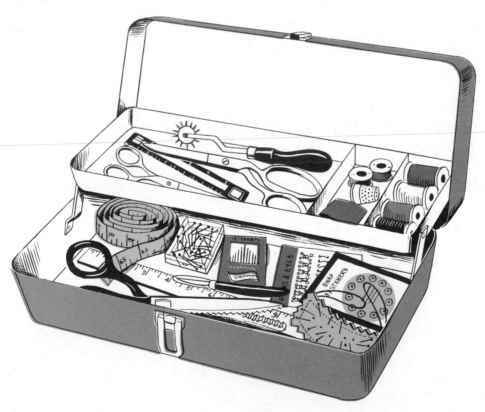

Storing small equipment

For a convenient and unusual type of small-equipment storage, try a fishing-tackle box. Hardware stores and sporting-goods stores have them. They may be purchased in attractive colors, such as green and blue, as well as in the more usual gray metal. Different sizes are available, too. This type of box has a top handle for easy carrying and compartments for separating small articles, and it does not crush or become soggy when wet. Also, shears, scissors, pins, and needles are stored safely. Cutting equipment is less likely to be damaged, nor will points and sharp edges be a hazard. A secure latch keeps a box of this type from dropping open unexpectedly. Safe and convenient equipment storage is a good-management practice. (See illustration on page 158.)

The Sewing Machine

There are a few basic things you will need to learn about sewing machines before you sew. *First,* it is essential that you learn to name machine parts correctly and to recognize them. Otherwise, it will be difficult for you to follow directions involving the operation of the machine. Also you cannot ask questions about the machine or answer them without an adequate vocabulary.

Although various types of machines differ somewhat in appearance each one has a threading arrangement with its related parts: a stitch regulator; a needle-thread tension regulator; a take-up lever; and a presser foot. The direction manual for your particular machine will help you identify its parts. (See illustration of machine parts, below.)

The principal sewing machine parts and their use

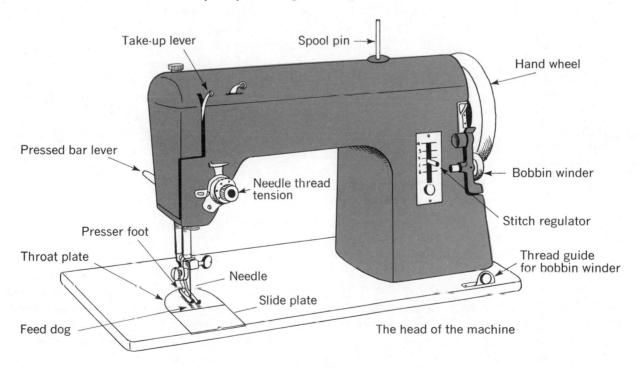

Take-up lever · Spool pin · Hand wheel · Pressed bar lever · Needle thread tension · Bobbin winder · Stitch regulator · Presser foot · Throat plate · Needle · Thread guide for bobbin winder · Feed dog · Slide plate · The head of the machine

Fabric Determines Machine Needle and Stitch Size

Fabric Type	Machine Needle Size	Machine Setting for Straight Stitching	
		Inside Seams	Top Stitch
Sheer	11 fine	12 to 15	15–18
Lightweight	11 or 14 fine or medium	12	14–16
Medium	14 medium	12	14–16
Medium heavy	16 medium coarse	10	12
Heavy	18 or 19 coarse	8	10

Second, you will need to learn how some parts can be adjusted, and how the parts affect the stitching. The stitch regulator controls stitch length and the direction of stitching. Learn how to adjust it for long and short stitches, as needed, and for stitching backward. Backstitching is used to reinforce the ends of plain seams, as well as for other tasks. Stitch length can be adjusted for different weights of fabrics, and for different types of sewing. You will need to adjust stitch length for machine basting, which is a temporary stitching with about 6 to 8 stitches per inch. Permanent machine stitches should be shorter. Changing the needle to a different size is a simple but important adjustment to be able to make. Also, learn to check the position of the needle each time you sew. If the needle is installed backwards it will cause stitching difficulty. Discard needles that are blunt or bent. (See the chart for machine stitch length and needle size related to fabric weight, above.)

The thread from the bobbin (under the slideplate) locks with the upper thread to make a stitch. The machine will make a perfect interlocked stitch when the tensions are correctly adjusted. Both the needle-thread tension and the bobbin tension should be the same. Skill and understanding of the sewing machine mechanism is necessary to make an accurate tension adjustment. Follow your teacher's instructions about whether or not to attempt to regulate tensions at any time.

The amount of pressure on the presser foot can be controlled also. Exact directions for this are included in your machine direction manual. This pressure, with which the fabric is held under the presser foot, is adjusted according to the thickness of the fabric, its slipperiness, and other characteristics that would affect how it can be carried along under the presser foot. (See illustrations "To regulate thread-handling parts" and "To reinforce seams with backstitching," page 161.)

160

Third, it is essential to learn how to thread the machine. Many things can cause poor stitching, but incorrect threading is often all or part of the cause. Nothing takes the fun out of sewing more quickly than a mass of tangled threads. And how discouraging it is to have a thread break, or to see the machine come unthreaded just as you start to stitch. Learn the needle-threading system for your machine, and how to wind the bobbin evenly. Use the same thread on the bobbin as in threading the needle. (See "If thread breaks in sewing machine" and "Avoid tangles when you begin to sew," pages 162 and 163.)

Fourth, you must learn how to start stitching; how to control the speed of the machine; and how to stop smoothly. Practice with a light touch on the knee or foot

To Regulate Thread Handling

Tension Adjustments

Tensions control the threads that interlock to form the sewing machine stitch. There are two tensions, the upper and lower. The upper tension controls the needle thread (shown in blue), while the lower tension controls the thread from the bobbin case or shuttle. A perfectly locked stitch can be formed only when the tensions on the needle and bobbin threads are in balance so that the two threads are drawn into the fabric to the same degree as illustrated below. The tensions should be heavy enough to pull the threads to the center of the fabric and make a good stitch.

 Both tensions correct.

 Loose upper tension. Tight lower tension.

 Tight upper tension. Loose lower tension.

To Reinforce Seams with Backstitching

1. Set stitch regulator for desired stitch length. Position needle into fabric about ½ inch from edge and seam width from right. Raise stitch regulator to reverse.

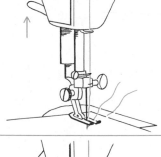

2. Back stitch to edge of fabric for reinforcement. Lower stitch regulator.

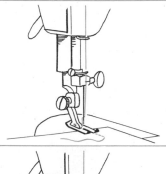

3. Stich to end of seam. Raise stitch regulator.

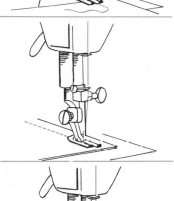

4. Back stitch to reinforce end of seam. Lower stitch regulator to forward stitching position.

5. With take-up lever at its highest point, raise presser foot, draw fabric back and cut threads on thread cutter.

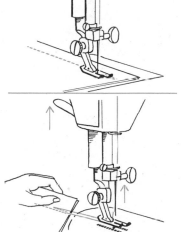

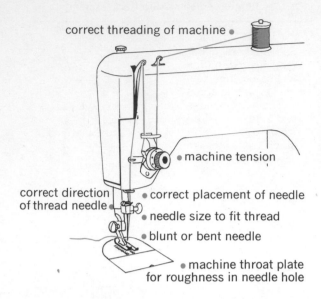

correct threading of machine

machine tension

correct direction of thread needle

correct placement of needle

needle size to fit thread

blunt or bent needle

machine throat plate for roughness in needle hole

stitching. Don't risk being grounded for hazardous machine operation.

And, *finally*, remember that all machine parts should be handled carefully. Forcing a part or using unnecessary pressure on any part may cause damage and put your machine out of order. Do your part in keeping your machine in good condition. (See "Sewing Suggestions," page 163.)

The sewing machine is the most valuable piece of equipment you will use when you sew. The ability to use it is the first step towards developing and improving your sewing skill. Take advantage of the planned classroom lessons and supervised practice sessions you will have at school to learn how to run the machine and take care of it. Almost immediately you will understand that knowing how to use a sewing machine is a practical skill useful in solving everyday homemaking problems. Later on if you plan to buy your own machine you will have a good basis for making a wise choice. Some knowledge of sewing machines and how to operate them will make you a better consumer.

control. Work for an even rate of speed; and run the machine only as fast as you are able to control the fabric under the presser foot. Practice until you can stop the machine exactly where you want it to stop. If you want to be a first-rate sewing-machine operator, avoid poor habits, such as reckless speeding and uncontrolled

Avoid Tangles When You Begin to Stitch

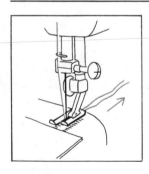 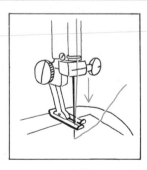 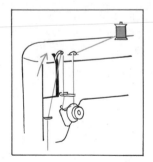 

1. Both thread ends should be pulled towards back of presser foot before stitching.

2. Lower the needle into the fabric before stitching in order to eliminate thread jamming.

3. Before and after stitching be sure take-up lever on machine is at highest point. This prevents thread from slipping out of needle, jamming or breaking.

4. Thread should be wound evenly on an empty bobbin. For perfectly balanced stitch use identical type thread for both upper threading and bobbin.

Breaking of Needle Might be Caused by:	1. Improper size of needle for thread and material. 2. Needle bent. 3. Pulling of material when stitching. 4. Needle striking improperly fastened presser foot or attachments. 5. Crossing too thick a seam with too small a needle.
Breaking of Needle Thread Might be Caused by:	1. A knot in needle thread. 2. Improper threading. 3. Upper tension too tight. 4. Needle not inserted in needle clamp as far as it will go. 5. Needle blunt or bent. 6. Needle in backwards. 7. Thread too coarse for needle. 8. Roughened hole in throat plate. 9. Improper arrangement of thread when starting to sew.
Breaking of Bobbin Thread Might be Caused by:	1. Improper threading of bobbin case. 2. Bobbin thread tension too tight. 3. A knot in bobbin thread.
Skipping of Stitches Might be Caused by:	1. Needle not inserted in needle clamp as far as it will go. 2. Needle in backwards. 3. Needle threaded incorrectly. Thread from long groove side to short groove side. 4. Needle blunt or bent. 5. Needle too small for thread. 6. Needle too short.
Puckered Seams Might be Caused by:	1. Tension too tight. 2. Stitch too long for material being sewn. 3. Wrong presser foot. Use only the presser foot provided for each particular machine, as they are, in some cases, not interchangeable. If machine runs heavily, clean and oil it.

IV. Patterns

Your Measurements and
Your Pattern Size

Probably the most important characteristic of a garment you sew for yourself is the way it fits you. If it fits you well, you will look attractive, be comfortable, and take pleasure in wearing it. How can you be assured of a well-fitted garment?

1. Select your correct pattern size.
2. Check your pattern fit before you sew.
3. Take time for fitting as you sew.

Actually, sewing clothing for yourself is shaping flat pieces of fabric to fit your individual body shape. Therefore, it is important for you to understand your particular shape.

In order to find your pattern type and size, you need to compare your body measurements with the measurements on a pattern size chart. (See the chart on the next page.) Take your body measurements over the clothes you expect to wear with the garment you plan to sew. For instance, measurements for blouses, dresses, and skirts should be taken over undergar-

163

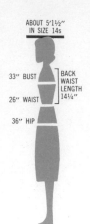

ABOUT 5'1½"
IN SIZE 14s

33" BUST
26" WAIST
36" HIP
BACK WAIST LENGTH 14¼"

Sub-Teen

Sub-Teen patterns are for a figure still growing but beginning to "mature", with more bust than the Girl.

Size	8s	10s	12s	14s
Bust	28	29	31	33
Waist	23	24	25	26
Hip	31	32	34	36
Back Waist Length	13½	13¾	14	14¼

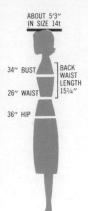

ABOUT 5'3"
IN SIZE 14t

34" BUST
26" WAIST
36" HIP
BACK WAIST LENGTH 15¼"

Teen

Teen patterns are designed for a figure more developed and taller than the Sub-Teen, but not as tall as the Junior figure.

Size	10t	12t	14t	16t
Bust	30	32	34	36
Waist	24	25	26	28
Hip	32	34	36	38
Back Waist Length	14¾	15	15¼	15½

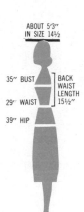

ABOUT 5'3"
IN SIZE 14½

35" BUST
29" WAIST
39" HIP
BACK WAIST LENGTH 15½"

Half-Size

For a fully developed figure, shorter than Miss-Woman, with narrower shoulders. Waist and hips are larger in proportion to bust.

Size	12½	14½	16½	18½	20½	22½
Bust	33	35	37	39	41	43
Waist	27	29	31	33	35	37½
Hip	37	39	41	43	45	47
Back Waist Length	15¼	15½	15¾	16	16¼	16½

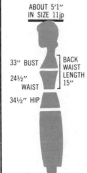

ABOUT 5'1"
IN SIZE 11jp

33" BUST
24½" WAIST
34½" HIP
BACK WAIST LENGTH 15"

Junior Petite

Junior Petite patterns are designed for a well developed figure which is diminutive in size. This is a size not an age group.

Size	3JP	5JP	7JP	9JP	11JP	13JP
Bust	31	31½	32	32½	33	33½
Waist	22½	23	23½	24	24½	25
Hip	32½	33	33½	34	34½	35
Back Waist Length	14	14¼	14½	14¾	15	15¼

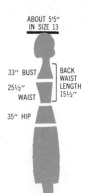

ABOUT 5'5"
IN SIZE 13

33" BUST
25½" WAIST
35" HIP
BACK WAIST LENGTH 15½"

Junior Miss

Junior Miss patterns are designed for the developed figure that is not as tall as the Miss.

Size	9	11	13	15
Bust	30½	31½	33	35
Waist	23½	24½	25½	27
Hip	32½	33½	35	37
Back Waist Length	15	15¼	15½	15¾

ABOUT 5'6"
IN SIZE 14

34" BUST
26" WAIST
36" HIP
BACK WAIST LENGTH 16¼"

Miss

Miss patterns are designed for a well-proportioned, fully developed figure that is taller than any of the other types.

Size	10	12	14	16	18	20
Bust	31	32	34	36	38	40
Waist	24	25	26	28	30	32
Hip	33	34	36	38	40	42
Back Waist Length	15¾	16	16¼	16½	16¾	17

Skirts, Slacks, & Shorts: Select by waist measurement or if hips are much larger in proportion to waist, select size by hip measurement

* Approved by the Measurements Standard Committee of the Pattern Industry.

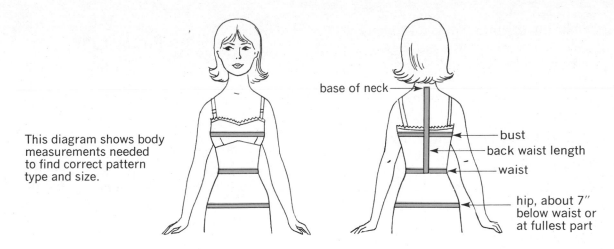

This diagram shows body measurements needed to find correct pattern type and size.

base of neck

bust

back waist length

waist

hip, about 7" below waist or at fullest part

ments. Or you might measure over a very lightweight dress that fits you well. But do not measure over heavy outer clothing, such as bulky sweaters and wool skirts, as this would add width and give incorrect measurements. Also, if you measure over garments which do not fit you well, you may not be accurate in measuring exact locations. For example, it may be difficult to find your correct waist location in a poorly fitted dress. A waist measure taken over a heavy waistband would not be accurate either.

It is helpful to tie a colored cord around your waist to show clearly where your waist is located. The string should be pulled securely, but not tight, and tied. Your waist can probably be defined as the smallest area between your bust and hips.

To determine pattern type and size you will need the following measurements: bustline; waist; back waist length (from base of neck to waist); and hips (about 7 inches below the waist or at the fullest part). Some other measures would be useful for checking pattern fit after you have purchased a pattern. Record shoulder length, front waist length, skirt length, and arm length. These measurements describe your figure.

Check Your Pattern Measurements

Your Personal Measurement Chart	Your Measurements	Pattern Measurements	Adjustment + or −
bust		*	
waist		*	
hips		*	
back waist length		*	
shoulder			
front skirt length			
back skirt length			
sleeve, shoulder to elbow			
sleeve, elbow to wrist			

* Use measurements on pattern envelope.

To obtain accurate measurements you will need to work with a partner. Record measurements immediately before you forget the numbers.

Pattern Types and Sizes

You will find that you need to consider figure types in determining your pattern size. Figure types are based on the amount of figure development, or physical maturity. Height and back waist length, as well as the bust, waist, and hip measurements, are some indications of physical maturity.

Girls differ in rate of physical development. You may have a different figure type from those of some of your classmates even though you are of about the same age. Depending on your individual measurements, you may find your particular figure type to be teen, junior, or perhaps misses. Two other figure types, girls and subteens, are for less mature figures. Another figure type, called women's, is for much more mature figures.

It is possible to use pattern shells to determine your correct pattern size. Pattern shells are basic patterns sewed of firm material. The advantage in trying on shells to determine your pattern size is that you can see yourself in an actual garment. The disadvantage of shells, for finding size, is that you may change size several times while you are growing rapidly. Therefore, you must remember to check your pattern size again every few months.

Patterns are planned with some allowance for ease. Ease, as used here, means an allowance of extra space in the garment for comfort, in addition to the actual amount of room needed by the body.

Buy the pattern type and size which corresponds most closely with your body measurements.

Checking Pattern Fit

Check the fit of your pattern by comparing your measurements with the corresponding measurements on your pattern. For example, compare your back and front waist lengths with the back and front waist lengths on your pattern. Also, compare your own skirt length and shoulder length with those on the pattern. Widths as well as lengths should be considered. Check pattern width at the bustline, waist, and hipline with your own measurements. Remember that good fit includes some ease for wearing comfort.

A second way that you may check your pattern is by fitting the pattern on your body. You will probably need some help to do this accurately. Put the pieces directly over the type of undergarment you expect to wear with the finished garment. Pin darts together in order to see how length and location of each will affect fit. Underarm darts at the bustline should be directed toward the fullest part of the bust, rather than above or below it. Also, bodice front darts at the waistline should point toward the bust.

Tie a cord around your waist to mark the exact location of your waistline, as you did in measuring your waist. The waistline seam of a pattern, either bodice or skirt pieces, may be matched to the cord.

Making Pattern Alterations

You may find that you need to make some minor alterations to improve the fit of your pattern. Changes may be necessary even though you bought the pattern type and size most like your individual body measurements.

A few very general alterations will be considered here. Most patterns include

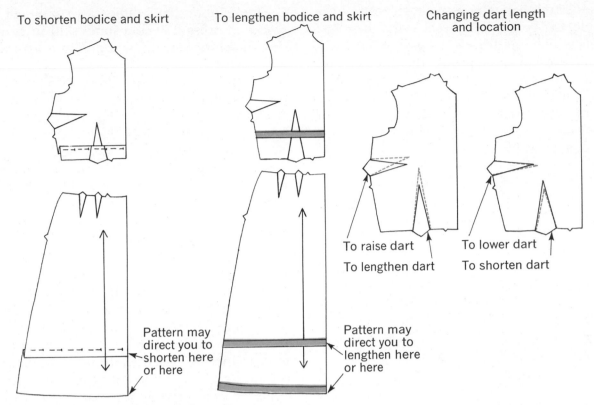

To shorten bodice and skirt

To lengthen bodice and skirt

Changing dart length and location

To raise dart
To lengthen dart

To lower dart
To shorten dart

Pattern may direct you to shorten here or here

Pattern may direct you to lengthen here or here

markings and directions for two types of alterations, lengthening and shortening. To lengthen a bodice, skirt, or sleeve, cut apart the pattern piece at the horizontal alteration line. Attach a strip of paper the width of the extra length needed. When lengthening the skirt, some additional length could be added to the bottom.

For shortening bodice, skirt, or sleeves, reverse the lengthening method. At the horizontal alteration line fold the pattern piece half the length you want to shorten it. Fasten the fold in place with pins or tape.

Darts may be lengthened or shortened by drawing the new length on the pattern. Also, the direction of the dart may be changed by drawing the new lines on the pattern. Draw from the base of the dart, using a ruler to keep lines straight.

V. Fabric and Thread

Choose your fabric carefully

Some fabrics are easier to work with than others, and therefore are good choices for beginners. Use plain colors rather than stripes, plaids, and prints. It takes experience to imagine the appearance of a finished garment sewed from plaids, stripes, or prints. These fabric designs require careful planning before cutting in order to have an attractive garment. As a result, much additional time may be needed to complete a project. Inexperienced sewers may find it better use of their time to learn how to use equip-

167

ment and to master some basic techniques. Later, if you prefer, work with these fabrics which require special pattern layouts.

A fabric which appears the same on both sides is easier to use than a fabric with a different inside and outside. To avoid errors, you must be especially alert in cutting and sewing fabrics which do not look the same on both sides.

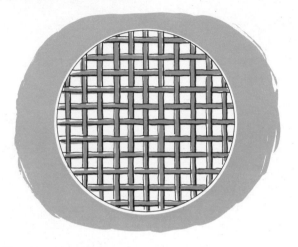

Closely woven fabric.
A good fabric for first projects. This material is less likely to stretch and ravel as you cut, sew and press. This firmer material will be easier to handle in pinning, cutting, and sewing.

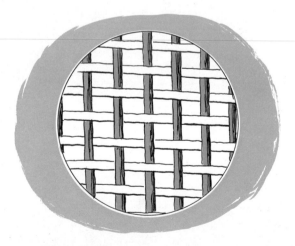

Loosely woven fabric.
A difficult fabric to handle. It is likely to stretch and ravel as you sew. You may have trouble pinning it securely.

Thick fabrics are difficult to pin, cut, sew, and press. Develop some skill in cutting, machine sewing, and pressing before you use these.

Closely woven fabrics are good choices for your first few projects. Raveling and stretching are likely to be less than in lossely woven materials. This type of fabric feels firm and easy to handle.

A closely woven fabric is one in which many yarns per square inch have been used in both the lengthwise and crosswise grainline of the fabric. When you look closely at a particular fabric, you can see these yarns running the length of the fabric and across it. Warp yarns form the lengthwise grainline of a fabric, and filling yarns make up the crosswise grainline. In order to understand this idea clearly, perhaps your class will have an opportunity to examine samples of cloth under a magnifying lens. When samples of cloth are enlarged for viewing this way, you can easily see differences in the number of yarns used in making different fabrics.

To summarize, we can say that the characteristics of a particular fabric will cause it to be easy or difficult to sew. You are likely to have success in your first sewing project if you select fabrics which are closely woven and non-bulky, which appear the same on both sides and are of a solid color.

Get the facts when you buy fabrics

Take time to study the information you find on the end of the bolt and on attached labels. Record useful information which you can use as you sew. For instance, you need to know the width of the fabric before you decide how much to buy. You will want to know the fiber content to avoid possible damage from incorrect iron temperatures when you press. How will the finished garment be cleaned? Is machine washing suggested? Should it be hand-washed? Or, must it be dry-cleaned?

How much shrinkage should you expect? Look for information about a preshrinking treatment. Sanforizing is a shrink-resistant finish used in the manufacture of cotton fabrics. Cotton fabrics which have had this preshrinking treatment may be expected to shrink less than one per cent.

Is the fabric color-fast? What does this tell you about washing the garment? Does the fabric have a wrinkle-resistant finish? Is a wrinkle-resistant, or minimum-care finish, important for the appearance and care of the garment?

Prepare before you sew

Some preparation of your fabric is usually necessary before you sew. *Pressing* is almost always needed for a smooth start. Pattern lay-out and cutting will be more accurate if there are no rough folds or wrinkles in the fabric.

Ends of the fabric should be straight, so that when it is folded for cutting, the grainline can be matched exactly on both thicknesses of the fabric. The ends can be straightened, if necessary, by cutting. Pull a thread as a guide for cutting straight across the material. Cut as close as possible to the end of the fabric.

The *grainline* in your fabric *should be straight* before you cut. The grainline is straight when lengthwise and crosswise yarns are perpendicular, or at right angles to each other. When the grainline is exactly straight, the fabric can be folded evenly. The corners of straight fabric form right angles. Use a table corner to check grainline accuracy. If some straightening is needed, it may be possible to correct this by pulling the fabric straight. Pull evenly, but firmly, on the bias until the lengthwise and crosswise yarns form right angles. (See pages 174 and 176 for a description of bias.)

Cotton with wash-and-wear finishes cannot be straightened by pulling the corners. Therefore, look at the grainline of the material carefully before you buy to be sure that it is straight. If you buy fabrics

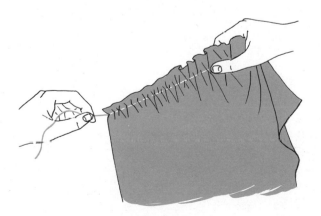

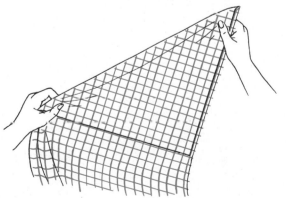

that have this finish but are slightly off-grain you must accept the idea that your finished garment may be slightly off-grain. You may have more satisfactory results in sewing fabrics with wash-and-wear finishes if you choose plain colors rather than prints, checks, or plaids. Slight irregularity in the grainline will not show as readily in a plain fabric.

If you are unsure about shrinkage in your fabric it will be worth the extra time needed to *preshrink* it. You can straighten your fabric at the same time. Use this procedure for cotton fabrics. First, straighten the ends by pulling a thread and cutting across the fabric along the crosswise grain. Fold the fabric lengthwise and pin or baste the ends. Soak it in lukewarm water until thoroughly wet. Squeeze out as much water as possible. Roll it in a bath towel to take out more water. Spread the fabric on a water-resistant table top. Use the table corner and side as a guide to straighten the ends and sides of the material. After it has dried, press it.

Choose appropriate thread and needle

Mercerized cotton thread, available in many colors, is suitable for sewing most cottons. Heavy-duty mercerized thread, as the term suggests, is used in sewing very coarse or thick fabrics. The mercerization process is used to give the thread additional strength and to make it possible to dye it more easily.

Non-mercerized cotton sewing thread can be purchased only in black and white. It is labeled so that small numbers indicate thread sizes suitable for heavy fabrics, and larger numbers indicate finer thread sizes suitable for lightweight and sheer materials. Non-mercerized cotton thread is satisfactory for cotton and linen fabrics.

In addition to cotton thread, both nylon and Dacron polyester thread are available. Although they are strong threads, they will melt at high temperatures. Therefore, they should not be used in sewing clothing which will be washed in very hot water

Fabric Determines Thread and Needle Size

Fabric type	Thread size	Needle size for hand sewing
Sheer—lawn, dimity, chiffon, voile, organdy	mercerized cotton A or 50 cotton (non-mercerized) 80–100 (black and white only)	9, 10
Synthetic sheers, Dacron polyester, nylon	silk 0 nylon	
Lightweight—gingham, chambray, percale	mercerized cotton A or 50 cotton (non-mercerized) 60–70 (black and white only) silk A or B	8, 9
Medium—broadcloth, poplin, pique, wool flannel, seersucker, wool jersey, corduroy, velveteen, sailcloth, very light weight denim	mercerized cotton A or 50 cotton (non-mercerized) 50–60 (black and white only) silk A or B	7, 8
Medium heavy—coating fabrics, heavy denim as for jeans, gabardine	mercerized cotton—heavy duty cotton (non-mercerized) 30–40 (black and white only)	6

* Non-mercerized cotton thread is suitable for sewing cotton and linen fabrics.

and ironed at a high temperature. They are meant to be used with fabrics which are made largely of man-made fibers.

Hand-sewing needles are made in different sizes for different uses. Your fabric determines the best needle size to use. Choose size 9 or 10 for very fine fabrics, and 7 or 8 for hand sewing on medium-weight materials. A packet of assorted sizes will equip you for most hand work. (See chart on page 170 for suggestions about choosing needles and thread.)

VI. Projects That Will Help You Learn as You Sew

Project No. 1
A Simple Blouse

Learning to handle fabrics
Interpreting a pattern
Transferring pattern markings
Stay-stitching
Making darts
Making facings
Attaching a facing at the neck seam line
Deciding which kind of hook-and-eye
    fastener to use

Project No. 2
An A-Line Skirt with Waistband

Learning to finish a seam
Making a zipper placket
Attaching a waistband—Method 1
Attaching a waistband—Method 2
Turning a hem
Controlling excess fullness in a hem

Project No. 3
A Blouse with Attached Collar,
Set-in Sleeves, and Buttonholes

Making an interfacing
(Attaching a collar)
Setting in sleeves
Making buttonholes
Putting on a patch pocket

Project No. 4
A Jumper with Waistline Seam
and Long Back Zipper Placket

Learning to handle a pile fabric
Joining skirt to bodice with waistline
    seam
Putting in a long back zipper placket
Finishing a hem with seam binding
Making a tailor's hem

Project Nos. 5 and 6
An Underlined Skirt and a Blouse—
Separates or an Outfit

Transferring pattern marks on to thick
    material
Underlining a skirt
Interfacing a waistband—Method 1
Interfacing a waistband—Method 2
Facing a no-waistband skirt at waistline
Finishing the waist of a no-waistband skirt
    —Method 1 (with an inside facing)
Finishing the waist of a no-waistband skirt
    —Method 2 (with grosgrain ribbon)
Putting in a seam pocket—Method 1
Putting in a seam pocket—Method 2

Project No. 7
A One-Piece Dress

Studying a one-piece dress before you plan
Making kimono sleeves
Making raglan sleeves

171

Project	New Sewing Skills	More Practice on These Skills
1. Blouse: sleeveless; collarless; no buttons; could be an overblouse Fabric suggestions: firmly woven cotton fabric; same both sides—broadcloth, chambray, percale; plain color Other suggestions: Select cap sleeves if you do not look well in a sleeveless garment. This blouse and the A-line skirt (Project 2) may be planned to be worn together.	fabric selection; straightening fabric; selecting correct pattern size; checking pattern fit; altering pattern, if needed interpreting pattern guide; laying pattern on fabric correctly; cutting with grainline; transferring pattern markings to fabric stay-stitching; making bust darts; making facings; understitching; pressing; making plain seams; making closure at neck	
2. A-line skirt with waistband Fabric suggestions: firmly woven cotton fabric; crisp for A-line shape—sailcloth, denim, poplin	making skirt zipper placket; making waistline darts; fitting at waist and hipline; attaching waistband; finishing seam—edge-stitched, (with or without pinking); finishing hem—turned and edge-stitched	selection of fabric; preparation of fabric selection of pattern; preparation of pattern interpretation of pattern guide; laying pattern on fabric correctly; cutting with grainline; transferring pattern markings to fabric stay-stitching; making a plain seam; pressing with grainline
3. Blouse with attached collar, set-in sleeves, and machine-made buttonholes Suggestions: This blouse could be planned to wear with the A-line skirt (Project 2) or jumper (Project 4). Alternative project for this blouse: housecoat with set-in sleeves, attached collar, and machine-made buttonholes	attaching collar; setting in sleeves; making buttonholes by machine; interfacing Optional: adding patch pocket to either blouse or housecoat	Same as above in Project 2
4. Jumper with waistline seam, long back zipper, and underlined skirt Alternative: This project could be omitted and waistline seam and long back zipper placket could be included in dress (Project 7). Underlining is included in Projects 5 and 6.	making waistline seam; making long back zipper placket; fitting at bustline, waistline, and hipline; finishing hem as suitable for fabric used; sewing on corduroy, a pile fabric Optional: underlining skirt to hold shape	Same as above in Project 2
5. Underlined skirt, which may be planned to combine with blouse (Project 6) as an outfit Fabric suggestions: wool flannel; wool and man-made fiber blends, as wool and nylon; corduroy Optional: You may want to select a design with no waistband	planning color, texture, lines of separates to make a well-coordinated outfit; underlining; choosing and making appropriate seam finishes; interfacing waistband Optional: finishing waist without waistband; putting pocket in seam; preparation of woolen fabrics, if wool is used	selection of fabric; preparation of fabric selection of pattern; preparation of pattern interpretation of pattern guide; laying pattern on fabric correctly; cutting with grainline; transferring pattern markings stay-stitching; pressing with grainline; making a plain seam making a skirt zipper placket; making a hem
6. Blouse, which may be planned to combine with Project 5 Optional: Underline blouse; choose fabric and pattern designs that are suitable with skirt. Alternative project for 5 and 6: a two-piece dress with both pieces underlined	underlining; making appropriate seam finishes Optional: putting in long back zipper; using wool, or wool-blend fabric	fabric selection; fabric preparation pattern selection; pattern preparation pattern guide interpretation; laying pattern on fabric correctly; cutting with grainline; transferring pattern markings stay-stitching; pressing with grainline; making a plain seam; finishing a seam interfacing; fit at bustline, waistline; set-in sleeves,
7. One-piece dress Fabric suggestions: for cool weather: wool flannel; wool and nylon flannel; corduroy; for warm weather: cotton broadcloth; pique; chambray	alteration of dress pattern; joining skirt to bodice; making a waistline seam (if jumper, Project 4, was omitted); fitting at bust, waist, and hipline; making appropriate seam finish Optional: Try either kimono or raglan sleeves, if you were successful with set-in sleeves (Project 3). Underline skirt, or both skirt and bodice, if appropriate.	Same as in Project 6

Your Guide to Sewing Skill

Vocabulary	Management Practices You May Learn	Applying Design Principles When You Sew
selvage, stay-stitch, understitch, interfacing, dart, open placket, tracing wheel, transfer, right angles, notches, alteration, crosswise fold, lengthwise grainline, crosswise grainline, names of sewing machine parts, facing—clip, trim, edge-stitching, baste stitching, directional stitching, measuring gauge, dressmaker's carbon, lengthwise fold, snap fasteners, hook-and-eye fasteners	To follow directions which make your work easier 1. Study pattern guide. 2. Understand directions before you begin. 3. Watch and listen during demonstrations. 4. Study charts and bulletin boards for helpful directions.	Will you consider your figure type and personal coloring when you select the **color** for your blouse and skirt? Do you want to **accent** your blouse or skirt by using contrasting colors? Can you apply ideas about good **proportion** when you plan skirt length?
lapped zipper placket slip-stitch pink seam finish fitted waistline curved seam	To learn correct use and care for small equipment 1. Use cutting shears to cut fabric only. 2. Store shears properly to prevent nicks, scratches, and dulled blades. 3. Protect table tops and other surfaces when you use tracing wheel. 4. Plan orderly storage for equipment.	
undercollar to ease (a sewing technique—a verb) set-in sleeve patch pocket attached collar machine-made buttonholes	To maintain sewing machine in good working condition 1. Learn to thread machine correctly. 2. Avoid sewing over pins. 3. Pull bobbin and top thread under presser foot to prevent knotting. 4. Store machine with fabric scrap under presser foot. 5. Follow instructions when you attempt to use attachments.	What type of skirt or jumper would you wear with your blouse to create **harmony** in your outfit? How does the size of a **pocket** and its location affect the over-all appearance of a garment? What design principles may help you decide? How might you use design principles to plan the number of **buttons,** their size, and arrangement?
bodice underlining zipper placket ease (a quality of fit—a noun) waistline stay	To make progress by using your time and energy well every day 1. Use all your class time every day. 2. Make minimum trips to use iron and other equipment. Store equipment near the place of use. Store sewing supplies within sight and easy reach. 3. Record progress as you finish each step. 4. Check pattern fit; alter accurately.	Is the **silhouette** of your jumper suited to your figure type? Did you consider the **color** and **texture** of your fabric in relation to your figure type? If you plan a **neutral** color jumper, have you thought of accenting it with a bright print blouse?
	To practice ways of saving your time and energy 1. If possible, adjust chairs and tables to best height for good posture. 2. Arrange large equipment to save steps and avoid crowding. 3. Maintain good posture to avoid tiring. 4. Plan orderly storage of small equipment to save time.	Can you recognize formal or informal **balance** in your blouse and skirt? Is there **harmony** in the combination of textures? Is a feeling of **rhythm** created by the lines of your skirt and blouse? If you plan to wear them as an outfit, are the lines of the skirt and blouse **harmonious?**
	To spend your money wisely when you sew 1. Buy correct yardage for your pattern. 2. Remember to prepare fabrics before cutting. 3. Study pattern layout to prevent cutting errors. 4. Help to make equipment last longer by proper use and care.	
waistline stay bound buttonholes	To check your progress through self-evaluation 1. Learn how to use a written check-list. 2. Compare your standards with those set by the class. 3. Enjoy continuous improvement with each project.	Did you consider principles of design in choosing your pattern? Can you recognize good **proportion** and **scale** in your completed dress? Does your sleeve length show good **proportion** in relation to arm length and body height? Is the width of your hem in good **proportion** to your height?

Project No. 1
A Simple Blouse

A good starting point for a beginner is a simple blouse. Choose a style without collar or sleeves. These can come later. Plan to make an open placket rather than a zipper placket or buttonholes.

What can you learn by making a simple blouse? You will be able to apply what you have learned about patterns and fabrics when you:

    select a blouse pattern for yourself
    check pattern fit
    alter the pattern, if necessary
    select and prepare a firm, washable fabric for sewing

You will take the first steps toward other skills by learning how to:

    handle a fabric
    interpret a pattern guide
    pin a pattern on the fabric, following grainline markings
    cut with the grainline
    transfer pattern markings to the fabric
    stay-stitch
    sew and press darts
    attach a facing
    make a plain seam

Choose a firmly woven fabric which appears to be the same on both sides. Broadcloth, chambray, or percale are good materials for your first project. You may want to plan the blouse so that it can be worn with the A-line skirt suggested in Project No. 2.

Learning to handle fabrics

Your completed garments will show how you cared for your fabric. Perhaps the most important thing to learn about fabric is how to fold, cut, pin, and press it WITHOUT STRETCHING! When you are able to do this well, you have taken a major step in learning to sew well.

To avoid stretching fabrics you must understand grainline. As was explained in Unit 5 (pages 81–144), all woven fabrics have grainlines. These fabrics are formed from yarns which are interlaced with each other in the weaving process. Warp yarns,

Woven fabric

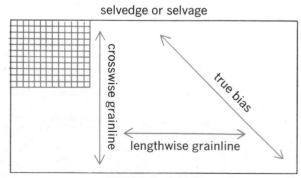

174

To avoid stretching your fabric, remember to

1. Lay out pattern with regard to grainline.

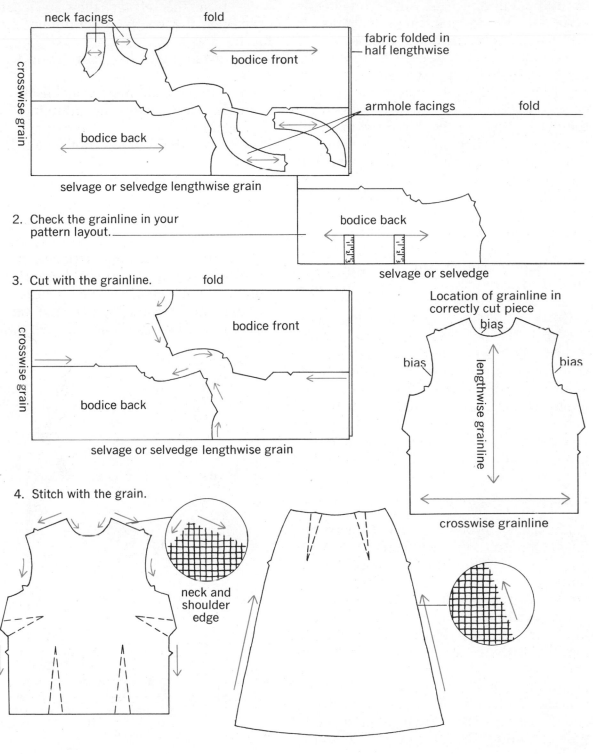

neck facings

fold

fabric folded in half lengthwise

bodice front

armhole facings

fold

crosswise grain

bodice back

selvage or selvedge lengthwise grain

2. Check the grainline in your pattern layout.

bodice back

selvage or selvedge

3. Cut with the grainline.

fold

bodice front

crosswise grain

bodice back

selvage or selvedge lengthwise grain

Location of grainline in correctly cut piece

bias

bias

bias

lengthwise grainline

crosswise grainline

4. Stitch with the grain.

neck and shoulder edge

175

which run the long length of a fabric parallel to the selvage, form the lengthwise grainline. Filling yarns, which run directly across the fabric from one selvage to the other, form the crosswise grainline.

The term "bias," as used in sewing, refers to a diagonal direction across the fabric. Bias edges stretch more easily than edges cut with the crosswise or lengthwise grainline. You can see this for yourself by cutting a bias edge on a scrap of material. Pull the bias edge and notice how much it stretches. Compare this to the amount you can stretch a straight-grain edge of the same length. There are, however, ways to control stretching on bias edges as you sew. Look and listen for ways to do this. By the time you finish your first project, you should be able to explain at least one procedure to reduce bias stretch.

Cutting, stitching, and pressing "with the grainline" is a basic idea to acquire. The phrase "with the grainline" is used several ways when sewing is discussed. When you stitch vertically you stitch with lengthwise grainline, or warp threads, of a woven fabric. When you stitch horizontally you stitch with the crosswise grainline, or filling threads, of a woven fabric.

Interpreting a pattern

Markings on your pattern tell you how to lay each pattern piece on your fabric with regard to grainline. Follow these pattern markings carefully, because this will give you the correct grainline in your completed garment. For example, a lengthwise grainline mark on a pattern piece should be laid parallel with the lengthwise grainline in your fabric. You can learn to check the grainline in your pattern layout if you recall that both ends of parallel lines are an equal distance from each other. Lengthwise grainline threads run parallel to the selvage. If both ends of the lengthwise grainline pattern marking are an equal distance from the selvage, they are located exactly on the lengthwise grainline in the fabric.

You avoid stretching your fabric when you:

cut with the grainline, not against it.

stitch seams with the grainline, not against it.

press with the grainline, not against it.

Transferring pattern markings

Transfer pattern markings to your material after you have finished cutting. A tracing wheel and dressmaker's carbon paper will transfer markings satisfactorily on most lightweight and washable fabrics. A dull table knife could be used instead of a tracing wheel. Use a light-colored carbon paper on white and light-colored fabrics.

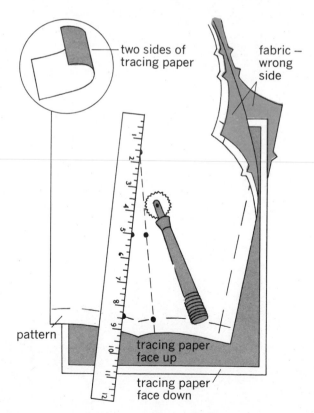

two sides of tracing paper

fabric — wrong side

pattern

tracing paper face up

tracing paper face down

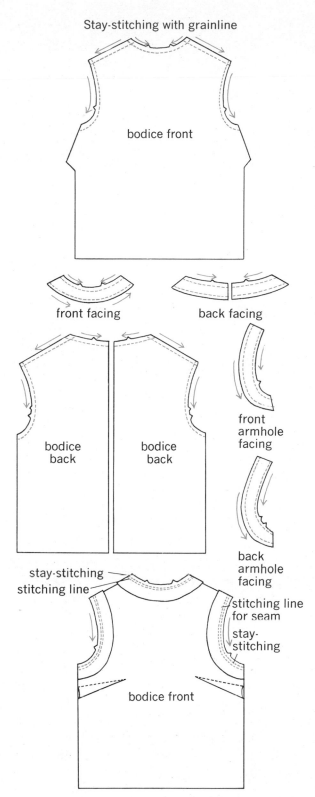

Stay-stitching with grainline

bodice front

front facing

back facing

bodice back

bodice back

front armhole facing

back armhole facing

stay-stitching
stitching line

stitching line for seam

stay-stitching

bodice front

For a simple blouse, mark darts and, perhaps, seam allowances. On other garments it may be useful to transfer other markings in addition to these. For example, the top of a sleeve will need to be marked for matching at shoulder seams. Pattern guides give suggestions about the markings you will need.

Arrange the carbon paper so that all markings will be on the *inside* of the garment when it is finished.

Stay-stitching

Stay-stitching is stitching to give additional strength to certain parts of a garment that are apt to stretch.

It is a machine stitching with 10 to 12 stitches per inch or the same stitch length that you will use in your seams. Stitch about ½ inch from the garment edge if your seam allowance is ⅝ inch. If it is located accurately, stay-stitching will not show on the outside of the garment.

The direction in which you stay-stitch is as important as where you place it. Stitch with the grainline, not against it. Stitching against the grainline encourages stretching and raveling.

Stay-stitch separate garment pieces, where needed, before you put your garment together. Stay-stitch curved areas or bias edges that you will join to another piece. This will hold the grainline in these areas securely while you work on the garment. Curved or bias areas tend to stretch easily, particularly in loosely woven material. A stay-stitch is usually needed at the neck where a facing will be attached; at the armhole where it will be joined to a sleeve or facing; at the skirt waist where a bodice, a waistband, or a facing will be attached; and at the shoulder. Also, some curved areas on small pieces are stay-stitched, such as facing pieces.

Making darts

Darts are basic construction details in most garments. They give shape to clothes; in other words, darts are planned to make flat pieces of fabric fit human figures. They are placed to give fit at the waist, shoulders, bustline, elbows, and neckline. Several different dart shapes may be used, depending on the design of the garment. Also, a dart may be stitched curved or straight, again depending on the design.

Stitch a dart to a sharp point by starting at the wide end and working toward the point. A blunt-ended dart causes wrinkles or bubbles on the outside.

To fasten the dart end, pull the threads to the inside and tie securely.

After a dart is stitched the fabric is no longer flat but molded into a curve. Therefore, press darts over the rounded surface of a pressing ham. Curved darts and darts in heavier fabrics are slashed and pressed open to avoid a lumpy appearance on the

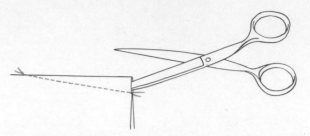

A curved dart is slashed open through the fold edge so it will lie flat.

outside. Double-pointed darts are clipped at the waist, and, sometimes, above and below the waist. This helps the waist area set smoothly on the figure.

Darts in lightweight washable garments are usually turned to one side and pressed, rather than slashed. Horizontal darts and slanted underarm darts are turned downward. Vertical darts in front are pressed toward the center front. Vertical darts in the back are pressed toward the center back.

Making facings

To "face" in clothing construction means to finish, or complete, an edge of a garment by enclosing the edge with a piece of fabric.

A sleeveless, collarless blouse pattern may include pattern pieces for cutting fitted facings to finish the neck edge and the armholes. When you look at your pattern pieces you may think that such peculiar shapes have no real use. Yet each one is essential to the complete design of the pattern. A fitted facing, when assembled for attaching, is shaped like the area that it will enclose, or complete. (See the diagram of the blouse and the armhole facings on page 182.)

Assemble the facings carefully, especially the armhole facings. Left and right armhole facings need to be assembled so that notches on the facings match notches in the armhole.

1. Stitch toward point.
   This is good. The dart is stitched to a sharp point.
2. This needs improvement. The blunt end will cause a wrinkle or bubble on the outside.

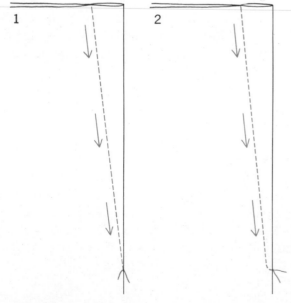

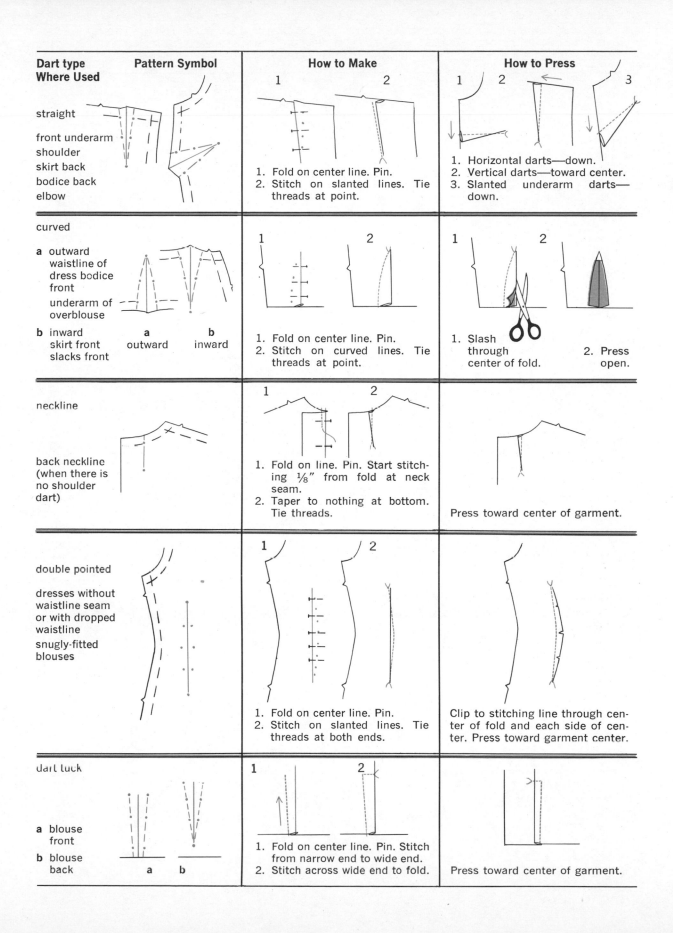

Dart type Where Used	Pattern Symbol	How to Make	How to Press
straight front underarm shoulder skirt back bodice back elbow		1 2 1. Fold on center line. Pin. 2. Stitch on slanted lines. Tie threads at point.	1 2 3 1. Horizontal darts—down. 2. Vertical darts—toward center. 3. Slanted underarm darts—down.
curved **a** outward waistline of dress bodice front underarm of overblouse **b** inward skirt front slacks front	**a** outward **b** inward	1 2 1. Fold on center line. Pin. 2. Stitch on curved lines. Tie threads at point.	1 2 1. Slash through center of fold. 2. Press open.
neckline back neckline (when there is no shoulder dart)		1 2 1. Fold on line. Pin. Start stitching ⅛″ from fold at neck seam. 2. Taper to nothing at bottom. Tie threads.	Press toward center of garment.
double pointed dresses without waistline seam or with dropped waistline snugly-fitted blouses		1 2 1. Fold on center line. Pin. 2. Stitch on slanted lines. Tie threads at both ends.	Clip to stitching line through center of fold and each side of center. Press toward garment center.
dart tuck **a** blouse front **b** blouse back	**a** **b**	1 2 1. Fold on center line. Pin. Stitch from narrow end to wide end. 2. Stitch across wide end to fold.	Press toward center of garment.

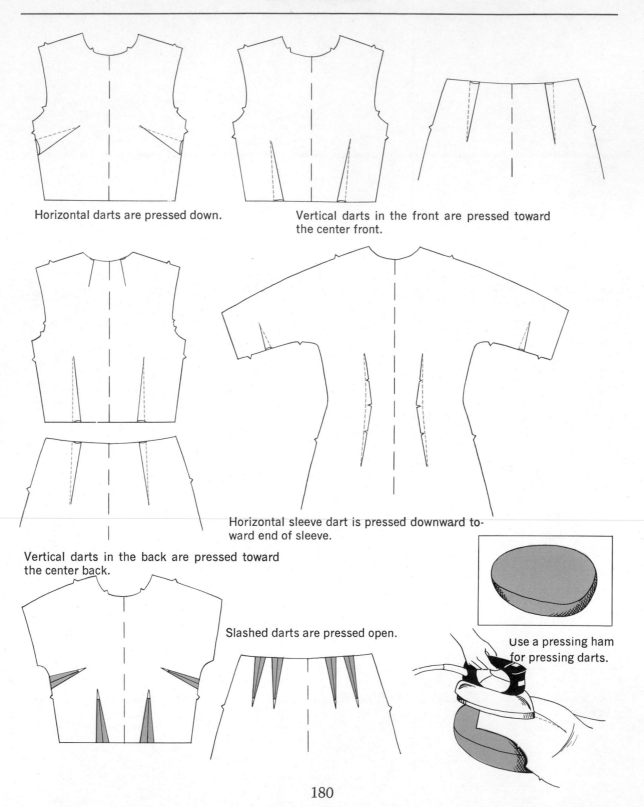

Horizontal darts are pressed down.

Vertical darts in the front are pressed toward the center front.

Vertical darts in the back are pressed toward the center back.

Horizontal sleeve dart is pressed downward toward end of sleeve.

Slashed darts are pressed open.

Use a pressing ham for pressing darts.

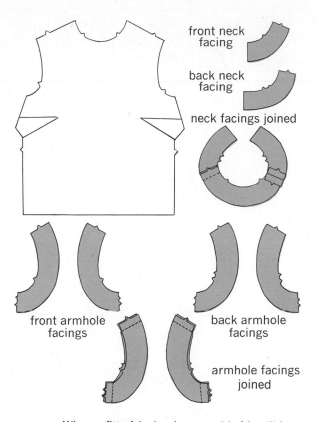

front neck facing

back neck facing

neck facings joined

front armhole facings

back armhole facings

armhole facings joined

When a fitted facing is assembled it will have the same shape as the area it will enclose (see above). Left and right armhole facings need to be assembled so that notches on the facings match notches in the armhole.

Finish facing edges after assembling, but before attaching them to the blouse. On washable garments, facing edges may be turned about ¼ inch or less and edge-stitched. To edge-stitch means to machine-stitch close to an edge. When machine-stitching a narrow turned edge, use the presser foot to guide the stitching line evenly about ⅛ inch from the edge. Edge-stitching a turned edge on a rounded shape, such as a facing, is easier if the ¼-inch turning line is marked with a machine stitch first. Also, the rounded edge can be clipped so that it will turn easily and lie flat. However a crease resistant fabric will resist turning even after clipping and will have to be pressed thoroughly.

Throughout all the steps these small rounded facing pieces should be handled lightly. The edge will be rippled if it has been stretched. A facing that has been marked, turned, and edge stitched carefully will not cause ridges to show outside the garment. The facing will fit exactly the area it encloses.

Steps for Finishing Rounded Facing Edges before Attaching

1. Make a regular machine stitch ¼ inch from the outside edge. Clip the edges in several places up to the ¼-inch stitching line.

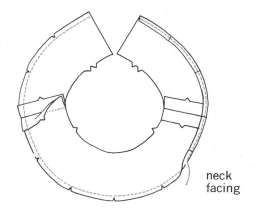

neck facing

2. Turn on the ¼-inch stitching line. Press; then machine-stitch about ⅛ inch from the turned edge. Use the presser foot to guide the stitching line.

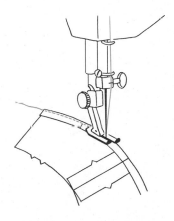

181

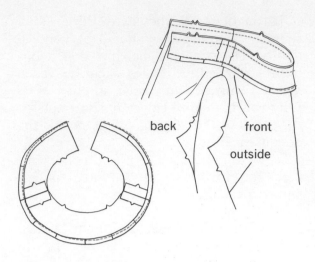

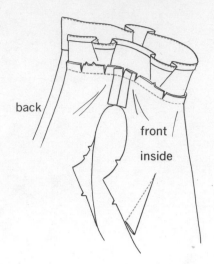

Neck facing. Shoulder seams on facing and garment are matched.

Finishing the raw facing edge makes the garment more durable, especially if the material ravels easily. The inside of the garment will look better if the raw edges have been concealed. A zig-zag machine stitch is satisfactory for both washable fabrics and thicker non-washable material, or seam binding can be used. If the fabric has a cross weave and doesn't seem to ravel, a machine stitch about ¼″ from the edge plus a pinked edge can be used.

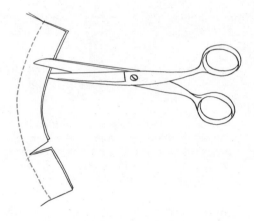

Armhole facing. Underarm seams on facing and garment are matched.

To clip is to cut into the seam allowance from edge to seam line. You "clip" a seam so the outer edges will spread to fit another section of the garment, or so a curved seam will lie flat when turned. Or you "clip" into a corner of a squared neckline or facing, so the seam can be turned.

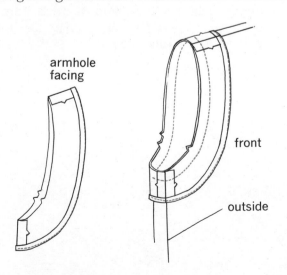

Attaching a facing at the neck seam line

Use the notches to match the grainline of your facing exactly with the grainline in the rest of your blouse. Shoulder seams can be used to match the neck facing to the blouse, and underarm seams can be used to match the armhole facings.

182

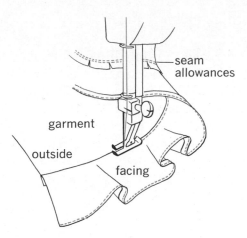

seam allowances

garment

outside

facing

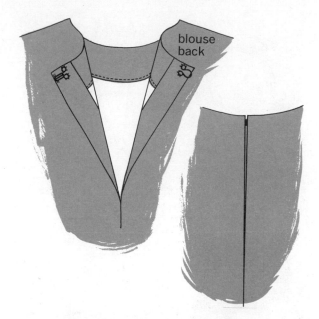

blouse back

Hook and round eye.
Use a hook and round eye on edges that do not overlap.

Sew facing pieces to your blouse at the seam allowance. Then, clip the allowance carefully almost the width of the seam allowance. This curved seam allowance is clipped so that it will lie flat when it is turned to the inside. Clipping can also make a single curved edge easier to turn. Clipping, you remember, was suggested before you tried to turn the edges of your facing. Use the points of sharp scissors. Practice clipping on a scrap until you can control the scissors. Careful control of your scissors is necessary to avoid cutting the seam.

In the diagram at the top of this column you will see the final step in attaching a facing to a neckline. This important step is called understitching. This final stitching keeps the facing from rolling to the outside of the garment where it might be seen. To do understitching on a neckline facing you proceed this way. Turn the seam allowance under the facing. Machine-stitch on top of the facing, very close to the seam and through all thicknesses of fabric. There will be a sharp edge where you turn the facing to the inside of the garment. With this treatment you can expect the facing to stay in place under the garment instead of popping into view. Facings that are well done add much to the appearance of a garment.

Deciding which kind of hook-and-eye fastener

Close the neck edge of an open placket with a hook-and-eye fastener. If the two placket edges meet, use a round eye. If the edges overlap, as in a waistband, use a straight eye. (See the diagram on page 190.)

Are you adding some new words to your vocabulary as you learn about these different sewing techniques? Can you list at least six or seven new words that you have learned as you have been developing some skill in using fabrics, patterns, and sewing equipment? Clothing construction, like all other skills, has a specialized vocabulary which you will learn to use gradually. Practice using the correct terms when you talk about your various projects in sewing. Learn to spell each term correctly. Review words and terms often. Build your vocabulary.

One reason for finishing seams is to prevent raveling and stretching. Threads on the edge of a seam tend to pull apart from each other as a garment is handled and worn. Also, washing and ironing causes unprotected seam threads to separate. Another reason for finishing seams is that the inside of the garment is neat when loose threads are controlled.

There are several satisfactory ways to finish plain seams. Before choosing the best finish, consider the thickness of the fabric. Also, look at the closeness of the yarns in the material. You will want to use a turned and edge-stitched finish only on a lightweight, closely woven material. Seam edges in a very thick fabric would be difficult or impossible to turn. In a very loosely woven material this finish might not hold threads securely. For thick and loosely woven materials, binding would probably be a better finish than turning and stitching.

Some of the finishes can be done rapidly but only with specialized equipment. For instance, a seam edge can be machine-zigzagged rather quickly, but a special attachment, or machine, is needed. A turned and edge-stitched finish, on the other hand, can be done on a regular straight-stitch sewing machine with no special equipment. Pinking shears are needed for the stitched-and-pinked edge. Overcasting can be done by hand and requires no special equipment.

Another thing to think about in deciding on your seam finish is the type of wear the garment will receive. Seams need to be finished securely in a garment that will be worn often and machine-washed. The type of finish that is possible will depend, too, on whether the material is slippery or easy to handle.

Project No. 2
An A-Line Skirt with Waistband

What might you learn from making an A-line skirt? You may learn how to:

finish plain seams
make a lapped skirt zipper placket
attach a waistband
hem a skirt

You need a crisp but firm fabric for an A-shaped skirt. The material should be heavier, with more body, than a blouse fabric. Choose sailcloth, denim, or poplin for a washable, unlined skirt. This skirt may be combined with a simple blouse to make an attractive casual outfit. Washable garments, especially ones to be machine-washed, are more durable if the seams are finished. There are several types of seam finishes for firm cotton fabrics.

You may need to try several finishes on a scrap of your material to find the most suitable one. (See the chart, "Finishes for Plain Seams" below, which compares several finishes for plain seams.)

Seam finishing requires additional time but the results in durability and appearance will be worthwhile. Look for seam finishes on ready-to-wear clothes when you shop. It is a sign of good construction.

Finishes for Plain Seams

Finish	Illustration	Fabric on which suitable	Advantages and disadvantages
Turned and edge-stitched		Good on lightweight, opaque materials—sailcloth, broadcloth, chambray Not good for thick fabrics or very loose weaves	If there are many seams, may take much time. Holds firmly.
Stitched and pinked		Good on lightweight, closely woven fabrics Not good for fabrics which ravel easily	Can be done quickly. Need pinking shears.
Machine zigzagged		Good for both lightweight cottons and heavier cottons, such as corduroy	Need special equipment. Good for quick reinforcement of seams in ready-to-wear. Secures seams well.
Overcast		Suitable for both lightweight and heavier fabrics	No special equipment needed. Could be used to reinforce seams on ready-to-wear if you do not have special equipment. May not hold so securely as other methods.
Bound		Good on heavier materials which cannot be turned and stitched.	May take more time than other methods.

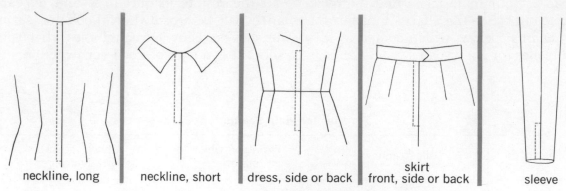

neckline, long | neckline, short | dress, side or back | skirt front, side or back | sleeve

Some of the many types of plackets for which a lapped application is used. Lapped zipper application can be used in any garment if it fits into the design and construction. Generally light to medium weight fabrics lend themselves best to lapped applications. They are most often preferred for reasons of ample coverage, reduced gapping at waistline and less possibility of a placket fold catching in the zipper in a center back application. There is no rule on which direction the lap or fold should face. Right-handed persons find that placement of the lap on the left side of the garment makes the zipper pull-tab more accessible; left-handed persons, a right-sided lap.

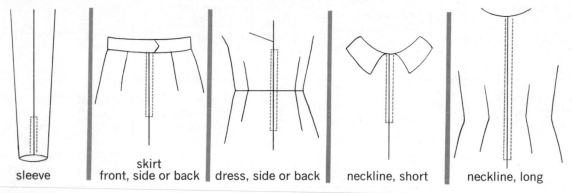

sleeve | skirt front, side or back | dress, side or back | neckline, short | neckline, long

Some of the many types of plackets for which a center application is used. Centered zipper application is used where the type of fabric or the design or construction of a garment requires a symmetrical appearance or less bulk of fabric in the placket area. Heavier or piled fabrics are best suited for such plackets. Centered applications are most often used when the design of the garment features plackets in a faced, slashed opening, slot-seamed wrist openings and box and inverted pleats.

We take for granted the many little conveniences we enjoy every day. Can you imagine a world without zippers? In the pre-zipper era plackets were fastened with buttons, snaps, hooks, and lacings. The development of a practical sliding closure with interlocking metal teeth is credited to Gideon Sundback who was associated with Talon Incorporated. He patented his invention in 1917. The word "zipper" was registered by the B. F. Goodrich Company in 1923 as a trademark for one of their new products, zippered galoshes. Today "zipper" is a common household term used when referring to all sliding closures with interlocking teeth.

The two types of zipper plackets are the lapped placket and the centered placket. Either type has advantages and can be used in several different places. The appearance of a centered placket depends on your ability to stitch each side exactly even, so that the placket is symmetrical. Careful stitching is necessary for a lapped placket also, as it should be the same width from the seam line along its entire length.

In a heavy fabric, a centered placket may appear less bulky than a lapped placket.

Regardless of the type of placket, the zipper should be completely covered, though a centered placket on a side seam, as in a skirt, may show the zipper when the wearer is seated. This is because the side seam folds and wrinkles somewhat due to the seated posture.

Select a zipper with some thought about your garment and the care you will give it. Both nylon and metal zippers are available. Nylon zippers are thinner and will add less bulk to a placket opening than metal ones. But special care is needed in pressing around a nylon zipper as the teeth may be damaged by a hot iron. Also machine washing at high temperatures may damage a nylon zipper. If the garment is to be hand-washed, this may not be a problem.

Zippers may be purchased in a variety of colors. You may be able to find one which matches your fabric color.

Attention to details such as matching or coordinating the fabric color, the thread color, and the color of the zipper contributes to giving your garment an appearance of high quality. We can summarize by saying that a good zipper placket will be smooth and even in width, and the zipper will be covered.

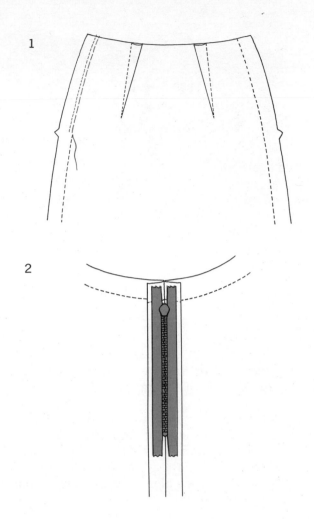

Lapped zipper placket in skirt

1. A side zipper placket is placed correctly on the left side. Stay-stitch the seam allowance the length of the zipper placket. Machine-baste the placket opening on the seam line. Press the seam open.

2. Check the placement of the zipper. Allow enough space at the top of the skirt for the waistband seam allowance plus an additional ¼ inch. This slight amount of extra space permits using the zipper tab easily.

3. Attach zipper foot. Adjust to right-hand side of needle. Open zipper. Place it face down on back seam allowance with teeth

187

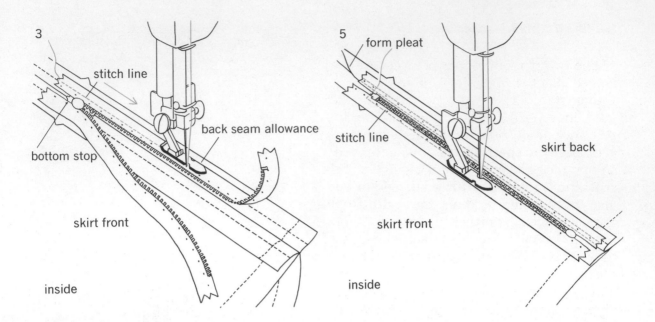

edge at seam line and bottom stop at lower end of basting. Sew through tape and back seam allowance only.

4. Adjust zipper foot to left-hand side of needle. Close zipper and turn face up. Finger or iron-press fabric away from zipper, thus making narrow fold in back seam allowance along zipper. Edge-stitch

on fold beginning at bottom end of tape; sew through fold and tape only.

5. Spread garment flat with zipper face down on front seam allowance, forming pleat at lower end of placket. Stitch across bottom and up along side of zipper, sewing through tape, seam allowance, and front of garment. Press.

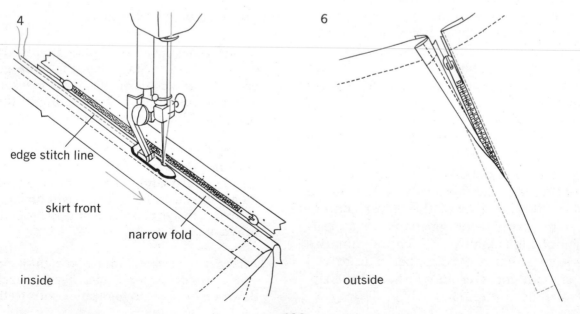

6. Remove machine basting from inside. Raise back seam allowance for easy access. Press placket on inside of garment. Place towel beneath placket and moistened press cloth over zipper. Hold iron lightly over placket. Allow steam to penetrate cloth. A tailor's ham is useful for protecting garment shape during steam pressing.

Tie thread ends on inside of garment.

Attaching a waistband—Method 1

These directions show how to attach a waistband with a final machine stitching on the outside.

1. Prepare the waistband by turning the seam allowance on the unnotched edge. Press and trim off to ¼ inch. The notches on the opposite side will be used to join the waistband to the skirt. Mark the location of the center front and center back of the waistband with thread, if you need some additional guides.

2. Work from the inside of the skirt. Pin the notched edge of the waistband to the skirt. Machine-stitch in place on the seam line.

3. Fold ends of waistband, right sides together. Machine-stitch across the ends.

4. Turn the waistband to the outside of the skirt. Pin the waistband in place, using the first machine stitch as a guide. Baste in place if you need to feel secure about this. Machine-stitch on the outside.

The finished waistband should be even in width all around. Check this by measuring before you stitch.

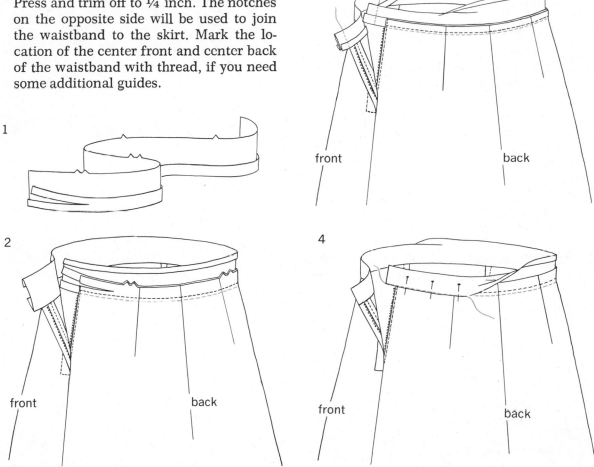

1

2
front   back

3
front   back

4
front   back

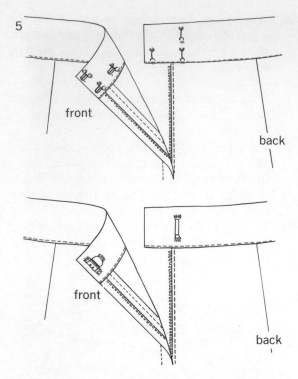

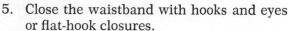

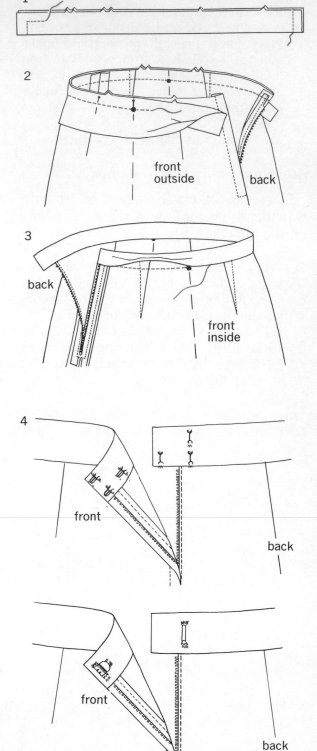

5. Close the waistband with hooks and eyes or flat-hook closures.

Attaching a waistband—Method 2

These directions show how to attach the waistband with a final hand stitch on the inside.

1. Assemble the waistband for attaching. Stitch the ends; then turn and press.

2. Work from the outside of the skirt. Match center front, center back, and side seams of the waistband to the skirt. Baste in place if you want to check the fit. Then, permanent-stitch at the seam line.

3. Turn the waistband to the inside. Make the final stitching by hand. A slip stitch would be a good hand stitch here.
The finished waistband should be the same width all around.

4. Close the waistband with hooks and eyes or with flat-hook closure.

190

Turning a hem

Study the illustrations.

Skirt length is marked from the floor with the person wearing the garment. You will need either a yardstick or a hem marker, and chalk or pins. This procedure can be done easily if you work in pairs, marking hems for each other.

Mark your hem this way:

Put on your garment and assume a good standing posture.

Experiment to find the best skirt length. Study the effects in a mirror.

When you have decided on the best skirt length, have your partner measure the hem location from the floor. Use pins or chalk marks every 2 inches around the skirt to give you a clearly marked line to use.

Take off the garment; turn at the marked line, and hand-baste about ¼ inch from the turned edge.

Press carefully at the turned edge.

Mark the width of the hem evenly, using a hem gauge or a ruler.

Cut away excess material.

If necessary, ease or shrink fullness before you proceed further. (See page 192.)

Finish, using the hem finish appropriate for the fabric. (See the chart on page 194 for suggestions about hem width and appropriate finishes.)

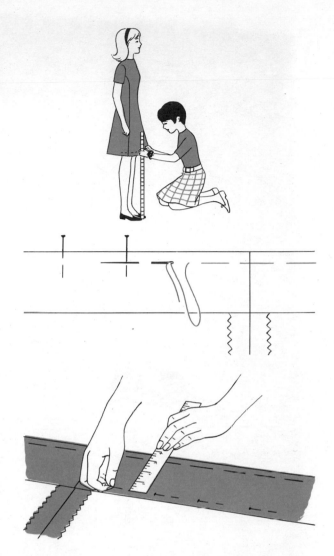

Controlling excess fullness in a hem

A necessary step in finishing a hem attractively is to make it lie flat on the area where it will rest when it is turned up. A gored or flared skirt will have more width at the bottom edge than farther up on the skirt. This type of excess fullness in a hem needs to be controlled so that it does not become visible puckers and pleats.

There are two ways to do this: by easing in the fullness to fit the area, or by shrinking the fullness. Easing is usually done if the fabric cannot be shrunk. This method is usually used on cottons and cotton blends. Shrinking is usually used on wool and wool man-made blends.

Before you try to work with fullness, the hem location should be marked, turned, and basted in place. The hem width should be marked and excess material cut away. Now you are ready to deal with the excess fullness. Proceed carefully.

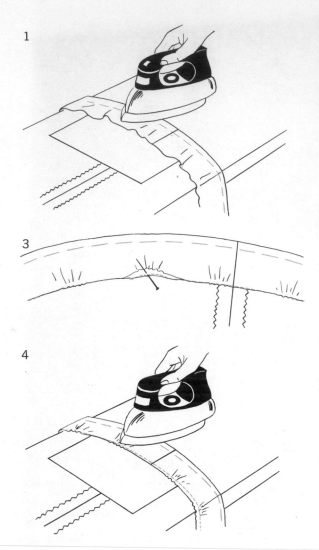

3. Pull up the thread on the underside carefully at each pressed pleat.
   Make a small gather at each pleat mark. This will ease the hem to fit the area it must cover.

4. Press to shrink out fullness at the gathered spots.
   In non-shrinkable fabric, press the gathers flat.

Continue with the hem finish.

Turned and stitched hem

1. Mark the hem location.

2. Turn the marked edge and baste.

3. Mark the hem width and trim away excess fabric.

4. Machine-stitch about ¼ inch from the cut edge of the hem.

5. Reduce the fullness if necessary.
   (See directions, in left column.)

6. Turn the edge on the ¼-inch stitching line.

7. Pin the hem in place.

8. Hand-stitch.
   (Slip-stitch is shown in the diagram.)

Follow these steps to ease or shrink hem fullness:

1. Press the hem to mark the location of the fullness. Place paper or press cloth between the hem and the garment to avoid press marks on the outside.
   Press the hem lightly, working upward from the fold.
   Form small pleats at even intervals where the fullness falls into ripples.

2. Machine-stitch at 10 stitches per inch at about ¼ inch below the cut edge.
   Leave the pleats flat as you stitch.

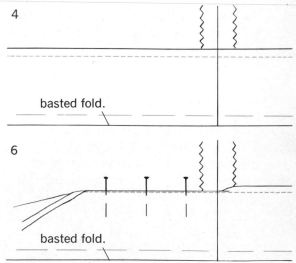

4

basted fold.

6

basted fold.

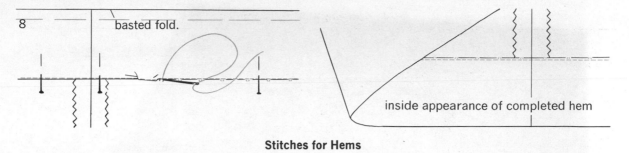

8 basted fold.

inside appearance of completed hem

Stitches for Hems

Begin at a side seam with knot hidden inside seam. Stitches taken on garment side must be very small (pick up one or two threads) and at least ¼" apart. **Do not pull thread tight.** Finish on hem or seam (never on garment side) with a few over-and-over stitches, ending with a loop or two. Clip thread, not too close.

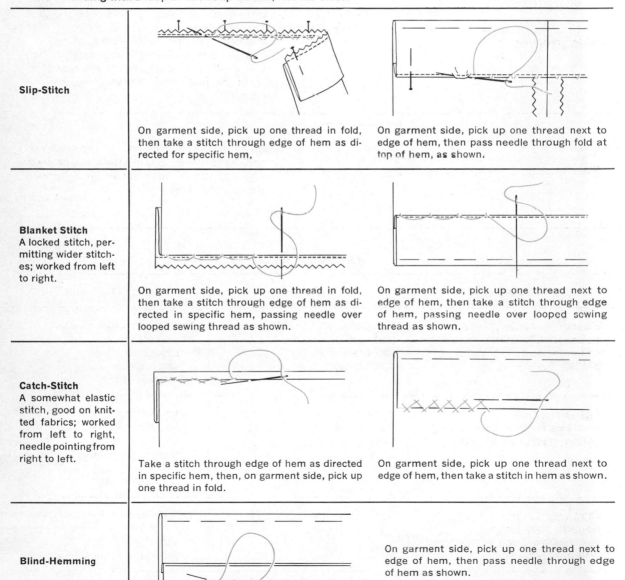

Slip-Stitch

On garment side, pick up one thread in fold, then take a stitch through edge of hem as directed for specific hem.

On garment side, pick up one thread next to edge of hem, then pass needle through fold at top of hem, as shown.

Blanket Stitch
A locked stitch, permitting wider stitches; worked from left to right.

On garment side, pick up one thread in fold, then take a stitch through edge of hem as directed in specific hem, passing needle over looped sewing thread as shown.

On garment side, pick up one thread next to edge of hem, then take a stitch through edge of hem, passing needle over looped sewing thread as shown.

Catch-Stitch
A somewhat elastic stitch, good on knitted fabrics; worked from left to right, needle pointing from right to left.

Take a stitch through edge of hem as directed in specific hem, then, on garment side, pick up one thread in fold.

On garment side, pick up one thread next to edge of hem, then take a stitch in hem as shown.

Blind-Hemming

On garment side, pick up one thread next to edge of hem, then pass needle through edge of hem as shown.

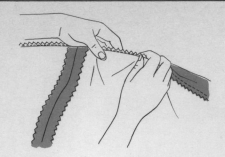

Inside Hemming

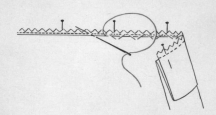

Turn hem back against right side of garment, making the fold in outer fabric even with machine stitching on a Tailor's or a Turned-and-Stitched Hem, or about 1/8" below edge of a hem with seam binding. . . . Pick up one thread in garment fold, then take a stitch through machine stitching or seam binding. Here shown on a Tailor's Hem.

Flat Hemming

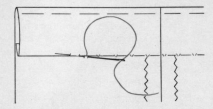

On garment side, pick up one thread next to hem edge, then pass needle through hem edge, as shown. Here shown on a Turned-and-Stitched Hem.

Fabrics and Hems

Fabric	Width of Hem	Hem Finish and Hand Stitch
Washable, medium-weight cotton, and cotton blends: sailcloth; poplin; broadcloth; pique	Approximately 2 to 2½ inches Garment design and skirt fullness should be considered	Turned and edge-stitched Hand stitch: *slip-stitch *catch-stitch *blanket stitch
Lightweight wool and wool-like fabrics, and heavier cotton, such as corduroy	Approximately 2 to 2½ inches Garment design and skirt fullness should be considered	Seam binding Hand stitch: *catch-stitch (inside hemming) *blind-hemming (flat hemming)
Coat fabrics (when you need to alter length) Also thick fabrics in skirts and dresses	Approximately 3 to 4 inches	Tailor's hem Hand stitch: *slip-stitch (inside hemming)

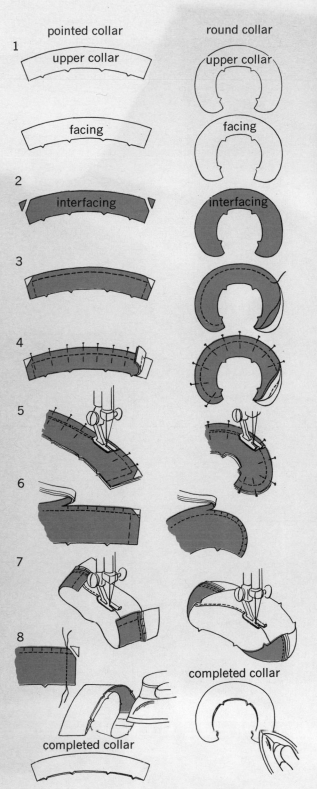

pointed collar

1

upper collar

facing

2

interfacing

3

4

5

6

7

8

completed collar

round collar

upper collar

facing

interfacing

completed collar

Project No. 3
A Blouse with Attached Collar, Set-in Sleeves, and Buttonholes

Making a simple blouse and skirt is an excellent way to get some experience in handling fabrics and patterns and in using equipment. You have learned to make darts and plain seams and to attach facings. Now you are ready for some new experiences in sewing. Select a blouse pattern which will guide you in learning to:

    assemble a collar
    attach a collar
    interface
    set in sleeves
    make buttonholes

If you want to try one thing more, add a patch pocket to this second blouse.

Assembling a collar

A one-piece collar which lies flat at the neck of the blouse when it is attached is a good type of collar for beginners to tackle. You will find many uses for this skill.

195

You will need to prepare three pieces before you are ready to assemble the collar for your blouse. *First,* prepare the upper collar and the facing by cutting these two pieces as directed on the pattern piece.

Second, prepare collar interfacing by cutting one additional layer the same size and shape as the upper collar and facing. Use a lightweight material such as batiste or lawn. If your blouse fabric is percale, broadcloth, chambray, or a fabric similar in feeling to one of these, cut the interfacing from the same material.

Third, using a stay-stitch, attach the interfacing piece to the wrong side of the facing piece.

Fourth, with right sides together pin the facing piece with the attached interfacing to the upper collar with right sides together.

Fifth, stitch the facing, upper collar, and interfacing together.

Sixth, trim off the seam allowance to about ⅜ inch. Then clip through the seam allowance to about ⅛ inch of the seam, making several clips per inch.

Seventh, understitch several inches along the center back of the collar on the facing side.

Eighth, turn the collar to the right side and press. Open the seam at the ends as far as possible. Then press the entire collar, being sure that the facing side does not show on the upper side of the collar.

Attaching a collar

First, fold the collar in half and mark the center back with a pin or thread.

Second, pin the collar to the neck edge of the blouse. Match the notches and the center back mark on the collar with a center back mark on the blouse.

Third, pin the facing pieces in place over the collar. See detailed instructions on

pages 182–184 for applying fitted blouse facing without a collar. The basic steps can be used to attach a fitted facing to the neckline of a blouse which opens in front and which has a collar.

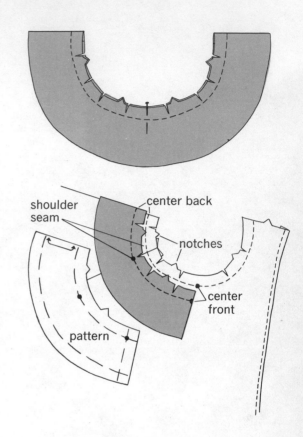

shoulder seam

center back

notches

center front

pattern

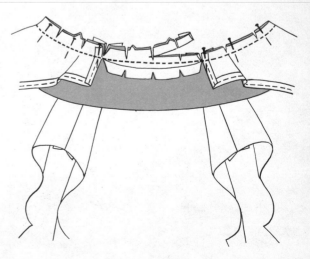

196

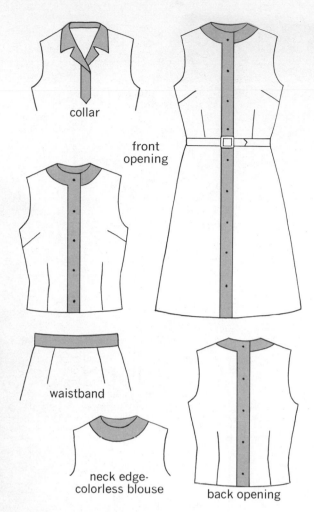

collar

front opening

waistband

neck edge-
colorless blouse

back opening

Interfacings in lightweight garments may be cut from the same fabric as the other parts of the garment. With prints, plaids, or stripes the fabric design on the interfacing might show through. Because of this a solid color or white would be a better choice. White cotton batiste, with either a soft or a crisp finish, is a suitable lightweight interfacing fabric. It can be used with lightweight cottons and with heavier fabrics. Remember to straighten it if necessary, and to shrink it before you cut.

Facing pattern pieces may be used to cut interfacings if separate pieces are not included in the pattern. Usually interfacings are cut on the same grainline as the facings and places they will interface, unless the pattern directs otherwise.

The outline of the interfacing should not be seen on the outside of the completed garment. Nor should any color or design

Making an interfacing

An interfacing is a hidden part of a garment which is meant to improve the outside appearance of the garment. It is a layer of fabric placed under a facing. Interfacings may be sewed into garments to hold the shape in certain areas. Or an interfacing may be used both to maintain shape and to reinforce an area. An example of this is an interfacing reinforcement under buttons and buttonholes where there is more strain from ordinary wear than in other parts. Interfacings may be needed in collars, waistbands, cuffs, armholes in sleeveless blouses, and neck edges of collarless blouses.

Blouse showing where interfacing should be attached to front pieces. This same procedure is used for both sides.

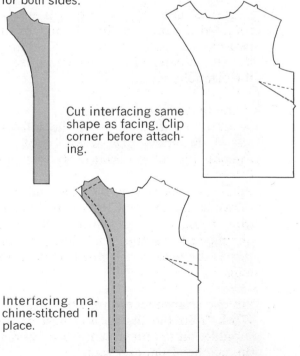

Cut interfacing same shape as facing. Clip corner before attaching.

Interfacing machine-stitched in place.

197

in the interfacing be visible through thin or loosely woven fabrics.

Directions for sewing an interfacing into a waistband are given on page 213. For interfacing a buttonhole area, see page 200; and for collar interfacing suggestions, see page 196.

Setting in sleeves

A sleeve is ready to be "set in" to the armhole after it has been assembled. Although you will find some variations in these steps, here are some suggestions to guide you in this process.

1. Machine-baste two rows of basting stitches around the cap of the sleeve. These stitches are used to ease the sleeve into a shape that will fit the armhole. Begin the stitching slightly beyond the notches. Put one row of stitches on the seam line. Place the second row about ¼ inch from the seam line toward the cut edge of the sleeve.

2. Begin to ease the sleeve cap into a rounded shape by pulling lightly on the two rows of basting stitches. Ease until the sleeve cap is about the same size as the armhole.

3. If the material can be shrunk, you may be able to shrink some of the fullness out of the sleeve cap. A wool fabric is the only type of material likely to shrink this way.
Place the sleeve cap over the end of a sleeve board. Steam lightly with a steam iron, using only the point of the iron. Shrink only to the seam line because this is the area which must fit the armhole.

4. Pin the shaped sleeve into the armhole. Work from the inside. Pin first at the shoulder, at the underarm seams, and at the notches front and back.

1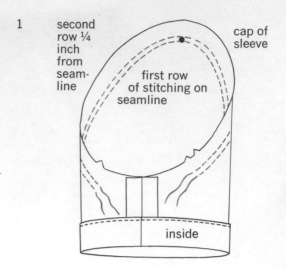

second row ¼ inch from seam-line

cap of sleeve

first row of stitching on seamline

inside

2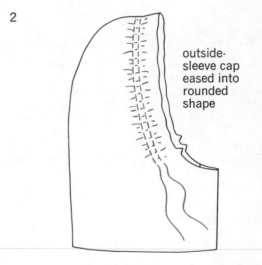

outside-sleeve cap eased into rounded shape

3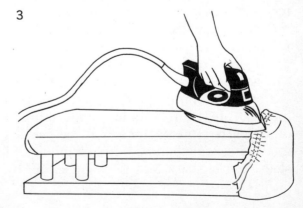

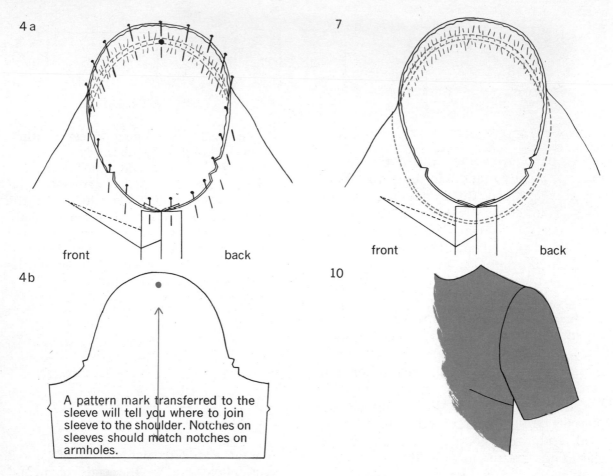

4 a

front   back

4 b

A pattern mark transferred to the sleeve will tell you where to join sleeve to the shoulder. Notches on sleeves should match notches on armholes.

7

front   back

10

Here is a good reason for cutting notches carefully: they are guides in assembling a garment.

Notice in the illustration that one notch is used to mark the place where the front of the sleeve joins the front of the armhole. Two notches are used at the back. This particular notching system is not used on all brands of patterns. It may be reversed, with two notches on the front and one at the back. Therefore, study your pattern to find the way notches are used to mark your particular pattern.

5. After the sleeve is eased into place by pinning, baste.

6. If you want to check the outside appearance before you stitch the sleeve in per-

manently, take time to try on the garment.

7. Machine-stitch along the seam line. Make a second stitching line, next to the first, around the underarm section between the notches. Work slowly to avoid puckers.

8. Clip the seam only if you need some extra ease in the armhole area.

9. Press the seam toward the inside of the sleeve. Use a sleeve board to press in the small area around the sleeve.

10. The outside of the sleeve should be smooth, free of puckers.
    The sleeve should be on straight grainline.

199

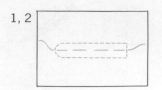
1, 2

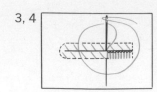
3, 4

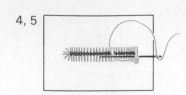
4, 5

Making Buttonholes

If you have ever examined the details on your ready-made clothing you have probably noticed differences in button-holes. Your coat may have fabric button-holes, but your washable clothes most likely have worked buttonholes.

Fabric buttonholes are constructed of fabric strips carefully cut and sewed in place. Considerable skill in handling small pieces of fabric and in controlling the sewing machine is necessary to make fabric buttonholes successfully. This is a technique you may want to learn after you have gained more skill in working with fabrics and equipment. Machine-made buttonholes can be made much faster than by hand and are stronger than handmade ones. They are made after the garment is completed. Always go over a machine-worked buttonhole a second time. It improves both appearance and wearing quality. Hand-worked buttonholes, like machine-made ones, are done after the garment is completed.

1. Mark the buttonhole on the straight grain.
2. Stitch around the mark, as shown, circling at end nearer garment edge.
3. Cut buttonhole on center mark and overcast the edges.
4. Work buttonhole stitch over the edges, working from right to left as follows:
   Start at straight end. Bring thread from needle eye around under needle point from right to left, forming a "purl." Place purl exactly on cut edge.
   At end toward garment edge, form a fan as shown, keeping the center stitch of the fan in line with the cut.
5. Make a bar at the end opposite the fan by taking several stitches across the end and working buttonhole stitch over the threads and through the garment cloth. (On vertical buttonholes fan is omitted and bar made at both ends. On such buttonholes, when stitching around the mark, stitch a plain rectangle.)

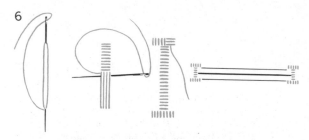
6

6. Bar tacks are often used at ends of worked buttonholes, or at the ends of bound pockets. Make 3 or 4 long stitches across ends of opening. Work overhand or buttonhole stitches over the long stitches, taking up a bit of the fabric with each stitch. Bars may also be made at the ends of the bar tack, forming a letter I as shown.

Worked buttonhole edges are stitched closely by hand or machine. Hand-worked buttonholes are made with a stitch appropriately called a buttonhole stitch. Also, they can be worked by using a zig-zag machine, or with a buttonhole attachment on a straight-stitch machine.

Worked buttonholes may be made on a blouse after it is otherwise complete. Attach an interfacing under the facing to reinforce the buttonhole area.

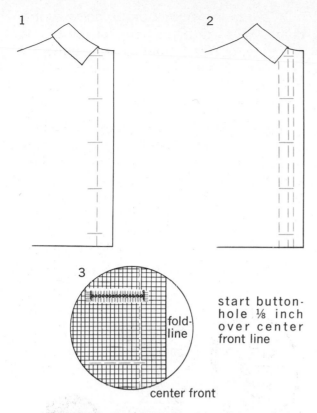

Marking the location of horizontal buttonholes must be done very carefully and accurately. Center front marking and horizontal line show buttonhole length and starting point. This is a minimum guide.

Mark the location for the buttonholes with thread. In girls' and women's clothing, buttonholes are made on the right side of a bodice front. Hand-baste or machine-baste through all layers—blouse front, interfacing, and facing. Horizontal buttonholes are correctly placed starting ⅛ inch over the center front toward the fold.

Mark the center front as a guide. This line can be used to locate the buttons which should be sewed on the center front. The center front line, plus horizontal stitches marking the length of the buttonholes, may be enough. If your eye needs more practice in judging distances accurately, make a second vertical line ⅛ inch over the center front toward the fold and a third vertical line to mark the opposite end of the buttonhole. If thread leaves small holes in your fabric, use as few basting marks on the outside front as possible. Perhaps only the center front marking and the horizontal stitches will be enough guides for you.

Buttonholes should follow the grainline exactly, unless they are purposely placed on the bias as a decorative trim. This is the reason why it is important to mark the location of the buttonholes before you make them.

The correct length to make buttonholes is the diameter of the button plus its thickness. Make a sample buttonhole on a scrap of fabric in order to check the size with the button.

The number of buttonholes and buttons to use on a particular garment is a design problem for you to solve. Usually, the pattern guide suggests the number of buttonholes to make. However, you may want to consider the type of button you expect to use and your measurement from neckline to waist before you decide on the number.

Buttons that close a garment at the center are sewed on opposite a horizontal buttonhole on the center front or back line. If the buttonhole is vertical, mark the upper end on the opposite side and sew on the button ⅛″ below this mark. If the closing is an off-center or slanted one, close the garment and put a pin through the end of the buttonhole nearer the edge if it is horizontal, or through the upper end if vertical. Then position the button ⅛″ from this mark. The location of buttons which have no matching buttonholes but are used for trimming, or for attaching an extra part of a garment, is indicated on patterns by small dots. On heavy fabrics, it is a good idea to use "heavy duty" or special "button" thread for sewing on buttons. The thread should be used double.

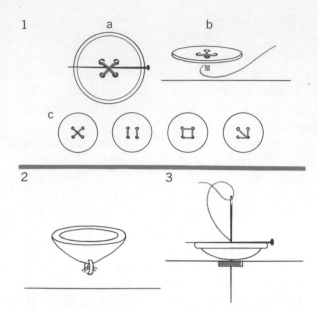

If you make worked buttonholes by machine, follow the directions for the zig-zag machine, or the buttonhole attachment to be used with a straight-stitch machine.

Putting on a patch pocket

A patch pocket is sewed to the outside of a garment. This type of pocket can be attached to either the bodice or the skirt. Whenever you plan the location of a patch pocket, you apply your knowledge of design principles. This type of pocket often becomes an accent, or center of interest. Therefore, where it will be placed is a matter which should be considered carefully.

1. A button which is to go through a buttonhole should have a shank or stem to allow room for the extra fabric between button and garment. When a button has no shank, place a heavy pin, toothpick or kitchen match on top of the button and sew over it. (Illustration a.) Then remove the pin and wind the thread under the button around the stitches, forming a stem. (Illustration b.) Fasten securely. If the button has four holes, there are decorative ways of sewing, as shown in Illustration c.

2. If the shank is metal or plastic, it is not necessary to sew over a pin unless the fabric is very thick. But if the shank is of cloth, then a thread stem should also be made. When sewing shank buttons, keep the stitches small and parallel to the edge of the fabric.

3. Buttons that will receive extra strain or are sewed on a single thickness of fabric should be reinforced. On the inside of the garment, directly under the button location, place a small flat button or a square of fabric and sew through button or fabric when attaching the outside button.

202

Planning the best size and shape for the pocket is also a design problem. Here you can use your knowledge of proportion and scale. Consider the area where the pocket will be placed, as well as the size of the person who will wear the garment.

Another design problem to be solved is the number of patch pockets to include. In some cases, one pocket may seem to be enough added design of this type. In other cases, two pockets may be used to create balance. (See illustrations, page 202.)

You can attach patch pockets by machine, using an edge-stitch, or you can use a hand slip-stitch. The machine edge-stitch can be seen on the outside and could be considered a decorative trim. The hand slip-stitch will not be visible when it is completed. The machine stitch is a faster method than the hand stitch. If the garment will be machine-washed, the machine stitch will be more durable.

Follow pattern instructions for making the pocket. These may show the top edge finished with a separate facing piece or the facing cut on as a part of a single pocket piece and then folded back.

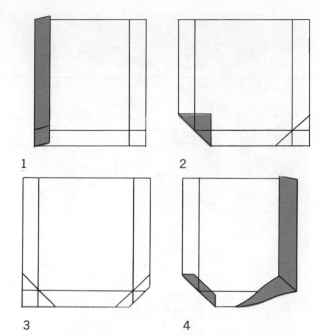

1 2

3 4

Mitering a square pocket or other squared details to be edge-stitched to garment. On the illustrations, the right side of the fabric is solid color, the wrong side is shaded.

1. Turn seam allowance inside. Press.

2. Press corners diagonally through creases.

3. Trim corners ⅛″ from diagonal creases.

4. Fold corners, edges inside on creases.

Mark the location for the pocket by basting around the area by hand or by machine. It is necessary to mark only the sides and bottom of the space.

This will give you an exact guide for placing the pocket straight on the grain line. As you become more aware of details in ready-to-wear clothes you may notice patch pockets on a variety of garments. They appear with variations in shape and size on dressier clothes made of better fabrics as well as casual clothes in the most durable material.

Machine edge-stitch is a decorative trim.

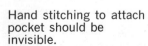

Hand stitching to attach pocket should be invisible.

203

A long zipper in the center back seam can be either applied with a lapped placket or centered on the seam. Make a centered zipper placket if you want to try a new technique. If not, use a lapped zipper placket again, as in the A-shaped skirt, Project No. 2. Directions for making a centered zipper placket are included with this project. Still another practice in applying a long back zipper is described in Project No. 7, the one-piece dress, page 219.

Learning to handle a pile fabric

Corduroy is a pile fabric, and is sometimes called a napped fabric. Pile fabrics have textures, or surface characteristics, which require some special procedures in cutting and sewing. The lengthwise ridges of tiny, cut yarns which identify corduroy are called wales. Wide-wale corduroy has fewer and wider ridges than pinwale corduroy. These cut yarns on the outside surface of corduroy run downward and feel smooth in one direction; in the opposite direction, they run upward and feel rough. Corduroy appears lighter in the direction where the pile runs down, and darker in the direction where it runs up. Therefore, in order to have an even appearance in a corduroy garment all pieces must be cut in the same direction. Usually, corduroy is cut with the pile running up, the direction that shows the color advantageously. If pieces are to be cut double, make a lengthwise fold. If a crosswise fold is used in cutting corduroy, the pile on the upper and lower side of the fabric will run in opposite directions. You will need more fabric to cut a garment from a pile fabric because of the one-direction layout you will need to use. The pattern envelope will tell you the yardage to buy for such fabrics. Also, a suggested pattern layout is included on pattern guide sheets.

Project No. 4
A Jumper with Waistline Seam and Long Back Zipper Placket

The sewing techniques you may learn as you make a jumper are useful also for making a dress. Let's consider some different techniques that you will have the opportunity to use in this project. You will learn to:

    cut and press corduroy, a pile fabric
    make a waistline seam
    put in a long back zipper placket
    finish a hem with seam binding

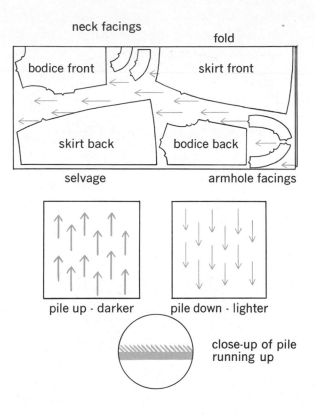

neck facings

fold

bodice front

skirt front

skirt back

bodice back

selvage

armhole facings

pile up - darker

pile down - lighter

close-up of pile running up

pile. Remember to press your completed garment on the wrong side, too. Brush a corduroy garment after pressing it. Brush downward, or in the direction in which the pile feels smooth. This will improve the appearance of the pile if some parts have been slightly crushed by pressing.

To summarize these ideas about corduroy: Corduroy is a pile fabric. It has a right and wrong side, and an up and down surface texture. Because of these characteristics, special care is needed in cutting, sewing, and pressing it.

Joining skirt to bodice with a waistline seam

Constructing a one-piece dress or jumper involves joining the skirt to the bodice with a waistline seam. This step can be handled easily if both parts are finished as much as possible before making the waist seam. Seams on both bodice and skirt should be pressed open and finished. Front waist darts should be pressed into place toward the center front. Back waist darts should be pressed toward the center back.

Check the waist fit of both the bodice and the skirt before you attempt to put them together. Each part should fit the waist, allowing enough ease for comfort as you sit or walk. Then you are ready to make the waistline seam.

First, pin the skirt to the bodice. Place the right side of the skirt and the right side of the bodice together. Match center backs, center fronts, side seams and darts. Pin the skirt to the bodice, easing any fullness in the skirt to fit the bodice.

Second, baste the bodice and skirt together on the seamline. As you baste check to be sure that darts are turned in the correct direction. Also, seams should be open unless your pattern indicates otherwise.

Cut corduroy with sharp cutting shears to avoid frayed edges. As you sew, it will be helpful to baste some joined edges that you might with other materials only pin. Corduroy, like other thick fabrics, should be sewed with a longer machine stitch than that used for lightweight cottons. Ten stitches per inch is about right.

Facings for a corduroy jumper might be cut from cotton broadcloth of the same color. Because of its thickness, a corduroy facing would add unnecessary bulk. Furthermore, the outline of a corduroy facing would be more likely to show on the outside than that of a lightweight facing. Understitching may easily be done on the broadcloth to hold the facing inside. Neat top-stitching is very difficult on corduroy.

Press corduroy on the wrong side. Use a steam iron if possible, and very gentle pressure in order to avoid flattening the

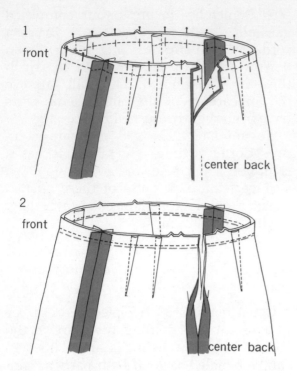

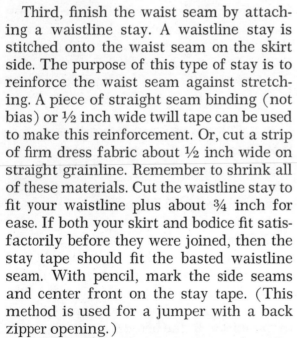

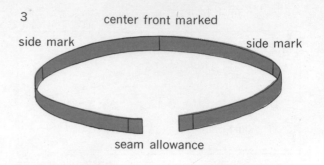

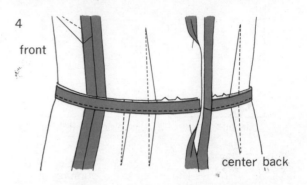

Third, finish the waist seam by attaching a waistline stay. A waistline stay is stitched onto the waist seam on the skirt side. The purpose of this type of stay is to reinforce the waist seam against stretching. A piece of straight seam binding (not bias) or ½ inch wide twill tape can be used to make this reinforcement. Or, cut a strip of firm dress fabric about ½ inch wide on straight grainline. Remember to shrink all of these materials. Cut the waistline stay to fit your waistline plus about ¾ inch for ease. If both your skirt and bodice fit satisfactorily before they were joined, then the stay tape should fit the basted waistline seam. With pencil, mark the side seams and center front on the stay tape. (This method is used for a jumper with a back zipper opening.)

Fourth, place the edge of the stay tape along the seam line. Pin the tape in place matching the markings on the tape with the side seams and center front of the jumper. Study the illustrations.

Use a regular machine stitch to attach the stay tape and to make a permanent waist seam in one step. Press the finished seam up. If the seam allowances seem bulky trim the bodice seam allowance back to ½ inch.

If your skirt has gathers you will find an alternate method more satisfactory. In this method the waistline stay is attached to the skirt before the skirt is joined to the bodice. The stay is used to help fit the skirt to your waistline.

An alternate method for attaching a waistline stay tape

If the skirt has pleats or gathers attach the stay tape to the skirt before joining the skirt to the bodice. The stay tape will be useful in obtaining a good fit at the waist as well as reinforcing the completed seam.

First, prepare the tape. (See direction three, "Joining Skirt to Bodice With a Waistline Stay"). Because the skirt will

206

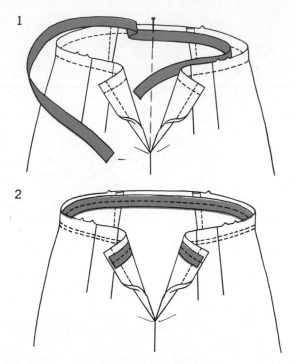

be eased to fit the stay tape, it is important to prepare the tape carefully. Remember to allow about ¾ inch for ease at the waistline when you determine the length of the tape. Mark the location of side seams, center front and center back. Use pins, chalk, dressmaker's marking pencil or a lead pencil.

Second, pin the tape inside the skirt matching the markings on the tape with the side seams, center front and center back of the skirt. Between these points, ease the skirt to fit the tape. You may find that it is necessary to adjust gathers, pleats or darts. However, if the stay tape was fitted accurately, then the skirt waistline should fit you well after it is eased to the stay tape.

Third, use a basting stitch to attach the stay tape to the skirt waist seam line. Then, you may want to try on the skirt for a final fitting before you join it to the bodice.

Fourth, proceed to pin the bodice and skirt together as directed in "Joining Skirt to bodice With a Waistline Seam."

Fifth, use a regular machine stitch to complete the waistline seam and permanently attach the waistline stay tape.

After the waistline seam is completed, there are a few last steps to be done on a one-piece dress or jumper. A zipper placket or buttonholes must be made. Last, the hem must be marked and finished.

Putting in a long back zipper placket

The zipper may be sewed in either before or after the neck facing is attached. In either case start by machine-basting the seam the length of the zipper placket. If the facing has been attached, continue the basting right on through the facing.

Plan the location of the zipper in relation to the top of the dress. Remember to allow enough space at the top of the dress for the seam allowance plus ¼ inch.

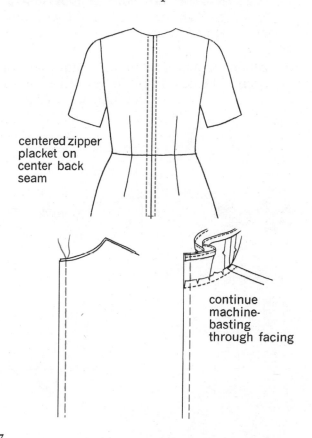

centered zipper placket on center back seam

continue machine-basting through facing

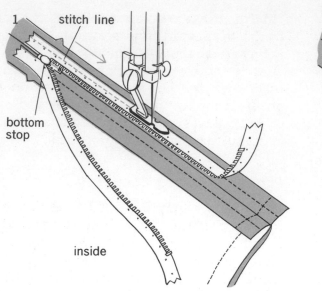

1. stitch line

bottom stop

inside

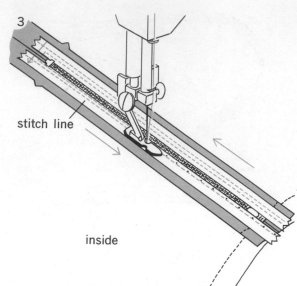

3. stitch line

inside

1. Attach zipper foot. Adjust to right-hand side of needle. Open zipper. Place it face down on one seam allowance with teeth edge at seam line and bottom stop at lower end of basting. Sew through tape and seam allowance only.

2. Adjust zipper foot to left-hand side of needle. Place other side of opened zipper on other seam allowance with edge of

teeth at seam line and pull-tab turned up. Begin stitching at turned-up pull-tab; sew through zipper tape and seam allowance only.

3. Close zipper. Spread garment flat. Begin stitching at neck edge; sew through tape, seam allowance, and garment, down one side, across bottom of zipper and up other side. Press.

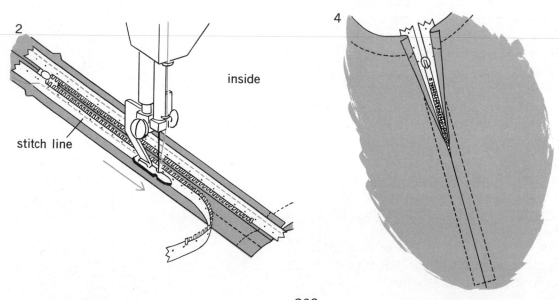

2. inside

stitch line

4.

hook and eye
fastener to close
centered placket

inside

outside

close-up view

4. Remove machine basting from seam. Clip machine basting every few stitches and remove carefully.

Press placket on inside of garment. Place towel beneath placket, and moistened press cloth over zipper. Hold iron lightly over placket. Allow steam to penetrate cloth. If placket seam is curved, a tailor's ham is useful for protecting garment shape during steam pressing.

Finishing a hem with seam binding

1. Mark the hem location.

2. Turn the hem at the marked line and baste.

3. Mark the hem width and trim away excess fabric.

4. If necessary, reduce the fullness by easing or shrinking. (See directions, p. 192.)

5. Use top stitching to attach the seam binding to the edge of the hem.

6. Pin the hem to the garment. For inside hemming, pin just below the seam binding.

7. Sew the hem to the garment with a slip-stitch, blanket stitch, or catch-stitch for inside hemming.
Use blind hemming or blanket stitch for flat hemming.

Today's fabrics with new fibers and finishes create sewing problems. You will find it difficult, if not impossible, to ease a fabric with a permanent press finish. Therefore, try making small darts to control hem fullness.

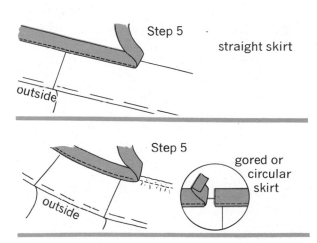

Step 5

straight skirt

outside

Step 5

outside

gored or circular skirt

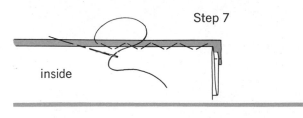

Step 7

inside

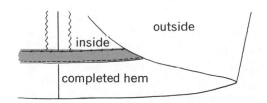

outside

inside

completed hem

209

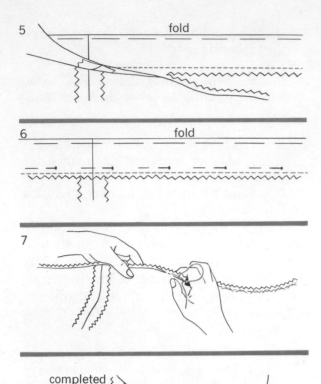

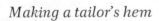

Making a tailor's hem

(Used for thick fabrics and for altering a coat hem)

1. Mark the hem location.

2. Turn the hem at the marked edge and baste.

3. Mark hem width and trim away excess fabric.

4. On a straight garment prepare the edge of the hem by machine stitching through one thickness of the fabric about ¼ inch from the cut hem edge. (If the garment is gored or full, reduce the fullness first, before machine-stitching.)

5. Pink the edge, or overcast the edge by hand.

6. Pin or baste the hem to the garment very near the machine-stitching line.

7. Sew with an inside hemming stitch, using the slip-stitch. Use the ¼-inch machine-stitching line as a guide to place hand stitches.

The care with which hand stitching is done on a garment adds to the attractiveness of that garment. Here are a few helpful suggestions about hand stitching. Use the needle size best suited to the weight of fabric, the size of thread, and the stitch to be made. Thread your needle with a thread length that is reasonably easy to handle. You want to avoid any knots and tangles as you work. A length of about 18 inches is enough even for a skillful seamstress to control well.

Do not pull your stitches so tightly that the fabric appears strained, drawn or puckered. This effect can be noticed on the outside by the slight ridge formed by too tight stitches. The outline of the completed hem should not be visible on the outside of the skirt. As you develop skill in stitching by hand, you will learn that the thread does not need to be pulled tightly in order to hold the fabric securely. In fact, slightly relaxed stitches are less likely to break under tension.

When hand stitching is done well, the stitches will be invisible on the right side. You will want to develop an ability to prick the yarns of the fabric so that the point of the needle does not go all the way through the fabric. This means that you must learn to judge the thickness of the various fabrics you sew. Only through careful practice can you gain some skill in hand stitching. Do not be discouraged if your first attempts are not perfect.

210

Project Nos. 5 and 6
An Underlined Skirt and a Blouse
—Separates or an Outfit

You are ready for this combination project after you have gained some skill in working with fabrics and equipment. Making a washable cotton skirt guided you in learning to stitch a lapped zipper placket; to apply a waistband; to finish plain seams; to mark and finish a hem. There are other techniques you may learn by making the type of skirt suggested for this project. You will face new challenges when you:

    work with fabrics of wool or a wool
      blend
    underline
    interface a waistband, *or* finish the waist
      edge with an inside facing
    attach a seam pocket

There are some choices to consider in planning this project. If you did not use corduroy for your jumper (Project No. 4), you may want to try this pile fabric now. Or use a plain-weave wool flannel or a wool blend.

The blouse may include more practice with machine-worked buttonholes, a zipper placket, a collar, or an interfacing. A cotton broadcloth blouse could be combined well with a corduroy skirt for a school outfit. If you make only the underlined skirt, it might be made of lightweight tweed and worn with a sweater.

Instead of a blouse and skirt, an alternative choice of a two-piece dress could include the same learnings. A two-piece corduroy dress would be appropriate for either school or dress-up wear. The skirt could be worn as a separate sometimes with a blouse or a sweater.

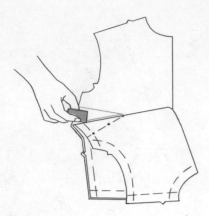

Transferring pattern marks on to thick material

Are you ready to try a different method to transfer pattern markings? Chalk and pins may be used to mark thicker fabrics such as corduroy. Put pins through the pattern and fabric at the marks to be transferred. Turn back the pattern and mark with chalk at the pin locations. If you need to mark two layers of fabric, just turn the fabric over and mark beside the pins. (See illustration above.)

Underlining a skirt

When attaching an underlining to a skirt, follow these steps:

1. Pin the underlining piece to the separate skirt pieces. Dart markings and seam markings, if you prefer, can be made on the underlining.

2. Baste the pieces together ½ inch from the edge. Whether you should hand-baste or machine-baste depends on your skill and on how easily the two fabrics can be handled together.

3. Pin, stitch, and press the darts with underlining in place.

4. Continue to assemble the skirt.

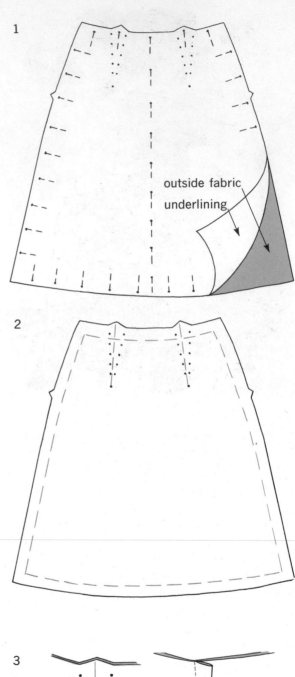

outside fabric
underlining

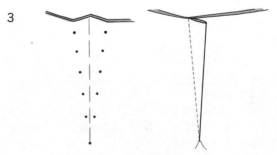

212

5

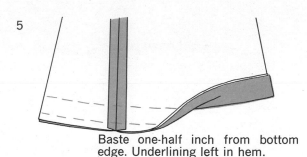

Baste one-half inch from bottom edge. Underlining left in hem.

Underlining cut away before hemming.

5. Hem. Baste the underlining to the hem after the hem width is marked, but before it is turned into place. This will hold the underlining in place inside the hem.

Or, here is a second way to treat the underlining when you hem.

Cut away the underling in the hem after the width is marked but before it is finished.

Advantages of underlining:

1. Underlining gives shape to clothing; the outside appearance of the garment will be better than if the underlining were not used.
2. The garment holds its original shape longer if the outside fabric is supported by underlining.
3. The inside of an underlined garment is attractive.
4. Underlining can cover scratchy fabrics which otherwise would be uncomfortable next to the skin.
5. Pattern markings can be put on the underlining rather than on the outside fabric.

6. The extra layer of fabric may add some warmth to winter garments.
7. The garment is less likely to wrinkle.

Disadvantages of underlining:

1. Underlining fabric adds expense.
2. Some additional time is needed to cut and attach underlinings.
3. Underlining may cause some warm-weather clothing to be uncomfortable.

In general, underlining improves the appearance and wearing quality of garments.

Interfacing a waistband—Method 1 (machine-stitched)

1. Cut the interfacing one half as wide as the waistband piece. Pin the interfacing to the waistband, matching notches. Machine-stitch the interfacing to the waistband ⅛ inch from the waistband fold and near the notched edge. If you stitch in the correct place, the upper stitching line will be hidden inside your waistband when it is turned.

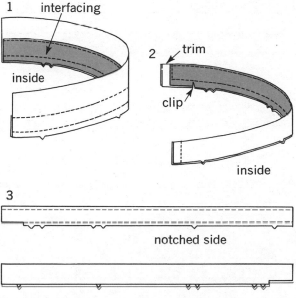

213

2. Fold the waistband with the right sides together. Stitch across the ends. Trim off the interfacing close to the end stitching.

3. Turn the waistband to the outside. It is now ready to attach to your skirt. Machine stitching shows on the notched side, which will be inside your skirt. No stitching should show on the outside of the waistband.

Interfacing a waistband—Method 2 (hand-stitched)

1. Cut the interfacing piece one half as wide as the waistband piece. Matching the notches, pin the interfacing to the inside of the waistband. Baste in place around the outer edge. Use a very loose catch stitch to attach the interfacing along the fold line of the waistband.

2. Fold the waistband, with the right sides together, and machine-stitch across the ends. Clip the interfacing close to the machine stitching.

3. Turn the waistband to the right side and press. The waistband is now ready to attach to the skirt.

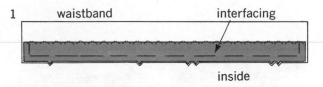

waistband   interfacing

inside

inside

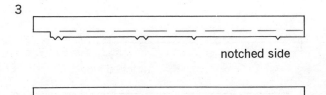

notched side

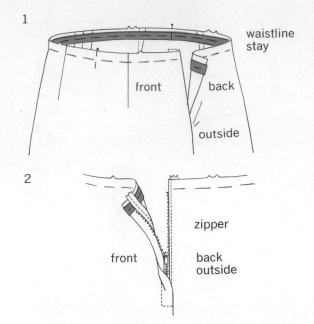

1

waistline stay

front   back

outside

2

zipper

front   back outside

The basting will show on the outside of the notched side. You remember that this is the side where the interfacing was attached. No stitching will show on the unnotched side.

(See Project 2 for two methods for *attaching* a waistband.)

Finishing the waist of a no-waistband skirt—Method 1 (with an inside facing)

Here are suggestions for finishing a skirt waistline with an inside facing:

1. Inside of the skirt baste a waistline stay to the waistline seam. The waistline stay should be cut to fit your waist. A mark center front, one center back, and one on the side of the stay will make it simpler to attach. The skirt top may be eased to fit the stay.

2. Make the zipper placket.

Now your skirt is ready for attaching the facing. Patterns are planned so that different pieces fit together perfectly. Fac-

214

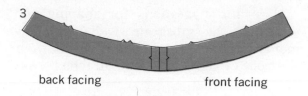

back facing   front facing

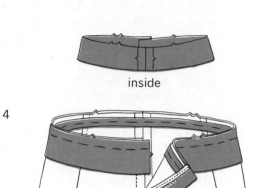

inside

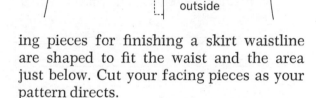

front back

outside

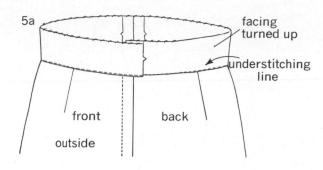

5a

facing turned up

understitching line

front back

outside

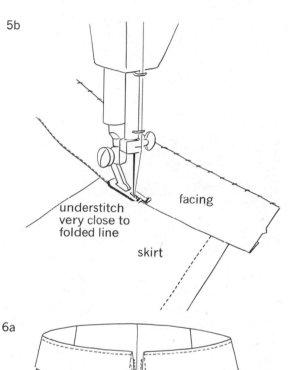

5b

understitch very close to folded line

facing

skirt

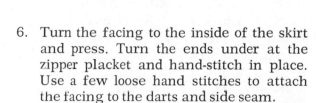

6a

front back

inside

ing pieces for finishing a skirt waistline are shaped to fit the waist and the area just below. Cut your facing pieces as your pattern directs.

3. Assemble facing pieces into a single unit. Finish the lower (larger) edge. The best method depends on your fabric. Turning and edge-stitching would be suitable for lightweight fabrics. Overcasting might be best for a heavier material. Do not finish the lower edge until you are sure the facing piece fits the waist area perfectly.

4. Work from the outside of your skirt. Pin, then baste, the facing to the waistline edge of the skirt. Check the fit at this point; then, finish the bottom edge of the facing. Machine-stitch in place. Catch the waistline stay in the stitching.

5. Turn the facing up and understitch. To understitch turn the seam allowance into the facing. Stitch on the facing piece close to where it joins the skirt. Stitch through all thicknesses of the fabric.

6. Turn the facing to the inside of the skirt and press. Turn the ends under at the zipper placket and hand-stitch in place. Use a few loose hand stitches to attach the facing to the darts and side seam.

With the facing in place the zipper ends about ¼ inch from the top of the skirt.

215

6b

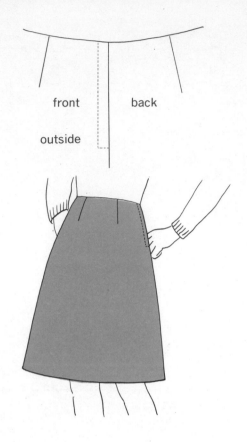

front | back

outside

On the outside, the waistband area will be smooth, with no pulling or wrinkles. There will be a sharp edge where the facing was pressed to the inside.

Finishing the waist of a no-waistband skirt —Method 2 (with grosgrain ribbon)

Grosgrain is a firm, closely woven fabric. It is heavy enough to hold the shape of the waist area; it will prevent stretching. You may be able to find grosgrain ribbon the exact width of your waistband pattern piece. If you are unable to find the exact width you need, buy wider ribbon and cut it to the correct width. Or you may be able to use a ribbon slightly narrower than your pattern piece. You need ribbon wide enough to make a ⅝-inch seam at the waist plus at least one inch to turn to the inside of your skirt.

Here are suggestions for shaping and attaching the grosgrain waistband. Remember that this band will be inside your skirt out of sight after it is attached.

1. Cut the band the correct length and width. Or use ribbon width as it is. Transfer pattern markings to the ribbon. These will show you how to shape the band and where to join it to the skirt.

2. Stitch small darts into the facing as marked on the pattern. Press all the darts in the same direction. These darts shape the band, or facing, so that it will fit the waist area. If the waist size of the skirt was changed in fitting, the band will need to be shaped accordingly.

3. Pin the smaller edge of the shaped ribbon to the skirt at the waistline seam mark, right sides together. The darts, which

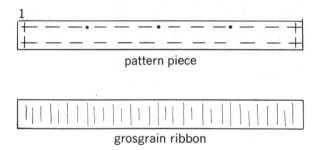

pattern piece

grosgrain ribbon

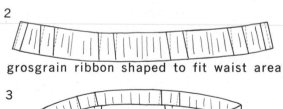

grosgrain ribbon shaped to fit waist area

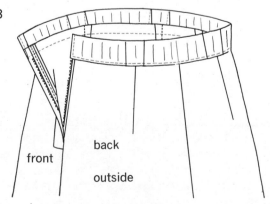

front | back

outside

show the inside of the shaped band will be outside. Use pattern markings as a guide to fit it on exactly. Ease the skirt slightly to fit the band. Turn under the ends of the band. Baste the band in place. Turn it under to check the fit; then, machine-stitch it in place.

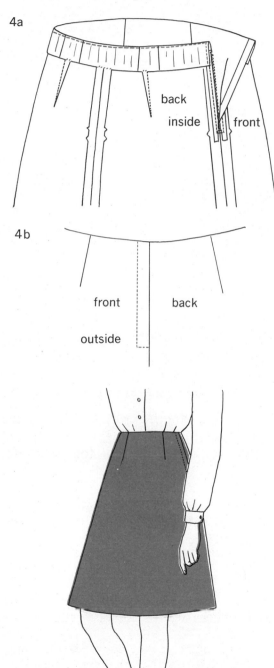

4. Press the band to the inside. Fasten it in place at the seams.

With the band in place the zipper ends about ¼ inch from the top of the skirt.

On the outside, the waistband area will be smooth, with no pulling or wrinkles. There will be a sharp edge where the grosgrain ribbon was pressed to the inside.

Putting in a seam pocket—Method 1

Cut and assemble the pocket. If your pattern does not include pieces for cutting a pocket you can easily make a pattern yourself. The diagram below shows the size and shape you need.

The straight edge: about 6½ inches long
Across the top: about 3¼ inches
Across at widest part: about 6 inches
Length at longest part: about 10½ inches

What materials should you use to cut the pocket pieces? You do not want the pocket shape to be outlined on the outside. Therefore you need to consider the thickness of the material. A firm cotton fabric would be satisfactory for a pocket in a corduroy skirt. For a light weight wool the underlining material would be satisfactory.

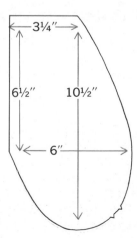

217

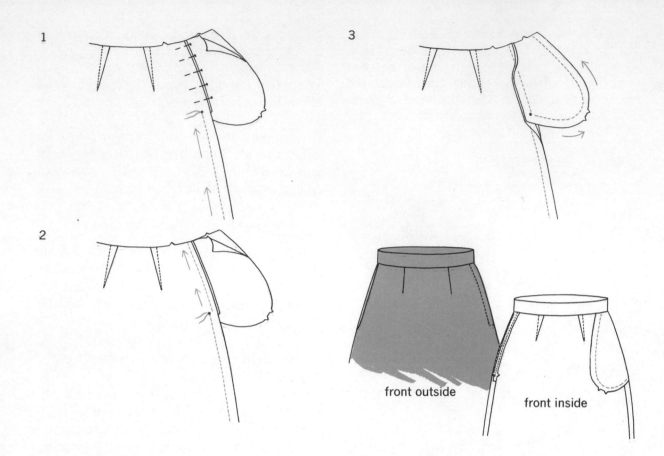

front outside

front inside

These steps show one method for joining the pocket to the skirt.

1. Stitch the side seam up to 6½ inches from the top of the skirt or the same length as the straight edge of the pocket. Pin one pocket piece, at the straight edge, to the front seam of the skirt and one to the back.

2. Stitch each side separately from the bottom of the pinning to the skirt top with a ⅜-inch seam.

3. Stitch the pocket pieces together with a ⅝-inch seam. Start the seam where the skirt seam ends. The pocket seam and the skirt seam should meet exactly. (This step will test your ability to stitch accurately.) Turn the completed pocket to the front and press.

When the waistband is attached, the raw edge of the pocket will be enclosed.

Putting in a seam pocket—Method 2

Let's look at another way to join a side-seam pocket to a skirt. Begin by cutting your pocket pieces; then follow these steps:

1. Assemble your pocket first. Stitch the curved outside edges together. Use a ⅝-inch seam allowance, and start 6½ inches down from the flat side of the pocket.

2. Prepare the skirt seam by stitching up to 6½ inches from the top. Press open.

3. Pin the open pocket edges to the open seam allowances of the skirt. Baste in

218

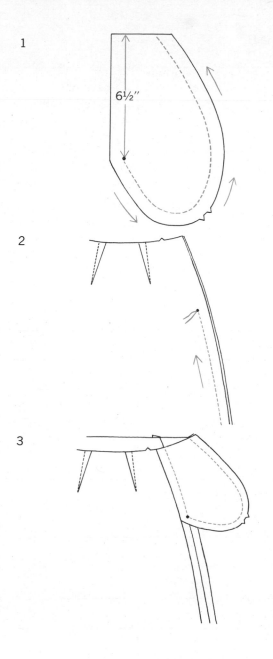

1

6½"

2

3

place if necessary, then machine-stitch. Turn the pocket pieces to the front of the skirt.

As you learn more about clothing construction techniques, you will discover that there is more than one way to accomplish some tasks. Usually each way has both advantages and disadvantages.

Project No. 7
A One-piece Dress

Before you make a plan for another sewing project, take time to look back and analyze your progress. What have you learned as you sewed? Have you made some new discoveries with each new garment? How well have you succeeded on previous projects? What new goals might you reach by sewing another garment?

Your own progress record may help you answer the question, What have I learned?

A one-piece dress is an ideal project for trying a few different techniques and for practicing more on the ones you have already tried. Use your progress record to plan according to your personal needs, but also to make it an experience in learning.

219

What Have I Learned?
Personal Progress Record

Skills	I have attempted this; results were good.	I have attempted this; more practice is needed.	I have not attempted this.
1. To select pattern size for myself			
2. To alter a pattern			
3. To cut with grainline			
4. To transfer pattern markings to fabrics			
5. To stay-stitch			
6. To make darts			
7. To make facings, including understitching			
8. To press			
9. To finish a plain seam			
10. To make a lapped zipper placket			
11. To make a centered zipper placket			
12. To finish a hem—turned and edge-stitched			
13. To finish a hem with seam binding			
14. To interface			
15. To attach a collar			
16. To set in sleeves			
17. To make machine-worked buttonholes			
18. To underline			
19. To interface a waistband			
20. To finish a waist with inside facing			
21. To make a patch pocket			
22. To make a seam pocket			
23. To make kimono sleeves			
24. To make raglan sleeves			
25. (list other skills you have learned.)			

What might you learn by making a one-piece dress? If you have not attempted these things yet, you may learn to:
   make a long back zipper placket
   make a waistline seam
   sew kimono sleeve *or* sew raglan sleeves
   underline a skirt, or both bodice and skirt
   finish a hem a different way
   attach a patch pocket or a seam pocket

Studying a one-piece dress before you plan

Before you begin, let's look closely at the inside and outside of a one-piece dress. Notice the techniques that have been used.

This dress, with the exception of the sleeves, has been underlined to maintain the A-shape of the skirt and the simple lines of the bodice. Underlining means that the lining fabric is attached to the outside fabric in the seams and darts. The skirt is underlined with a special underlining fabric, which is somewhat crisp. This fabric, which will hold the shape of the skirt well, is too crisp for the shape of the bodice. Therefore, batiste, with a soft feel, has been used in the bodice. This adds more body to the outside fabric but not crispness.

Seam binding was sewed into the waistline seam to serve as a stay, and to reduce stretch at the waist. The waist seam with the binding attached was turned upward before the back zipper placket was made.

Notice that the horizontal darts at the bustline are pressed downward. The vertical darts at the waistline in both the bodice and skirt are pressed toward the center front. This helps to give the dress shape and contour.

The neck facing was understitched. Can you point to the place where the understitching should be located? What is the reason for understitching?

The neck facing has been finished by edge-stitching and pinking. The plain-weave wool flannel fabric does not ravel easily and it will be dry-cleaned. Edge-stitching and pinking are an adequate finish for the facing.

The seams were finished by pinking only. Edge-stitching could have been done in addition to pinking.

The sleeve seams have been clipped at the underarm area. This may not always be necessary in order to have the sleeve fit well. You may want to clip at the underarm only if the fabric is bulky, or if you feel that you need a little extra ease around the armhole for a comfortable fit.

The excess fullness in the hem was shrunk out after it was turned so that it would lie flat. The hem was finished with seam binding.

An attractive garment is the result of the care and attention that has been used in completing each detail. This is true for ready-made clothes and those you sew.

221

Here is the outside view of the one-piece dress. Inside details affect the outside appearance. One of the most important characteristics of a dress is the way it fits. You will have learned much about clothing construction techniques when you can present yourself in an attractive dress that you have made.

Skillful work shows in this dress at these check points:

Shoulder seams end at the shoulders.

The set-in sleeve is free of puckers.

The bust darts point toward the bust.

The waistline seam is located at the waistline.

The darts at the waist are straight and are directed toward the full part of the body; the length of the darts is good in relation to the height of the wearer.

The hem does not show on the outside; it is parallel to the floor.

The understitching holds the neck facing inside.

The dress hangs evenly on the body.

There is enough ease for comfort.

You, too, will have an attractive, well-fitted dress if you:

take body measurements accurately

use body measurements to choose the best pattern type and size for your figure

check the fit of your pattern before you sew

make necessary pattern changes carefully

follow grainline marking when you cut, using sharp cutting shears

press with the grainline as you sew

Although many construction details are shown in these illustrations, they are only sketches. You may want to examine an actual dress also, in order to study construction details further. Look at some ready-made dresses as well as hand-made ones.

When you are ready to make your plan for your dress ask yourself:

What do I expect to learn?

What standards will I try to reach?

Making kimono sleeves

Kimono sleeves are cut on a garment as a part of the bodice. In this type of design a sharp curve is formed by the underarm seam. The curved section should be clipped in order to give enough ease under the arms. Because this is an area where there is apt to be strain, it is necessary to reinforce the clipped area. Otherwise the seam may not be strong enough to withstand the strain.

There are several ways to reinforce the curved underarm seam. One satisfactory way is to make a zig-zag machine stitch along the seam. Start by clipping the seam carefully in several places. Press the seam open. Since this is a very curved edge, try

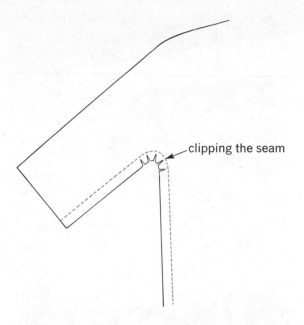

clipping the seam

There is another way to reinforce a clipped seam which does not require special equipment, as the zig-zag stitch does. Sew a strip of seam binding on the seam in the curved area. You may want to baste it in place first, using the stitches on the underside of the seam as a guide. The stitches which hold the seam binding in place permanently should follow the seam exactly. Clip along the curve and press the seam open.

Making raglan sleeves

pressing it over a pressing ham rather than on the flat surface of the ironing board. Make the machine stitch on the inside of the garment. The stitch should follow the seam line exactly. Of course, thread and fabric should match.

A raglan sleeve is a sleeve in which the sleeve pieces are cut to include the shoulder area. The sleeves are attached to the front and back bodice pieces before the side seams are made. This is a good style for sewing bonded fabrics, those with durable press finish, and thick materials that make it difficult to ease a sleeve into an armhole.

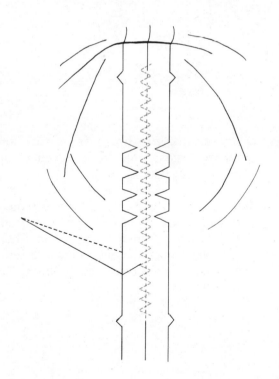

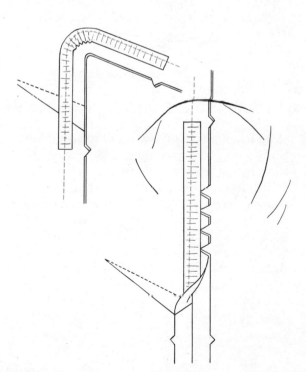

223

Suggested Learning Experiences

1. "She manages to get so many things done. She is a good manager. How does she manage to accomplish so much?" These familiar comments suggest that a good manager can be recognized and described. The management process starts when you recognize that you have a goal to reach, a problem to solve, or a task to finish. When you are able to plan how to use your energy, equipment, ability, and other resources to finish your work and reach your goal, you are involved in the management process.

Are you a good manager? Let's consider some ways that good management can lead to success when you sew. Study the following illustrations. And then, using the questions as guides, discuss each illustration. Look at each illustration carefully.

A. 1. What information did this girl bring to the store in order to choose her fabric and sewing notions wisely?
   2. When is a fabric "on sale" or at "special price" a bargain or a good choice? When is it not a good choice?
   3. Why select thread, buttons, and other notions when you select your fabric?

B. 1. What useful information about the fabric is this girl recording before she leaves the store?
   2. Why bother to write this information—why not just try to remember it?
   3. How will this information be helpful in sewing and in caring for the finished garment?
   4. What problems or difficulties might you have without complete information about the fabric you buy?

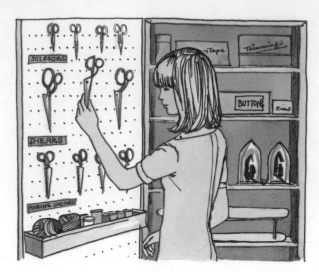 

C. 1. Does the way the cutting shears are stored show that safety was considered? Explain.
2. Are the shears stored so that the blades are protected against chips and scratches? Explain.
3. How is the table protected against damage by the tracing wheel points?
4. Why is it good management to store equipment so that it is easily reached, yet protected against damage, and so that it is not a hazard?
5. Explain or demonstrate how other pieces of sewing equipment should be stored.

D. 1. Why take time to get ready to work?
2. How much time is reasonable to spend in assembling equipment and materials before you begin? How much time should be spent in putting away and cleaning up?
3. How will an orderly work area affect your work? Does it make any difference whether a working area is orderly?

E. 1. What specific kinds of directions can this girl expect to find on her pattern guide?
2. What other sources of help are visible in the classroom?
3. Why is it good use of time to study directions as you sew?
4. From what resources in your classroom might you obtain answers to your questions?

F. 1. What suggestions can you make for improving this girl's work habits?
2. Why is she likely to become tired soon?
3. Why is it important to share equipment fairly in the classroom?

G. 1. Why is good posture important when you sew?
2. Is good posture a good management practice? Explain.
3. Demonstrate good posture as you work at the machine and at the table.
4. What are some consequences or results of poor posture as you sew?

H. 1. When is it important to allow time for fitting as you sew a garment?
2. Why is it good time management to take time for fitting as you sew?
3. Notice the girl in the completed garment. What must she do now if she wants to have her garment fit well?

I. 1. Why take time to check your own progress?
    2. How many ways to evaluate your own work are included in the illustration?
    3. How can a check list be used to determine whether you are making progress?

2. Plan an exhibit of easy-to-sew fabrics, or "fabrics for beginners" based on ideas from this unit and other sources.

3. Review vocabulary as you learn each new sewing technique.

4. Make a "question-box" or "problem-box." Write good questions and deposit them in the box to help your teacher know the special problems you are having with your work. Your teacher could have a short answering session once a week.

5. Share questions and answers through a bulletin board such as this:

Write questions on a piece of paper. Leave space on the paper for the answer. Or write questions and leave space on the bulletin board for answers to be pinned below the questions. (Also, the teacher might use this technique as a way to conduct oral review. The teacher and the pupils might write important questions; post them ahead of review day so they can be used as guides for studying; then use the questions to center interest on the reviews.)

6. Two paper-and-pencil quizzes using diagrams follow this page.
    Quiz No. 1 is planned to be used with Project No. 1, the sleeveless, collarless blouse.
    Quiz No. 2 is planned to be used with Project No. 2, the A-line skirt with waistband.

Quiz No. 1

Review what you have learned about pattern layout, grainline, and cutting.

Study the following diagram and answer the questions.

229

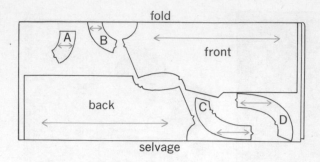

Blouse pattern
A, B—neck facings
C, D—armhole facings
Fabric is 36 inches wide.

1. Is the fabric folded with the lengthwise grainline or the crosswise grainline? How can you tell?
2. Are A and B placed on the lengthwise or crosswise grainline?
3. Are A and B placed on the same grainline as the back and the front pieces?
4. How many back pieces will be cut from this pattern layout? How many front pieces? How can you tell?
5. How wide would a pattern layout be if 36-inch-wide fabric was folded in half as this diagram shows?

Quiz No. 2

Review what you have learned about pattern layout, grainline, and cutting.
Study this diagram and answer questions.

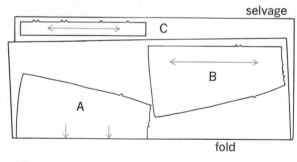

Skirt pattern
A—skirt front
B—skirt back
C—waistband

1. How many pieces of A will be cut from this layout? How many pieces of B? of C?
2. Explain what you could do to be sure that each pattern piece is placed exactly on the straight grainline of the fabric?
3. If this pattern layout is followed, will all pieces be cut on the same grainline?
4. If you cut "with the grainline," how would you cut the outer edges of A and B—from top to bottom, or from bottom to top?

References for Pupils and Teachers

Johnson, Hildegarde, Barbara Clawson, and Sarah Shoffner, *Sewing Step-by-Step*, a complete program of instruction on the sewing machine, patterns, and construction techniques. Ginn and Company, Boston, 1967.

McCall's Easy Sewing Book (1965). McCall Corporation, 230 Park Avenue, New York 10017.

Simplicity Sewing Book (1965). Simplicity Pattern Co., Inc., 200 Madison Avenue, New York 10016.

References for Teachers

Bane, Allyne, *Creative Clothing Construction*, Second Edition, McGraw-Hill Book Co., New York, 1966.

Bishop, Edna Bryte, and Marjorie Stotler Arch, *The Bishop Method of Clothing Construction*, Revised Edition. J. B. Lippincott Co., Philadelphia, 1966.

Professional Sewing Tips, Better Homes and Gardens, Creative Sewing Library. Meredith Publishing Co., New York, 1966.

Teacher's Textbook of Machine Sewing, Form 1876 (1960). The Singer Sewing Machine Co., Singer Building, 149 Broadway, New York 10001.

UNIT EIGHT

More Uses For Your Sewing Skills — Alterations and Repairs

I. Is It Ready to Wear?

Why Learn to Alter Ready-to-Wear Clothes?

Question: When is a ready-to-wear garment not a ready-to-wear garment for you?

Answer: When you are not willing to wear the garment until it is altered so that, for you, it is more comfortable, more becoming, or both.

This question and its answer describe a very modern problem, and a very practical problem, that you will need to learn how to solve. You may plan to buy all, or most, of your clothes ready-made. However, it is not likely that all the ready-to-wear clothes you need, or prefer to buy, will fit you satisfactorily. Mass-produced garments are not constructed for a particular individual, but each girl and woman has her own individual figure characteristics. Therefore, each girl or woman who expects to get wearing satisfaction from ready-to-wear garments may need to change them slightly, or much, to fit her particular characteristics.

Is it wise for you to purchase a garment that needs alteration? Sometimes you cannot avoid it. If you actually need a particular garment in order to be adequately clothed, you will have to select it from the available choices. The fact that it is not always possible to purchase clothing which fits satisfactorily may be enough reason for you to develop your alteration skills.

Have you considered how useful and satisfying your sewing skills could be in adapting your ready-to-wear clothes? If the cost of having several necessary alterations done for you is added to the original price of the garment, a low-priced garment may become an expensive one. Furthermore, alteration service is not provided by every retail clothing store, and alteration services by individuals or dressmaking shops may not be available in your community.

As you grow in your ability to select ready-to-wear clothes you will acquire your own standards of appearance and fit. If you are dependent on someone else to provide your alteration service, you must accept the standard that is available. Your sewing skills will permit you to develop self-reliance in fitting and maintaining your own clothes. Later, your skill may become a valuable resource in altering ready-to-wear clothing for an entire family.

If you have successfully constructed a few garments, you probably already have some skills that could be applied to alter-

ing your ready-mades. Your answers to the following questions will help you summarize your present skills and your ideas about alterations.

1. Do you already have some sewing skills that might be used in making alterations? Can you describe some of these skills?
2. Is it important to you that your clothes fit well? Why?
3. What would you like to learn about improving ready-to-wear garments for yourself?
4. How much time are you willing to devote to learning about altering ready-mades?

How Can You Decide What Garments Can Be Altered?

Construction details and the fabric will tell you if a garment can be altered. What clues can construction details give you? Seam allowances should be adequate for easing out, if this is needed. When seam allowances are left too narrow by alteration, they will not be durable. If skirt or sleeves need more length, look for enough hem width to "let down." If there isn't enough material to let down, you will need at least enough excess width to attach a facing.

Darts might need to be lengthened, shortened, or moved to improve fit. Moving a dart is a difficult alteration for a sewer with little experience. And even if there is someone else who might make this alteration for you, you will need to decide if the alteration is possible. Two clues will tell you if dart changes are possible. If dart ends have been marked by small punch holes, then alterations are limited. If the darts have been slashed and pressed open in the manufacturing process,

changes will be limited, or perhaps impossible. If you find that dart alterations are needed, examine the inside of the garment before you decide to buy it, to see whether the needed alterations are possible.

For good fit and appearance, grainline is as important in ready-to-wear clothes as in those you construct for yourself. If a garment has been cut off grain it may not be advisable to spend time on alterations. Consider other choices. Only an experienced and very skilled sewer can deal with the problem of altering a garment that has been cut off grain. Furthermore, it may not be possible to correct the difficulty at all.

What will the fabric tell you about alterations? A loosely woven fabric is likely to stretch as a result of much handling. A firmly woven fabric will be better able to withstand alterations which require ripping and restitching seams.

A fabric which ravels easily is difficult to handle. However, if no other improvement is needed, the garment could be made more durable by finishing the seams.

Permanent holes are left in some fabric when stitches are removed. It is not always possible to determine whether or not this will happen just by examining the fabric, but it is most likely to occur on fabrics with wrinkle-resistant or wash-and-wear finishes.

Another problem in garments that need to be altered is permanent creases. One of the advantages of some of the man-made fibers is that creases can be heat-set. This means that at a high temperature pleats or other desirable creases can be shaped into the fabric. Wash-and-wear finishes also cause fabrics to hold pressed-in creases rather persistently. This may be a disadvantage in some types of alteration. For example, the permanent crease made by pressing the original hemline is a problem if the skirt must be lengthened.

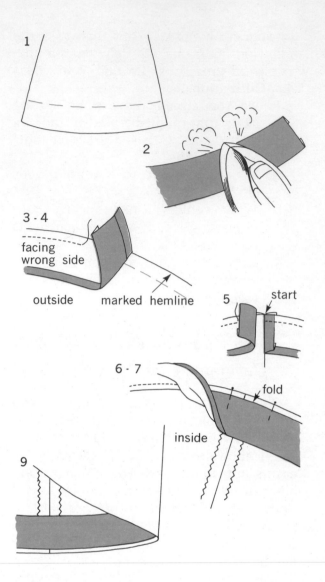

How Can You Improve the Fit or Adapt the Design to Yourself?

Changing skirt length

Skirt length is one of the most readily noticed marks of good fit and current style. It may be the only difference between an attractive, comfortable garment and one that is not. Even if you alter nothing else, ability to mark and finish a hem may well be a skill worth developing. If you have already constructed a skirt for yourself, you have had some experience in marking a hem. In altering skirt length, follow the steps for regular hemming. Start by taking out the present hem and marking the new hem length. (For steps in making a hem see "Learning as You Sew," pages 191–194.)

Lengthening a skirt may involve a different type of problem from shortening one. There is not always sufficient fabric to extend the length by a regular hemming procedure. When there is not enough fabric at the bottom to make a hem, a skirt may be finished with a facing. Ready-made hem facings may be purchased in a variety of colors. Taffeta facing is suitable for wool and wool-blend skirts. Cotton facing is most satisfactory for cottons and cotton blend fabrics.

Directions for Applying Prepared Hem Facing

1. Prepare the skirt by marking the hem line with a basting stitch.

2. Prepared hem facing is applied without shaping to a straight skirt. For facing a flared skirt or one with a definite bias bottom, prepare the facing by steam-pressing it into the curved shape of the hem.

3. Open one folded edge of the prepared facing and match it to the bottom edge of the skirt. Place the right side of the facing to the right side of skirt. Pin the facing to the skirt, starting one end of the facing at a seam line in the skirt.

4. Stitch the facing to the hem using the crease in the facing as a guide.

5. Overlap the ends slightly to close the facing ends.

6. Using the marked hem line as a guide, turn the facing to the inside.

7. Pin, then baste the fold in place as you would for regular hemming.

8. Hand-stitch the facing in place, using a slip stitch as for flat hemming. Do not pull the stitches tight or the outline of the facing will be visible on the outside.

9. The completed facing should lie smooth inside. Outside, the outline of the facing should not be visible.

Lengthening a skirt may present other special problems. A hem crease may have been heat-set permanently if the skirt is made of a man-made fabric. Polyesters, nylons, and acrylics are examples of man-made fibers in which pressed creases are apt to be permanent. Whether you are al-

tering a new garment or an older garment, you will need to determine whether or not a permanent crease was made where the hem was first turned. In older garments the turned edge may show wear. If some of the threads are worn through, the crease may be very noticeable. Or the fabric which was turned under the garment may no longer be exactly the same color as the outer side. In this case the old hem area will be clearly marked by its different color.

Regardless of the reason, any evidence of the old hem will detract from the appearance of a lengthened skirt. If appearance will affect the use of the garment, you may want to plan a suitable way to cover the evidence of the old hemline. You might use a fabric trim or decorative stitchery, keeping in mind that the trim should be related to the rest of the garment design. (See the illustrations below.)

235

Changing sleeve length

Not only does wearing comfort depend on sleeve length, but sleeve lengths, like skirt lengths, affect the overall appearance and style of a garment. And as with skirt length, it is usually easier to shorten than to lengthen a sleeve. The problem of additional fabric to "let down" must be considered whenever more length is needed. Just as a skirt can be lengthened by attaching a facing, a sleeve may be extended in the same way. Long sleeves in a coat, jacket, or dress may be lengthened by adding cuffs, however this is a complex alteration.

If permanent creases have been made in the fabric, the creases might be concealed by decorative trim. However, if the garment's use will not be affected by the creases, this will be no problem. This may be true of casual clothes. Whether a garment is useful to you after it has been altered to fit depends on your willingness to wear it.

Changing decorative trim

Perhaps the simplest type of change to make in ready-to-wear garments is either the adding or the removing of decorative trim. In planning this type of alteration, design principles should be applied—proportion and scale, emphasis, balance, and rhythm. For instance, belt width may be studied in terms of proportion and scale. If a wide belt is out of proportion for your measurements, you could replace it with a narrower belt or remove it altogether.

Attached trim, such as buttons or a belt, may provide poorly located accents. These accents could be relocated to provide a more suitable accent for your particular figure. The same type of alteration is possible for false pocket tabs which have been attached as trim.

Consider balance and rhythm in the design of the garment. Too much trim applied to a particular article of clothing may give a spotty appearance. Too many

different shapes used together may result in the same effect. The over-all appearance of a garment is produced by the combination of parts. Therefore, if you study the design of the entire garment you may be able to see how changing a part may improve the over-all appearance and make it more pleasing to you.

A change of decorative trim may make it possible to combine a garment successfully with clothes you already have. Buttons which are too ornate could be replaced with plainer buttons on a blouse to make it more suitable for school wear. The colors of added belts, pins, and buttons in a particular garment may limit the way it can be satisfactorily combined with other clothes. It might be possible, and desirable, to remove colored trim which limits the use of the garment.

Can you think of other ways to improve the appearance or add to the usefulness of ready-to-wear garments by adding, or taking away, or changing attached trim?

Adjusting the skirt waistband

A waistband which fits too closely, or one which is too wide, is likely to roll into wrinkled layers of fabric at the waist. A waistband which has become uncomfortably snug may be removed by ripping the waist seam. Work carefully, just as you would for any ripping, to avoid stretching the fabric or cutting threads.

When re-attaching the waistband, allow for a small amount of additional ease by reducing the size of the underlap and easing the skirt to the slightly longer waist allowance in the waistband. If the reduced underlap is too small to permit closing the waistband securely, it is possible to add an extension of fabric on the waistband before it is replaced.

Before you purchase a skirt, examine the waistband to determine whether it can be changed. Also, when you make a skirt you might plan for an adequate underlay to take care of this type of possible alteration.

237

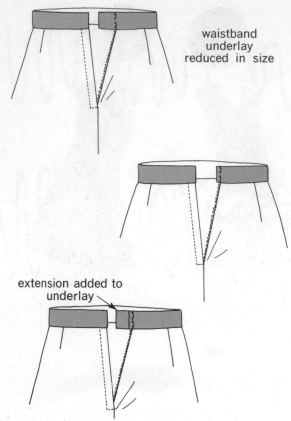

waistband
underlay
reduced in size

extension added to
underlay

extension added to provide for secure closing.

Waistband underlay reduced in size.
Extension added to underlay to provide for secure closing.

The fit of the skirt at the waist and immediately below the waist may be so snug that refitting the waistband does not provide enough change. The skirt waist circumference may need to be changed before the waistband is re-attached. This type of alteration will be more difficult. It will involve removing the zipper and changing seams and darts.

Instead of replacing the original waistband, the waist seam could be finished with an inside facing. This facing would be attached at the same seam line where the waistband was joined to the skirt. A problem may occur if the seam allowance

has been clipped too closely to the seam line. In this case, to avoid a weakened seam, stitch the new seam just outside the old one. (See "Learning as You Sew," pages 214–216, for directions on inside skirt facing.)

Making dress alterations that require more skill

Unless you are very skilled it may be unwise for you to attempt certain types of alterations. Some of these more difficult alterations are described below.

Changing the location of the waistline seam in a one-piece dress is a complex alteration, requiring several separate steps. If there is a zipper at either the side or back, it must be removed first. If the dress has a front or back button closing that extends to the waist or beyond it, the buttonholes nearest the waist will probably be affected. The location of the new waist seam must be marked. Both bodice and skirt may need to be refitted at the waist before the new waistline seam is sewed, for a bodice that is too short or too long is uncomfortable and makes the garment look incorrectly fitted. Your success with this type of alteration will depend on your patience in dealing with each of the necessary steps, with the time you have available, and with your ability to handle fabric and equipment.

Skirt seam allowances may be either increased or decreased in order to provide more or less ease in the skirt. This alteration, like changing bodice length, consists of several steps. Remember that altering skirt seams involves removing a side or back zipper, and a waistband or waist facing. Usually, the hem will need to be taken out, and after the seams have been changed, it may have to be marked again before it can be finished.

Merely ripping the seams and restitching them with larger or smaller allowances may not result in an improved fit. In a fitted skirt, you may require additional ease only at the front or at the back rather than ease evenly divided between front and back. If you are not symmetrical, each side may require a different seam allowance. In order actually to improve the fit, you may need to mark and pin each seam individually.

Adding a gusset is another alteration which is likely to be difficult for less-experienced sewers. A *gusset* is a small piece of fabric set into the underarm area. A kimono-sleeve bodice which needs some additional ease will fit more comfortably if a gusset is added. To do this successfully you need adequate skill to control the sewing machine while you work on a small area. Also, it is helpful to have enough patience to work carefully on a small area.

Adding a gusset to a ready-to-wear garment includes the problem of finding a piece of matching fabric. It may be possible to buy the matching fabric that is needed. Otherwise, a piece of unessential fabric might be found on the garment. Seam pockets, for example, could be removed and the material used. If the skirt length can be shortened, the excess fabric that is cut away there could be used. (See the directions for making a gusset on page 240.)

Changing slip length

When your slip length is coordinated with your outer garments, your outer clothes fit better and look better. If a slip is too long, it sags below the skirt. If it is too short, it fails to provide an adequate lining for your skirt.

Changing a slip length may be a simple procedure if the bottom has been finished

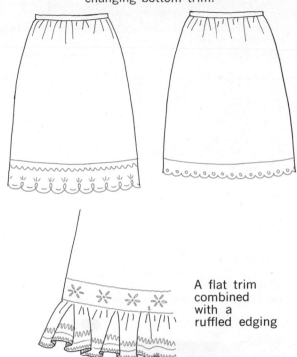

Increase or decrease slip length by changing bottom trim.

A flat trim combined with a ruffled edging

by attached lace or embroidered edging. These types of trims can be removed and replaced with either wider or narrower edging as needed. A satisfactory adjustment of a few inches in length may be made this way. Laces or other edges should be replaced with a similar edging which differs only in width. For example, replace nylon lace with nylon lace. When altering a cotton slip, replace cotton lace or cotton batiste embroidered edging with a similar type.

You may like to use your imagination to combine two decorative trims attractively to finish the bottom of the slip. For example, a flat eyelet trim could be combined with ruffled edging. Attach the new edging by using either a hand stitch, or a machine zig-zag stitch. (See the diagram, on page 241, showing the whipping stitch for attaching lace by hand.)

239

How to Set in a Gusset

A gusset put into a kimono sleeve results in a trimmer, closer-to-the-body fit plus greater ease of movement. A two-piece gusset, such as is demonstrated here, is generally considered easier to insert than a one-piece.

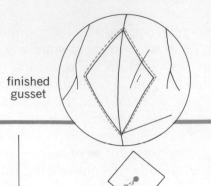

finished gusset

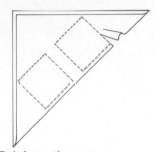

1. Reinforce the corner.
    Cut four 2″ bias squares, one for reinforcing each of the four slashes.

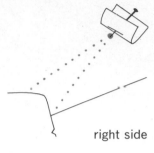

right side

On right side of bodice front, pin center of one square over point where stitching lines meet.

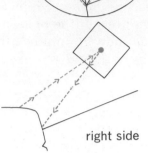

right side

Stitch along stitching lines right through the square, pivoting the work at the point.

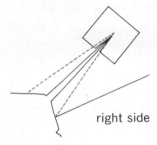

right side

2. Turn the point.
    Slash between stitched lines all the way to the point. But do not clip through the point.

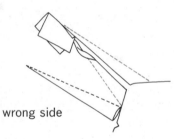

wrong side

Turn the square through the slash to the wrong side of the garment, and press.

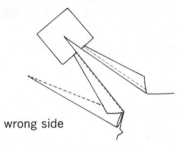

wrong side

Turn and press edges of slash to wrong side, letting stitching line roll slightly to inside.

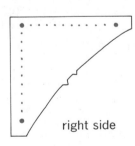

right side

3. Insert the gusset.
    On right side of gusset, mark dots and seam lines.

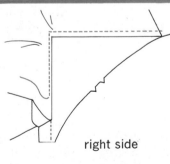

right side

Lay wrong side of slash over right side of gusset. Pin slash point to gusset point and edges of slash to seam lines. Topstitch.

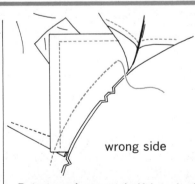

wrong side

Put second gusset half into bodice back. Then stitch side and underarm seams in one continuous operation. This joins the gusset pieces.

240

Joining lace to hemmed edge. Work from right to left. With lace toward you, catch one hem thread and lace edge together with whipping stitches. Or join flat with machine zigzag.

How Might You Make It More Durable?

Strengthening fasteners— hooks, snaps, buttons, and buttonholes

When you buy ready-to-wear clothing do you examine the fasteners? Snaps, buttons, and hook-and-eye fasteners are useful only when they are securely attached. A few additional stitches may be all that is necessary to hold them more firmly.

Would additional fasteners improve the appearance of the closings? Perhaps a firmer closing depends on more fasteners at the neck or waistband. Is a larger fastener needed where there will be much strain? In this case, small-size snaps and hooks can be replaced by larger ones. For example, coats, heavy skirts, and sportswear may need heavier fasteners.

Plastic buttons may be damaged beyond use if they are washed in hot water or ironed at high temperatures. Therefore, if the garment has plastic buttons and will receive this type of care, more durable buttons are necessary. Also, some types of buttons cannot be dry-cleaned satisfactorily. Your dry-cleaner can tell you whether or not a particular button is likely to survive the dry-cleaning process. Button size, of course, depends on the buttonhole. But you can probably get buttons of the same size as the original ones but made of more durable material.

A reinforcement may be sewed under the button location. If the garment will be worn frequently or if the fabric is loosely woven, this is a worthwhile procedure. Sew a small flat button underneath each outer button area in order to strengthen coat and jacket closings. Stitch through both buttons at the same time. Make a shank under the outer button to provide enough room for the thickness of the buttonhole. This prevents the button from pressing into the fabric when the garment is buttoned. A small piece of washable fabric is suitable for reinforcing a lightweight, washable article. This type of reinforcement may be specially useful on a washable garment which does not have interfacing under the buttons. (See "Learning as You Sew," pages 202–203, for directions on attaching buttons and reinforcements.)

Are the worked buttonholes in the garment stitched closely? If threads are too sparse, the buttonhole will probably stretch easily from ordinary wear. As a result, the

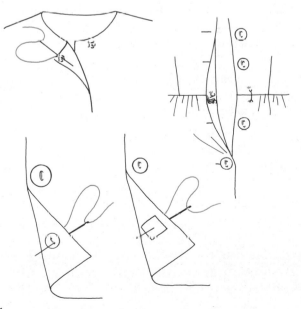

fabric will soon tear unless it is made more durable. Buttonholes may be reworked by hand. There is no need to remove the original stitches. Use a matching thread. Stitch closely, covering the fabric around the buttonhole completely. (See "Learning as You Sew," pages 200–201, for hand-worked buttonholes.)

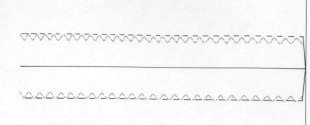

Reinforcing seams

The waist seam in a one-piece dress can be reinforced by sewing a stay into the seam. Just restitching the seam with smaller stitches would increase the durability. (For directions for attaching a waistline stay, see "Learning as You Sew," pages 206–207.)

The underarm seam of a kimono sleeve might also be reinforced against strain. When you construct a garment, this type of reinforcement might be done as a step in assembling the bodice. The same procedures could be used on a ready-to-wear garment. (For directions for reinforcing a kimono sleeve, see "Learning as You Sew," pages 222–223.)

If you are more skilled and very patient, you may want to insert a gusset instead of reinforcing the kimono-sleeve seam. This detail would provide some extra ease and reduce the strain. (See directions for inserting a gusset, as shown in illustrations on page 240.)

You will want to examine all seams for too-large stitches and hanging threads. Tie loose threads securely and cut them off close to the seam. It might be worthwhile for you to restitch some seams, particularly if the garment will be worn and washed frequently. The quality of a low cost garment can be increased rather quickly by reinforcing the stitching in the seams. This is something even a beginner at clothing construction can do.

Finishing plain seams

Normal wear will cause plain seams to ravel. If the material ravels easily the seam allowances will soon be frayed. Too much raveling will weaken the seam. A garment will be useful longer if plain seams are finished before it is worn. The fabric and the use of the garment determine the best finish. A machine zig-zag stitch would be a quick seam finish if you have access to this type of equipment. Also, machine edge-stitching would take very little time. Either of these methods would be satisfactory for

242

a washable garment. If you have no machine available, hand overcasting would be another solution. For thick fabrics either overcasting or binding is suitable. (See "Finishes for Plain Seams," page 185.)

Adding a sewed-in coat hanger

A coat or jacket may become misshapen across the shoulders when it must be hung on a hook in a school locker every day. A pointed hook may damage the lining and perhaps cause stitches which hold the lining to the outer fabric to break at the neckline. One way you can protect your school coat or jacket is by sewing a lightweight chain hanger at the neckline. This type of chain may be attached by a hand stitch at the eyelet ends. Some ready-to-wear coats and jackets made for rugged wear have this feature. (See illustrations, page 242.)

Instead of a specially designed chain, you might use other materials such as braid or twill tape.

II. Can You Repair Your Clothes?

What looks so sad as a sock with a hole in its heel—and another in the toe? What cries for help louder than a button hanging by a single, shredded thread? What looks more neglected than a sagging hem line? Holes, missing buttons, and rips add up to a careless appearance.

You find pleasure in buying attractive clothes which enhance your appearance. It is a challenge to your clothing construction skills to keep these clothes in top condition.

One way you can share in family clothes care is to take responsibility for your own clothing repairs. Also, by repairing only your own clothes you may better understand the time needed to repair clothes adequately for a family.

You can expect clothes that you wear frequently to require some occasional repairs. A few stitches at the right time may help you avoid major repairs later. Give immediate attention to minor tears, broken seams, and worn places.

Some types of repairs can be done equally well either by hand or at the sewing machine. However, it is helpful to have some skill in making ordinary repairs using only a thread and needle. All too frequently the damage needs weekly attention. It is not always possible to depend on the convenience of a sewing machine. Many persons find handwork to be relaxing. It can actually be more of a quiet recreation than a chore to be done.

243

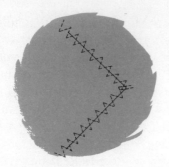

Tear repaired with zig-zag machine stitch. Place a piece of fabric underneath and stitch it to the torn area in order to reinforce it.

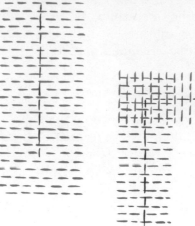
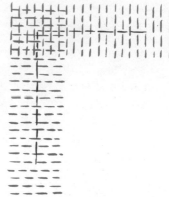

Straight-tear hand darn and corner hand darn. These illustrations show how stitches are placed parallel to each other. The corner tear shows darning stitches on both lengthwise and crosswise grainline to duplicate the weave.

Darns and other patches

A tear in a woven fabric can be mended quickly by using a *zig-zag sewing-machine stitch*. Cut a piece of fabric the shape of the tear and stitch it underneath the tear for reinforcement. Use a lightweight fabric the same color as that of the garment. Close the tear by stitching across the torn edges. Follow machine directions for correct stitch setting.

Hand darning is another satisfactory way to mend tears and holes in your clothes. Darning is a method of repairing a hole or tear by which broken yarns are covered by new yarns anchored in the fabric on either side of the tear. Use this type of mend for holes in the toes of your socks and stockings, and in plain-weave fabrics in which individual yarns can be seen clearly.

Mending a tear is a different type of problem from darning a small hole. When mending a tear the yarns in the fabric must be replaced in both the lengthwise and crosswise directions. Study the fabric weave and attempt to duplicate it as closely as possible. Darning stitches which replace broken lengthwise yarns should run parallel to other lengthwise yarns. Likewise, new stitches on the crosswise grainline should be parallel to other crosswise yarns. This is what is meant by duplicating the original weave. Following the grainline is as important to satisfactory mending as it is in constructing clothes. Do not pull the thread at the end of each row of stitches. Instead, keep the stitches somewhat loose to avoid puckering. How closely you should place stitches in darning depends on the closeness of the weave in the fabric. In a washable garment stitches should be not quite so close as those in the fabric. The patch may shrink when washed causing a puckered spot if the stitches were too close.

A good mend should blend into the fabric around it, making no rough spots or ridges. Use no knots in beginning or ending the darn. Use darning thread of the same weight as the yarns in the fabric. In better fabric it might be possible to use yarns raveled from the fabric. If the fabric color can be matched exactly the patch will blend with the garment color.

244

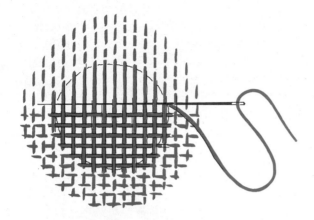

Darning small holes in woven fabric. This presents a different type of problem than mending a tear. The yarns in the fabric must be duplicated in both the lengthwise and crosswise directions.

In mending a tear on a flat area of the garment a piece of thin fabric might be basted underneath it. Darn the fabric reinforcement to the garment by stitching through it. It would be helpful to practice on scraps of fabric and socks to develop some skill in darning before you attempt a major repair.

We can summarize these ideas about darning by saying that skill in darning has several uses and that each use involves different problems. Straight tears, corner tears, and holes in woven fabrics require slightly different applications of darning. Mending holes in socks is a still different problem because it involves knitted fabric and usually rounded areas.

So called *"iron-on" patches* are sometimes useful. They are available in several common woven fabrics, including denim, broadcloth, and corduroy. Also, for repairing socks, pajamas, and other knit items,

soft knit patches may be purchased. Both types of fabric patches are available in a variety of colors. The main advantage of this type of patch is that it may save time in clothes repair.

The precut patch is laid on the place to be mended. When heat and pressure are applied on the prepared patch it is bonded, or fused, to the garment by an adhesive on the back of the patch. Follow directions for the correct ironing temperature and for the time that heat and pressure should be applied. If properly applied, iron-on repairs may be expected to withstand either dry-cleaning or washing, as labeled.

When and where these patches might be best used depends on the type of garments and the expected wear. In choosing the type of patch to use, the fabric construction and texture must be considered. For satisfactory results, put like fabrics together. Use a woven fabric patch only on a woven fabric and a knit patch on knit articles. Use a corduroy patch only on a cor-

How to Darn a Sock. (Shows how to hold the sock, as for darning in a rounded area.)

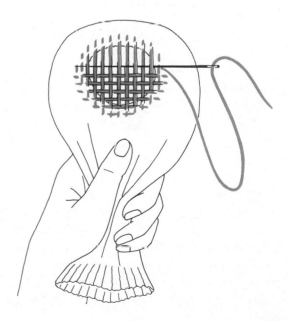

245

duroy garment and a denim patch only with denim. If a patch of the same fabric as the garment cannot be obtained, one of similar texture and weight can sometimes be used satisfactorily. Broadcloth patches, for example, might be used with other firmly woven, plain-weave fabrics as well as on broadcloth.

Consider color, too, in selecting a patch. If the patch cannot be matched exactly with the garment, the mend is likely to be easily noticed. Decorative patches of contrasting colors or textures, meant to be appliques, may be used effectively for some mending. The patches are precut into decorative shapes. The result is the addition of a trim as well as a patch. Whether or not this is suitable depends upon the type of garment and its expected use. The shape and color of the added trim should be considered in relation to the rest of the garment design. As in any other type of mending, consider how this type of repair will affect the appearance of the garment. Ap-

pearance and durability are usually equally important in repairing outer garments.

There are times when it is wise to pay for clothing repair services. Some department stores and tailoring shops make available re-weaving services. The cost of this type of mending service may be worthwhile in order to extend the usefulness of a damaged garment. An expert will be able to replace yarns in a woven fabric so that the mend will not be noticed.

Fasteners again

You can expect that buttons, snaps, and hook-and-eye closures will need repair occasionally. One of the ways you might begin to assume regular responsibility for repairing your own clothes is with small, but important, details such as these. Develop the habit of checking fasteners when you put away your clothes. Make the repair immediately and the article will be ready for the next wearing. Use the same procedures to repair fastenings as those you used to reinforce them in your new garments. (See "How Might You Make It More Durable?" page 241.)

Hem lines

What looks more neglected than a sagging hem line? You can repair a hem easily. First remove broken stitches. Then pin the detached section back into place. Using matching thread, repair the damage with a hemming stitch. (For suggestions on hemming stitches, see "Learning as You Sew," pages 193–194.)

Make it a clothes-care habit to check the hem as soon as you take off a skirt. If it needs restitching do it immediately before you forget it. Otherwise, put it among your urgent chores to be done. As you learn this simple routine you can prevent more of your hemline emergencies.

Suggested Learning Experiences

Bulletin Boards and Exhibits

1. Make a bulletin-board display or an exhibit showing ideas for altering ready-to-wear garments. Clipped illustrations might be used with appropriate comments. Use "before" and "after" illustrations if these are available.
2. Make a bulletin-board display or an exhibit showing ways to reinforce new garments. Use real garments, samples, or illustrations.
3. Make a bulletin-board display or an exhibit which explains the steps in a frequently used repair.
4. Arrange an exhibit of supplies for clothing repairs. Materials might include prepared hem facing, buttonhole twist, iron-on patches, and darning needles.

Laboratory

5. Plan laboratory sessions in which you learn how to darn, and how to patch a tear or rip. If some class members do not have garments which need repair, perhaps other class members could bring several articles to repair. Or collect items for repair from a childrens' home or a home for the aged. Consult your guidance counselor, your school nurse, or teacher for information about other sources of clothing to repair.
6. Plan laboratory sessions during which sewing skills are used to alter ready-to-wear garments. Each class member may plan an individual project for improving the appearance or durability of a ready-to-wear garment. Afterwards, have an exhibit or modeling session to explain the "before" and "after" condition of each garment. Determine the dollar and cent value of your work by finding out the probable cost of each type of alteration. Also keep a record of the time required to complete each project.

Demonstrations

7. Instead of individual projects and supervised laboratory work, plan one or more demonstrations on ready-to-wear alterations.

Individual Reports or Group Reports

8. Find out the cost of several types of alterations by inquiring from retail stores, dressmakers, tailor shops, dry-cleaners. Compare the information to see if the cost of a particular alteration is the same regardless of where it is done.
   Compare the cost of several types of common alterations. Which are most expensive? least expensive?
   Discuss these questions: How much is it worth to me to be able to make simple alterations and repairs on my own clothes?
   How much is it worth to a family if the homemaker has some skill in alteration and repair.

Home Experiences

9. Make a plan for repairing your own clothes. If your mother, or another adult family member, has always done this for you, plan to assume some of this responsibility. Find information about the type of repairs you need to make. Plan a specific time to work on this each week. Keep a record of the type of repairs you attempt during half a semester, or an entire semester.

Future Homemakers of America

10. Plan a chapter meeting in which clothing is repaired so that it might be donated to a charitable agency for distribution. Ask your chapter advisor to help you plan such a project.

A Practical Examination

11. Individually, or in small groups, examine one or more ready-to-wear garments to determine how the appearance or durability of each might be improved. Report results of your study to the group.

References for Pupils

(*Available from the Superintendent of Documents, U.S. Government Printing Office, Washington, D.C. 20402.)

How to Make Belts and Hems, Singer Sewing Library, Book No. 112 (1960). The Singer Sewing Machine Co., Singer Building, 149 Broadway, New York 10001.

How to Mend and Refit, Singer Sewing Library, Book No. 117 (1960). The Singer Sewing Machine Co., Singer Building, 149 Broadway, New York 10001.

LEWIS, DORA S., MABEL GOODE BOWERS, and MARIETTA KETTUNEN, "Altering Ready-mades and Remodeling Old Clothes," in *Clothing Construction and Wardrobe Planning*, pp. 318–324. The Macmillan Company, New York, 1960.

*THOMPSON, KATHLEEN, "Mending" in *Consumers All, The Yearbook of Agriculture, 1965*, pp. 385–390, U.S. Department of Agriculture, Washington, D.C.

References for Teachers

(*Available from the Superintendent of Documents, U.S. Government Printing Office, Washington, D.C. 20402.)

BISHOP, EDNA BRYTE, and MARJORIE STOTLER ARCH, "Alterations of Ready-to-Wear," pp. 18–38 in *Fashion Sewing by the Bishop Method*. J. B. Lippincott Company, Philadelphia, Pa., 1962.

BROCKMAN, HELEN L., "The Effective Use of Trimming," in *The Theory of Fashion and Design*, Chapter 11, pp. 265–299 (A good explanation of the how and why of trim on ready-to-wear garments). John Wiley & Sons, Inc., New York, 1965.

Clothing Repairs, Home and Garden Bulletin No. 107 (1965), U.S. Department of Agriculture, Washington, D.C.

"Improving Ready-to-Wear Clothes," in *Better Homes and Garden Sewing Book*, pp. 295–300. Meredith Publishing Co., Des Moines, 1961.

JOHNSON, MARY, *Mary Johnson's Guide to Altering and Restyling Ready-made Clothes*. E. P. Dutton & Co., Inc., New York, 1964.

SIEMAN, ESTHER (Extension Clothing Specialist), "Fitting Principles Applied to Selection and Alteration of Ready-to-Wear," p. 20 in *The Principles of Fitting*. University of Illinois, College of Agriculture and Home Economics, Urbana, Ill., 1962.

UNIT NINE

Vocations Which Require
Clothing and Textiles
Knowledge

I. Two Jobs Rather Than One

At some time probably every girl stops to wonder what her adult life will be like. There was a time when every girl planned to be a homemaker. When she married she expected to have a full-time job in managing a home and rearing a family. Formerly, most homemakers found homemaking to be a full-time vocation. There were no electrical conveniences to give help in housework. Housekeeping chores required much tedious physical effort.

Today, homemakers use many automatic appliances to do their work. Food can be purchased either partly prepared or completely ready for the table. It is no longer necessary to preserve food by canning—unless, of course, the homemaker prefers to do so. However, she may also choose from a variety of commercially frozen and canned foods. Clothes care is no longer a chore. Wrinkle-resistant clothing and automatic washers are in common use. Ideas about homemaking as a vocation are changing. It is no longer considered a full-time job for all women.

Beliefs about women's abilities and interests have changed, too. Sixty years ago most teen-age girls could not expect to have enough education to work outside the home except as unskilled laborers. Now, if she prefers, a girl can prepare herself for paid employment as well as for homemaking.

Women's interests and abilities are not restricted to the home. Women have proven their abilities in teaching, nursing, business, and retail selling. Women work as secretaries, doctors, taxi-drivers, bank cashiers, lawyers, clothes designers, skilled factory workers, university professors, bus drivers, and policewomen.

In 1965 one-third of all employed workers were women. In 1920 only 20 per cent, or one-fifth, of all workers were women.

The trend is toward increasing numbers of employed women. On this trend is based the prediction that eight of every ten girls will be employed as a paid worker at some time. Furthermore, young women today can expect to work for wages outside the home for twenty years or more of their adult lives.[1]

Consider, too, that three out of five of all employed women workers are married. Were you aware that so many homemakers today have this "dual role"? Since "dual" means two, this says that employed homemakers have two roles. They are both homemakers and employed workers.

What does all this mean? Should you prepare yourself for paid employment as well as for homemaking? How will you prepare yourself? You have a big decision ahead.

Most girls plan to be homemakers. Others plan careers in professions and other occupations. They may delay marriage until their education is under way. And a few may not marry at all. However, it is becoming more common for a girl to prepare herself to be both a homemaker and a paid worker. Each role, that of a homemaker and that of a paid employee, includes responsibilities and satisfactions.

Expert homemaking skills are particularly important to the homemaker who must spend part of her day away from her home. Home economics classes can help prepare girls by teaching some basic knowledge about homemaking.

II. What Can You Do Now to Prepare for a Vocation?

Develop General Traits and Abilities

The time when you will be an employee may seem to be far in the future. You cannot predict exactly the type of work you will have, nor the place where you will work. On the other hand, your day-to-day activities now help to determine your future opportunities. In today's complex world, employment requires preparation.

One thing you can do now is to develop some general traits and abilities. What are some characteristics on which success depends? Perhaps enthusiasm is one. Take an active interest in your school, classes, associates, the persons who help you every day, and yourself.

[1] Figures from *U.S. Bureau of the Census, Statistical Abstract of the United States, 1965* (86th edition), Washington, D.C., and *American Women, Report of the President's Commission on the Status of Women,* 1963. Superintendent of Documents, Washington, D.C.

Learn about Vocations

Another thing you can do now is investigate vocations which interest you. Study vocations systematically so that you can compare their advantages and disadvantages. Start by making a list of questions that you might ask. For instance, here are three questions that are important in considering any occupation:

1. What is the job like?
2. What are the working conditions?
3. What kind of preparation or special training is required?

What is the job like? You would want to know the usual activities you could expect. Does the work involve selling, sewing, assisting others with clothes care, thinking of new ideas, teaching, operating a machine, typing, or other activities?

What are the working conditions? Where would you work? Is the job available only in a large city? Are the working hours fairly routine or irregular? Some otherwise exciting and interesting jobs include irregular working hours. Not all conditions in any job are ideal. Is travel a

Develop your skills in reading and writing. There are few jobs in which these skills are not essential. These basic skills are necessary for school studies too.

Reliability or dependability is an essential trait that results from many small actions. Dependability means being prompt every day. Reliability is being prepared for class every day, too. Dependability is willingness to carry through on a special task or assignment. Your success in school now is related to your dependability. Later, your success on a job might be closely related to this same important trait—dependability.

In the following section, notice the traits and abilities required for the different jobs. Two successful young women tell about their work. Another tells how she is preparing for a career. Each developed some useful traits and abilities along the way toward success.

regular part of the job? Would you be required to spend days or even weeks away from your home? Again, a job which includes exciting and interesting activities may also involve extensive travel. This might be considered either an advantage or a disadvantage depending on the conditions you prefer.

What kind of preparation or special training is required for the job you want to do? A high-school education and willingness to keep on learning are sufficient preparation for some types of work. A college degree is required preparation for other occupations. Occupational training, available in vocational and technical schools, is necessary for other types of work. Whatever the preparation necessary for the job, a willingness to keep on learning after you are on the job is important, whether you are a high-school graduate or a college graduate—or neither.

III. Some Vocations for You to Consider

If you enjoy learning about clothing, fabrics, and fibers, you may find a vocation suited to these interests. This unit is planned to help you explore some occupations in which a knowledge of clothing is either essential or helpful. Possibly you will gain some new ideas about careers.

The selection of the occupational areas discussed in this unit is not meant to give a complete picture. Several different types of jobs are described, but only a few are presented in detail. Others are not included at all. It is hoped that you will be encouraged to further investigate jobs in clothing and fabrics.

Retail Selling

Joyce Barger Poling is the manager of a specialty clothing store. She attended high school at Evansville, Indiana, and she earned a B.A. degree in Home Economics at Indiana University, Bloomington, Indiana. Her views about retail selling are revealed in her own story about her job.

"I am the manager of a small women's specialty shop. Because the store is located near the entrance to Indiana University, we cater to the college student and career girl. A typical day begins by opening the door, assigning projects to employees, checking stock to see in which areas we may be low, eating lunch, reading and answering mail, planning window and case displays, supervising selling, checking out the cash register, closing the store and making the bank deposit.

"Advertising is a usual part of the job, too. We may plan to feature a certain brand of sports clothes. Perhaps we will use some of the new sweater-and-skirt sets

253

on the mannequins in the window. We may decide to run an advertisement in the newspaper. The display cases will need to be coordinated with the colors in the window theme. We might decide it would be fun to have some members of our high-school board model this brand of clothing informally in the store. Often there are style shows to be organized, special promotions, hiring and firing. And really, who knows what may be next? That's part of the excitement in retailing.

"Generally, I have a sales meeting every two weeks. At that time we discuss fashion trends, customer requests, air our grievances and resolve to be better sales-people. One of the girls may want to add a customer to our special calling list. Another may feel we are lacking a type of merchandise or that we're missing sales because we are not enthusiastic about selling or friendly to our customers.

"In retailing we work at a fast pace, a pace perhaps quickened by the growth of mass media in the last decade. Television, an example of mass media, has brought fashion news almost instantly to everyone who wants it. Because fashion is changing more quickly, it is important to be versatile and personable. You must be ready to meet many people and assess each person's individual needs. After showing the customer a few items, you must be able to ascertain her likes and dislikes. One soon finds that each customer is unique and one must discover her preferences.

"Change is one of the advantages of retailing. No day is like another. There is much opportunity to be creative. If you like clothes and working with the public, retailing may be for you. There are some disadvantages, however. Often working hours are long. Before Christmas the store is open every night until nine for four weeks. Though you think you may enjoy working with customers, sometimes it can be tedious and you may find yourself forcing that smile! Women in retailing who are steady, dependable employees usually have as good chances for advancement as men. Women who work irregularly because of home responsibilities cannot expect the same advancement opportunities.

"Retailing is more than displaying and selling clothes. The merchandise must be processed when it arrives. This process is called receiving. At this time the merchandise is inspected, marked off the order, ticketed, pressed and put into stock.

"After merchandise is in stock, it is very important to see that it remains neat and orderly. In most stores much time is spent taking care of the stock. Fragile fabrics and light-colored clothes must be covered. Loose buttons must be secured and merchandise placed in its proper size range.

"I did not gear myself specifically to retailing although it was one of my main interests when I was younger. Like many college freshmen I switched my major many times before happily discovering Home Economics. During college I thought, with my home economics background, it would be fun to go into interior design or fine arts. One of the nice things about a degree in Home Economics is its versatility as background for many areas.

"My first years in high school were busy and a little confusing. As a freshman in high school, I attended modeling school because I was so awkward. My mother felt I should not wear high heels or make-up until I could wear them properly. Being rather small I soon began modeling clothing for trunk showings at local stores. Generally salesmen's samples for trunk showings are very small. Through this experience I met Mrs. Foster, a sportswear buyer for Schultz's in Evansville. Mrs. Foster asked me to help with Schultz's Madamoiselle College Board and Style Show for high-school seniors. She encouraged me to participate in contests sponsored by magazines, leading to careers in retailing.

"Many of my college courses have been a help in preparation for my job. It is surprising how many things I learned then that I use every day now. A course like 'History of Costume' may give you information you need to understand fashion changes. A course in the 'Principles of Design' may help you plan a better window, change the format of an advertisement, or channel your creativity more effectively.

"With a knowledge of textiles you can explain to customers why certain fabrics have the characteristics they do. Perhaps a student is planning to spend the summer abroad in a language program. She will need clothing that is packable and washable, and requires little ironing. With a textile background you will be able to guide her buying.

"French seems to be the language of fashion although not everyone may agree. I personally feel it has been an aid. Something else that I have found important is a thorough understanding of a good etiquette book. It gives information about what should be worn to an afternoon wedding, a luncheon, etc. How can I sell fashion goods for special occasions without knowing something of appropriate dress?

"Retailing, particularly the merchandising area, offers many opportunities for aggressive, dedicated women. Generally, large department stores are interested in college graduates for participating in their executive training programs. Who knows, you might become a buyer, merchandise manager, or even president of the company."

Joyce Barger Poling
Bloomington, Indiana

255

This is retail selling from a store manager's viewpoint. The story points out the importance of working successfully with other people.

A high school education is minimum preparation for many types of retail selling jobs which do not include managerial responsibilities. There are many different jobs in large stores. This may be an occupational area that you will want to study further.

Teaching

Teaching is a challenging job. If you are a good student and you like to be at school, you might want to consider this occupational field. Basically, teaching consists of helping individuals learn. During one day a teacher may be in charge of from three to five classes. She should expect to be surrounded by pupils the greater part of a typical school day. Therefore, it is an advantage to be both patient and energetic.

A home economics teacher may specialize in teaching clothing courses, or she may teach several areas of home economics, one of which might be clothing. Clothing courses might include the study of natural and man-made fibers, of how fabrics are made, of fabric finishes, sewing techniques, and the buying of clothing. There is much opportunity to use original ideas in the classroom. Thinking of new ways to teach something is one way to be original.

Four or five years of college preparation are required to become a qualified teacher. Even after a teacher has completed her minimum college preparation, she continues to learn. She keeps herself informed about new developments in clothing, in fibers and fabrics, by attending meetings, by reading, and by enrolling in advanced courses during the summer. This need to

keep informed is an advantage outside the classroom as well as in. As a teacher gains new knowledge she will have it to use in her home and personal life as well as in the classroom.

Care and Maintenance of Clothing

The care and maintenance of clothing is a major business in our country. Commercial dry-cleaning plants offer the public an essential service. High standards in personal appearance are important to success in many occupations. Also, clean and pressed clothing are expected standards of dress for numerous social occasions.

There are various jobs within the dry-cleaning business. Clothes must be received, sorted, and spotted. Workers are

An attendant may expect to deal with an assortment of problems every day. She must be able to tell customers the correct way to load a washing machine. Customers' questions may range from what is the best water temperature for certain fabrics to what kinds of clothes to wash together and the amount of detergent to use.

Of course, tact and courtesy in assisting customers is essential. Also, a neat appearance and an enthusiasm for helping others are useful.

The study of textiles in high school home economics classes could provide a foundation for you in this type of work.

Dressmaking and Alteration

In this age of ready-to-wear clothing skilled seamstresses are still in demand as alteration experts and dressmakers. Why is this so? Many persons want well-fitted clothes, but they have neither the time to sew nor the sewing skill.

This is an occupation for girls who enjoy sewing and working with fabrics and clothing. There are opportunities for skilled sewers to work in either cities or smaller communities. Large department stores usually maintain alteration departments for the convenience of their customers. Custom dressmaker shops make garments to order for their clientele. Such shops, which may be located in cities or small towns, may also handle alterations. There are opportunities for good seamstresses to work in their own homes filling orders for alterations, or in sewing complete garments. Some dry-cleaning shops employ skilled sewers to make alterations.

The major qualification for employment as a dressmaker or alteration expert is better-than-average sewing skill. An expert sewer is a skilled craftsman. A knowledge

needed to operate machines. Clothes must be pressed and returned to customers. Each task requires handling and treating clothing. Some jobs are routine. A worker who likes routine tasks may become a very skilled and valuable employee. Providing a quality service can be satisfying.

Commercial laundry plants also offer clothes-care services to the public. Again, different types of jobs are involved.

Coin-operated laundries are well established in both large cities and small towns. This is a relatively new type of business but one which seems to be providing a needed service for individuals and families. Managers and attendants in coin-operated laundries need a general knowledge of clothing, washing products, and washing equipment. A knowledge of fibers and fabrics commonly used in clothing is especially necessary.

257

of the different fabrics and their characteristics is essential. It is just as necessary to develop skill in fitting as skill in sewing. A seamstress must be prepared to work on different types of garments, such as coats, suits, dresses, and skirts. Both speed and accuracy in sewing are important. In order to work profitably a paid seamstress must be able to complete projects rapidly.

There are several ways to prepare for paid employment in dressmaking and alteration. Many high school home economics courses may include some work in clothing construction. In these courses it is also possible to obtain a basic knowledge of the natural and man-made fibers, fabrics, and their characteristics.

Some vocational and technical high schools have intensive courses in dressmaking. Private trade schools also offer advanced courses in clothing construction. Adult evening courses in public schools are still another way to obtain this type of vocational training.

You can explore your own interest in this vocation by experimenting on clothes you sew for yourself. Be willing to try new techniques and use different fabrics. When you have enough skill, get some experience sewing for other persons. Learn where to obtain information about new fabrics, sewing techniques, and equipment. You will need to keep up to date about trends in clothing and fabrics.

Field Home Economist for Private Business

Young women with college-level training in home economics can qualify for interesting careers in the business world. Miss Jeanne Golly works in New York City as a field home economist for the J. C. Penney Company. In her own story she explains what a field home economist does and how she prepared herself for this kind of job.

"My home is San Antonio, Texas. I was graduated from Alamo Heights High School in 1959. My graduating class numbered about 250 students. During high school I pursued a college preparatory curriculum. My high-school schedule included four years of Homemaking.

"I was active in many phases of school life—student council, service organizations, pep squad, National Honor Society, and Future Homemakers of America. My interest in FHA began during my freshman year in high school. As I grew older, I accepted increasing responsibility in the organization. I served my chapter in various capacities, from committee member to president of the chapter for two years in succession. I also served as a district president of the Texas Association during my senior year.

"I believe that many of my personal characteristics, which I have been able to develop, have contributed greatly to any amount of success I have enjoyed. These characteristics include leadership ability, self-confidence, and initiative. Two other traits which have been helpful in my work are maturity of judgment and self-acceptance.

"I was graduated from the University of Texas in 1963 with a Bachelor of Science degree in Home Economics Education. My minor areas of study were science and textiles and clothing. Again, I was extremely active in many phases of campus life. My activities included student government, service organizations, and the University of Texas Home Economics Club chapter. I served my chapter in many capacities, from committee member to chapter president for two years. I also served in a statewide capacity as parliamentarian, and then president of the Texas Home Economics College Chapter of the American Home Economics Association.

"It was during my undergraduate years that I became interested in advanced study in home economics. This interest prompted me to enroll in graduate school at Michigan State University, East Lansing, Michigan, in 1964. I was graduated from Michigan State University in 1966 with a Master of Arts degree in Textiles, Clothing,

and Retailing. Graduate school was a very challenging experience for me.

"I have been fortunate to have had the opportunity to hold a variety of positions related to my interests in home economics. During high school I served as a student assistant in the Homemaking Department and in the Nursery School. During undergraduate college days I served as a student assistant in the Department of Home Economics. I also served as an Apprentice Home Economist for the utility company in San Antonio for the summers before my junior and senior years in college.

"After graduation from the University of Texas I accepted a position as a 7th grade homemaking teacher in the Austin Public School System where I taught for one school year. During graduate school I was an assistant instructor in the Department of Textiles, Clothing, and Related Arts. From this work I gained additional teaching experience, this time on the college level.

"I believe that all of the various experiences I have had during high school, college, and graduate school, and other experiences outside of the realm of formal education, have helped prepare me for the job I hold today. I am an educator working in business. My title is Field Home Economist for J. C. Penney Company. My major role is that of planning, organizing, and presenting programs of professional interest to groups of home economics teachers throughout the United States. I work closely with local educators and businessmen.

"My job is challenging, stimulating, creative, and richly rewarding. It enables me to make certain valuable contributions to the profession of home economics and to education in general. It requires a thorough knowledge of home economics. Teaching ability is important, too. Other personal qualities are necessary, such as public-speaking ability, self-confidence and self-discipline, and ability to get along with others. Also important is the desire to make the world a better place to live.

"My office is in the J. C. Penney building in New York City. However, the job takes me away from the office about forty-two weeks out of the year. Days are rarely "typical," for I could be involved in any or all of the activities related to presenting a program to home economics educators anywhere in the country. The satisfactions I derive from my job are many. Perhaps the two greatest are a feeling of contributing in a small way to the professions of home economics and education, and the satisfying relationships with the people for whom I work and with whom I work. I believe that opportunities for the future are limited only by failure to grow and develop as challenges arise."

Jeanne Golly
New York City

Design and Production of Theater Costumes

Individuals who understand clothing make an important contribution in the entertainment field. Designing and constructing costumes for theater productions are occupations in which a knowledge of clothing is essential. If you like plays and the excitement of play production, this may be a future for you. Mary Anne Pope is a senior student at Indiana University majoring in Home Economics. Actually, her carefully selected college courses are preparing her for two careers—theater costume production and Home Economics teaching. Read Mary Anne's story, which tells how her vocational interests are being developed.

"There were about one thousand students in the high school I attended. I grew up in a town of about 20,000 approximately forty miles from Chicago. I enjoyed school and took part in a wide variety of activities throughout my high-school years. During my freshman and sophomore years my ambition was to become a nurse and I joined the Future Nurses Club. Later, when I considered teaching as a career, I became a member of the Future Teachers Club. I assisted in a history class for one semester of my senior year as a cadet teacher. I also belonged to the Latin and Booster clubs. Another of my numerous activities was working on the high-school yearbook as photo editor.

"I followed a general academic curriculum, taking college preparatory courses.

"Outside of school my interests included camping, music, swimming, and sewing. I was a member of Girl Scouts throughout high school and look back upon my experiences with much satisfaction. Through scouts I worked in the hospital my sophomore and junior years and took several camping trips. A highlight of my scouting activities was a seventeen-day bus trip through the eastern states the summer before my sophomore year. Every night we would stay at a different camp site. We camped on the battlefield at Gettysburg and then went on to Annapolis, Washington, D.C., Williamsburg, and the Smoky Mountain National Park.

"I enjoy all kinds of good music. During high school I continued piano lessons, took courses in music appreciation and theory, and became a member of the *a cappella* choir my senior year. As a college student, I still enjoy music and look forward to the time I can continue my camping interest.

"The summer before my junior year I took a senior life-saving course and helped teach swimming at a nearby beach. After high school I became a water-safety instructor. During one summer I worked as a life guard and swimming instructor. My biggest problem is finding time to do all I would like to do. In the future I plan on taking modeling and judo lessons. As time permits, I plan to learn how to water-ski, sail a boat, and fly a plane. I want to continue to explore fields that interest me. New ideas and open-mindedness are important to me.

"I started preparing myself for a career in costuming long before I considered it as a future vocation. I have always considered clothing a hobby. For my twelfth birthday I received a sewing machine from my parents. I immediately set to work learning how to sew by my trial-and-error method. In seventh and eighth grade home economics classes I learned sewing techniques. I had to correct poor habits I had picked up in the preceding year. I had not been cutting garments out correctly and therefore my seams were uneven.

"Many times during my high-school years I was called upon by my younger sisters to produce costumes for various events. I made Greek and Roman costumes, Elizabethan, Puritan, and Hawaiian dresses, and angel, can-can, and roaring 20's outfits for plays, parties, and Scout events. I enjoyed making these costumes and tried to be as original as possible when constructing them.

"When I was a senior I took another course in clothing construction. I was interested in costuming at the time, and since I was working in the high school library, I decided to see what books were available on costuming. To my disappointment, one book was all I could find on the subject.

"Because of my interest in clothing, I chose the field of home economics as a major when entering college. It seems strange now that I did not consider costuming as a career before my junior year in college. Because of my interest in clothing I received valuable information from my Textiles course on types of fabric and their properties, such as drapability and durability. Flat Pattern Design course furnished me with information on how to design various collars, yokes, necklines, and sleeves.

"When I finally had time to select courses other than my requirements in college, I enrolled in a course in costuming. I enjoyed the course and saw possibilities for an interesting future. Since then, I have become very interested in stage costume production as a career.

"Last semester I took a course in advanced stage costume. I received a basic overview of what may be involved in a career in costuming. This course includes the study of the basic history of dress. Students design costumes for specific plays, such as *Henry IV* and *The Beggar's Opera*. Students in the course also help produce costumes by working in the costume laboratory. They are responsible for the care and maintenance of costumes for the run of a play given in the university theater.

"This semester I am taking Introduction to Dramatic Production. The course includes analyzing plays and basic fundamentals of scenery, lighting, and costuming. This course is helping me to see costuming in relationship to other technical aspects included in staging a play. Just a knowledge of how to design costumes is not enough. A costume maker must take into consideration what effect stage lights and different types of settings will have on a costume.

"A career in costuming may include one or all of the following types of activities: costume design, costume construction, and maintenance of costumes during a show. The different jobs may have a variety of titles. A person may be called a seamstress, a wardrobe mistress, or a costume designer, according to the duties involved in a specific job. A seamstress would be responsible for cutting out, sewing together, and fitting of costumes. The wardrobe mistress would help performers dress, make necessary repairs, and see to the cleaning of costumes during and after the run of the show. Costume designers prepare drawings of costumes and may supervise their construction.

"A career in costuming gives an individual the opportunity to work with talented, imaginative people. There is little time in costume design to become bored from a monotonous routine. Something new and interesting is happening daily to challenge one's creative abilities. Often a career in costuming will involve longer hours than a nine-to-five job. Nights may be taken up with last-minute construction and working during rehearsals and shows. Costuming, like some other types of interesting work, does not always include regular hours. The irregular hours may be a disadvantage to the person who likes routine.

"Trained costume makers are needed by theaters throughout the country. Costumers are specialists who may be employed either in educational theater or in the professional theater. Opera, musicals, and plays are examples of entertainment forms produced. Educational theaters are usually located on college campuses where there are Speech and Theater Departments. Unlike the professional theater, classroom learning is a part in the educational theater. Professional theater refers to an occupational field.

"An individual with good training would have no trouble finding a job in the educational theater. A costumer in an educational theater may have teaching responsibilities as well as regular costuming duties. The usual beginning salary for an individual with a master's degree is around $5500 on the college level. Costuming in professional theater is highly competitive. It is difficult to find a good beginning job and the salary is low. One may begin as an understudy of an established costumer. Advancement is very possible when an individual is interested and willing to work hard at his job. Skills in clothing construction and fitting will help the beginning costumer advance. Ability and training in costume design are important to a successful career.

"Today many of my high-school activities and interests are continuing to play a part in my everyday life. My interest in clothing took me into the field of home economics where I am now working toward my bachelor's degree and teaching certificate. In the future I plan to work toward my master's degree in the field of Speech and Theater, specializing in costuming. At this time I do not know whether I will want a career in the educational or professional theater."

Mary Anne Pope
Senior, Indiana University
Bloomington, Indiana

Suggested Learning Experiences

Individual or Group Projects

1. How do workers "get started" in jobs? Let each class member ask an employee how he developed an interest in the work. Ask the worker how he was led into his type of work. Share information through group discussion.

2. Invite a member of the local Home Economics Association to tell the class about job opportunities in the clothing field. If there is no local Home Economics group, write to the state president for help. Your Home Economics teacher is a good resource for this type of information, too. However, you may want more than one viewpoint.

3. Ask a young woman who has a dual role of homemaker/wage-earner to tell satisfactions she finds in such an arrangement. Also, ask her to describe problems an employed homemaker may need to solve.

4. If possible, take a field trip to a clothing industry in your community. Find information about the specific types of jobs you will see.

5. Do you have a hobby or special interest that could lead to employment in the clothing industry? Share your hobbies and interests in an exhibit.

6. Future Homemakers of America. Consult your *National Program of Work 1965–69.* See "Project: Jobs, Careers, and You" for suggested activities.

Individual or Group Reports

7. Find out whether there are courses leading to employment in the clothing industry offered in public vocational schools in your area. Also, obtain information about private vocational schools with courses in clothing skills and fashion design. The guidance counselor may be able to help on this.

8. Brainstorm. Can you think of new jobs or types of work we may have by the year 2000? In what new ways will the human needs of clothing, housing, and food be provided? What new products will we need and want? What new services will we need and want?

9. Ask your civics teacher to help you find information on jobs in your community which require knowledge of clothing and fabrics or which involve working directly with clothing or fabrics. Plan individual or group reports.

10. Invite your art teacher to explain how art knowledge and skill is useful in clothing occupations.

References for Pupils

(*Available from the Superintendent of Documents, U.S. Government Printing Office, Washington, D.C. 20402.)

BAIRD, GLADYS A., "Is the Fashion Business for You?" *What's New in Home Economics*, Vol. 28, No. 5 (May–June 1964), pp. 34–37.

*"Careers for Women in Retailing," Women's Bureau Bulletin 271 (1963), U.S. Department of Labor, Washington, D.C.

"Fashion Artistry," in "You and Your Career," *Co-ed Magazine*, Vol. 10, No. 7 (March 1965), p. 18.

Future Jobs for High School Girls, Pamphlet No. 7 (revised 1966), Women's Bureau, U.S. Department of Labor, Washington, D.C.

Home Economics Has a Career for You in Textiles and Clothing, American Home Economics Association, Washington, D.C., 1963.

LEWIS, DORA, MABEL GOODE BOWERS, and MARIETTA KETTUNEN, *Clothing Construction and Wardrobe Planning*. The Macmillan Company, New York, 1960. Chapter 20: "Careers in Clothing in Fashion," pp. 536–553.

OERKE, BESS V., *Dress*. Chas. A. Bennett Co., Inc., Peoria, Ill., 1960. Chapter 14: "Careers in Home Economics," pp. 563–570.

RATHBONE, LUCY, ELIZABETH TARPLEY, MARJORIE EAST, and NELL GILES AHERN, *Fashions and Fabrics*. Houghton Mifflin Company, Boston, 1962. "Careers in Fashions and Fabrics," pp. 493–510.

SPLAVER, SARAH, *Your Career if You're Not Going to College*. Julian Messner, Inc., New York, 1963.

SUGARMAN, DANIEL A., and ROLLIE HOCHSTEIN, "What It Means To Be A Girl Now!" *Seventeen*, Vol. 25, No. 5 (May 1966), pp. 172–173, 254–257.

WHITCOMB, HELEN, and ROSALIND LANG, *Charm: A Career Girl's Guide to Business and Personal Success*. McGraw-Hill Book Company, Inc. (Gregg Division), New York, 1964.

References for Teachers

(*Available from the Superintendent of Documents, U.S. Government Printing Office, Washington, D.C. 20402.)

American Women: Report of the President's Commission on the Status of Women, 1963, Superintendent of Documents, U.S. Government Printing Office, Washington, D.C. Statistics concerning women workers and predictions about future employment of women; graphs showing trends in proportion of employed women in the work force.

BRADFIELD, VELMA S., MILDRED M. HUBER, and JOHN A. TAFT, *Occupations Related to Home Economics: A Guide for Counselors*, Bulletin of the California State Department of Education, Vol. 30, No. 8 (1961), California State Department of Education, Sacramento, Calif.

*Careers for Women in Retailing," Women's Bureau Bulletin 271 (1963), U.S. Department of Labor, Washington, D.C.

CLAYTON, NANALEE, "Stay: Skilled Training Applied to Youth," *What's New in Home Economics*, Vol. 29, No. 6 (September 1965), pp. 44, 46.

Clothing Maintenance Specialist: A Suggested Training Program, a Manpower Development and Training Program, Division of Vocational and Technical Education, Office of Education, U.S. Department of Health, Education, and Welfare, Washington, D.C., 1964.

JANSSEN, PETER A., "Threads of Fashion," *American Education*, Vol. 1, No. 10 (November 1965), pp. 9–11.

PURGRASKI, CAROLYN, "Job Pretraining," *Practical Forecast*, Vol. 9, No. 9 (May 1964), pp. 14–15, 31.

Index

C

D

271

Weight control, 31, 32–33
Women as job-holders, 250–251
Woof yarns, *see* Weft yarns
Wool, 93
    fibers of, 90
    finishes used on, 126
    labeling of, 104
    pressing of, 120, 144
    washing of, 106, 120, 121, 137
    See also Wool clothing

Wool clothing, care of, 106, 145
    protection of, from moths, 148
    See also Wool
Wool Products Labeling Act of 1939, 104

Z

Zefran, 106
Zippers, 186–188, 207–209

ABCDEFGHIJ 0698
PRINTED IN THE UNITED STATES OF AMERICA